THE COLLEGE STUDENT

THE COLLEGE STUDENT
READING AND STUDY SKILLS

EDWARD SPARGO

This text used to be called *The Now Student*. It is essentially unchanged, but has been given a new title and new photographs to maintain its appeal to today's college freshmen.

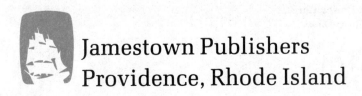
Jamestown Publishers
Providence, Rhode Island

THE COLLEGE STUDENT
Reading and Study Skills

Catalog No. 811
Copyright ©1977 by Jamestown Publishers,
Inc. The special contents of this edition
copyright ©1983.

Cover Design by Deborah Hulsey Christie
Text Design by Stephen R. Anthony

Printed in the United States
BB 83 84 85 86 9 8 7 6 5 4 3 2 1
ISBN 0-89061-357-5

Preface

The College Student functions three ways in developing students' reading and study skills: (1) It is an instructional text. Each of twenty-five lessons deals with a particular reading or study skill and presents specific techniques for developing it. (2) It promotes faster, more efficient reading with increased comprehension. Each lesson is a timed reading selection of 1500 words followed by a comprehension test. Students are encouraged to chart their progress in reading speed as well as in comprehension. (3) It provides opportunities to practice new skills. Each lesson is followed by an appropriate exercise which encourages students to use the skills and techniques discussed.

The text emphasizes sequential procedures which students can use at once to become more proficient in performing daily assignments. The language is concrete and readable; the word choice and structure reflect the author's intent to present useful information in its most understandable form. The design and organization are consistent and regular from one lesson to the next so that students soon become comfortable with an easily recognized format that is stimulating but not threatening.

One of the most useful features of the text is the *cloze* comprehension tests which follow each lesson. These are discussed at length in the Instructor's Guide.

Certain practice exercises contain excerpts from *30 Ways to Get Ahead at College* by Joseph L. Lennon, O.P., Vice President of Providence College, to whom the author is grateful.

The photographs appearing in the text and on the cover were taken at the Bristol campus of Roger Williams College in Rhode Island.

The author is most indebted to Raymond H. Harris for his assistance in rewriting and editing this Revised Edition.

E.S.

Contents

> Read the introduction before beginning any work. It explains how the selections are organized and what procedures to use to gain maximum benefit from your program of reading and study improvement.

Introduction to the Student

The further you go in school the more challenges you face, and the higher people's expectations of you become. You are expected to learn independently — to rely more on your reading in the learning process and less on your teachers. You are expected to manage your own time and assume more of the responsibility for your own education. In order to do this, you must have the necessary reading and study skills.

The skills you need for academic success are discussed in the following selections. If you will read each selection carefully and practice the suggested techniques, you will soon find yourself becoming a more efficient student and a faster, more capable learner.

USING THE TEXT

The effectiveness of any textbook depends upon how well it is used. Here are some suggestions for using this text.

1. **Preview Each Selection.** Before reading, take a minute or two to preview. As a study skill, *previewing* will be discussed fully in the text; but for now, preview by reading the title, the introductory statement in the box preceding the selection, and the headings throughout the selection.

This simple procedure will help you to read each lesson more efficiently. Knowing what is coming helps you to organize as you read and improves your understanding.

2. **Time Your Reading.** Just before starting to read, glance at the clock and make note of your starting time. If your instructor is timing the class, he will indicate when to begin reading. At the end of the selection, note your reading time in minutes and seconds. Turn to the table on page 254 and convert your time to a words-per-minute rate. Find the time on the table that is closest to your actual reading time. Record these scores in

the box at the end of each selection. We want you to keep a record of your reading rate throughout the text so that you will be able to see your improvement as it occurs.

3. **Do the Comprehension Tests.** Two comprehension tests follow each selection. One measures your understanding of material from the beginning of the selection, and the other, material from the end of the selection. Together, they will show you how well you understand the entire selection.

Although the tests resemble familiar fill-in exercises, they are actually a relatively new, highly effective reading test called a *cloze test*. Cloze tests have been found to be ideally suited to check your understanding of the kind of factual material that is presented in this book.

In order to receive credit on the cloze tests, you should fill a blank with the exact word that has been removed. However, in some situations instructors will allow you to take credit for very close synonyms. Be sure to check to find out which procedure your instructor prefers to follow.

Because it is sometimes impossible to determine for sure what the missing word is, the tests are quite demanding and not the simple exercise they first appear to be. Nevertheless, if you read the selection attentively, it is not difficult to achieve a high score. Every blank need not be correctly filled to score 100 percent comprehension.

Correct your tests by referring to the answer key at the end of the book. Credit yourself with two points for each correctly filled blank and record the scores for both tests in the box at the end of the selection. A conversion table on page 254 lets you convert your total cloze score to a comprehension percentage, which you will also record in the box.

Graphs are provided in the back of the book on which you can plot your reading rate and comprehension percentage for each selection. Trends and improvements can be readily seen when plotted on a graph.

4. **Complete Practice Exercises.** Following most of the selections there are exercises that provide opportunities to practice using the suggestions you have just read about. Needless to say, if you expect your improvement to last and become part of your study habits, you must practice the new techniques. The exercises have been designed to start you off.

Some of the selections are followed by questions that should be discussed in class or among small groups of students. If this is not possible, however, think each question through by yourself. By seeking answers to these questions, you may become more proficient in finding answers to personal study problems.

The text provides the means for you to improve your reading and study skills; so resolve now to give it the serious attention it deserves, and, in this way, to make the time you spend on schoolwork more satisfying and rewarding.

Every student brings both strengths and weaknesses to the job of learning. Your attitude, reading skills and study habits all contribute to your success or failure as a student. Diagnosing your strengths and weaknesses now and taking advantage of your school's remedial programs and counseling will put you on the right track to academic success.

Diagnosing Strengths and Weaknesses

If you were to begin a new job tomorrow, you would bring with you some basic strengths and weaknesses. Success or failure in your work would depend, to a great extent, on your ability to use your strengths and weaknesses to best advantage.

Of utmost importance is your attitude. A person who begins a job convinced that he isn't going to like it or sure that he is going to fail is exhibiting a weakness which can only hinder his success. On the other hand, a person who is secure in his belief that he is probably as capable of doing the work as anyone else and who is willing to make a cheerful attempt at it possesses a certain strength of purpose. Chances are he will do well.

Having the prerequisite skills for a particular job is a strength. Lacking those skills is obviously a weakness. A bookkeeper who can't add or a carpenter who can't cut a straight line with a saw are hopeless cases.

This book has been designed to help you capitalize on the strengths and overcome the weaknesses that you bring to the job of learning. But in order to measure your development, you must first take stock of where you stand now. As we get further along in the book, we'll be dealing in some detail with specific processes for developing and strengthening learning skills. However, as a beginning, you should pause to examine your present strengths and weaknesses in three areas that are critical to your success or failure in school: your attitude, your reading and communication skills, and your study habits.

ATTITUDE

In his book *Why College Students Fail*, Dr. Robert Pitcher has defined underachieving as *underbelieving* in oneself. If you approach a subject convinced that it's too difficult for you and that you will surely fail, chances are you will prove yourself right. Low self-concept is one of the most destructive forces in a student's life and the most formidable obstacle to learning. Expectation of success and a willingness to try, on the other hand, are a student's greatest strengths.

Perhaps one of the most useful concepts you can acquire as you set out to improve your academic performance is that you don't have to be a "genius" to succeed in school. You will find it quite safe to assume that you can do as well as anyone else if you will use your strong points and work to improve your weak ones. All schools, both high schools and colleges, are geared to the needs of average people. And usually, a hardworking average student will outperform a lazy "genius" every time. Some students have a habit of rationalizing the success of others and their own lack of success by saying, "I'm just not the academic type. I'm no genius and I'm not a grind like he is."

There are precious few geniuses among successful students. By and large, successful students are very average, ordinary people who make the most of whatever they have to bring to the task of learning.

An old cliché says: *Nothing succeeds like success*. Unfortunately, the opposite is also true: *Nothing fails like failure*. Once you have established a negative attitude, it feeds on itself until you become convinced that you can do nothing right and there's no use in trying. If, after taking honest stock of your attitude, you recognize a persistent lack of confidence in your ability to do well in school, you must resolve at once to change your outlook. If you can't do this by yourself, you should seek help from school counselors or from an understanding friend or relative. Many schools have specialists on their staff who deal with just this sort of problem because they recognize that

self-esteem and a healthy self-concept are important assets to learning.

READING AND COMMUNICATING

By now, you probably know in a general way if you are a good reader, a poor reader, or just fair. However, this should be part of the inventory of your strengths and weaknesses. It has been demonstrated time and again that good reading skills, learning and success in school go hand-in-hand.

So it is essential that you find out at once if your reading skills are up to dealing with the material you will be expected to learn from now on. If your reading skills are weak, you must take steps to improve them. If you read well, you should want to read better and to become a more versatile reader than you are now. You can use the reading skills inventory that follows this selection as a first step toward analyzing your reading.

Reading becomes more demanding as you go further in school. Not only do you encounter more difficult material, but you also are expected to read actively. That is, you are expected to evaluate and understand what you read, as well as absorb the information presented. Reading for learning is the sum of reading for information *and* reading for understanding. You should find out which skills you have now that will work for you in that direction, which you must strengthen, and which you must acquire.

If after taking an honest inventory of your reading skills you find you need help, seek it out. Your counselors can direct you. Most high schools and colleges, and many public and private community facilities, offer help in reading. Also, they are prepared to analyze your reading skills and prescribe a suitable remedial program for your needs. Don't shy away from help fearing that you will be branded stupid or inferior. The reason that reading clinics have been established on every progressive high school and college campus is that there is so much need for them. If you have a reading problem or you feel the need of a program to improve your reading skills, get help. You won't be alone.

On the other side of the coin, you must be able to communicate the knowledge you gain through reading. The saddest and most often heard complaint from students is: "I know it, but I can't explain it."

Sometimes, just improving reading and study habits solves this problem. Building vocabulary increases the number of words you have available to explain what you know. One of the selections later in this book deals with writing effectively, but if you recognize that you have a hard core problem, you should seek help. Again, most schools recognize writing deficiency as a common problem among students and provide facilities for diagnosis and help.

Faulty vision and substandard hearing are often causes of reading and communication difficulties that should not be overlooked. An eye test and a hearing test are essential parts of your inventory of strengths and weaknesses. Even if you have normal vision and hearing, you should check to make sure that you are using these precious learning receptors properly and not abusing them. A checklist is included at the end of this selection to direct your attention to possible trouble. However, your eyes and ears should be checked by a specialist periodically throughout your school career, and periodically afterward, so that the earliest signs of trouble may be noticed and attended to.

STUDY SKILLS

Some students have an intuitive feeling for doing the right things when they study. Other students stumble

into correct methods through trial and error. Unfortunately, the vast majority of students just don't know how to study efficiently and they suffer needlessly because of it. The problem? Usually no one has bothered to tell them the "tricks of the trade."

Use the study skills inventory following this selection to find out what you know about studying in general and about your own study habits in particular. Many of the selections in this book deal with specific study skills; you're told very explicitly *how to study*, and exercises are provided to help you get on the right track. But after that you are on your own; what you do with the suggestions is up to you.

We spoke earlier of attitudes. As you progress in high school and go from high school to college, you continually find yourself with new freedoms and new responsibilities that you must cope with. Consequently, the sooner that childhood attitudes give way to the demands of adulthood, the better off you will be. You are expected to shift your attitude from short-range to long-range goals and to understand the need for studying. You are suddenly in a serious situation, and your attitude must become more serious accordingly. In short, you are expected to mature.

If you mean to succeed in school, you must begin to consider why you are in school and for whose benefit. If you are in school only because you have to be there, because it's fashionable in your group, or because your parents insist on it, chances are you won't last long and you won't do very well. You won't have the motivation to study or the will to put up with the work it entails. For you to study effectively, your attitude must be that you are in school to learn because you feel that's what you ought to be doing and because it fits your long-range goals. Only then will the effort required to study seem worthwhile.

_____: Reading Time

_____: Reading Rate

_____: Score, Test A

_____: Score, Test B

_____: Total Score

_____%: Comprehension

COMPREHENSION TEST 1-A

Directions: The following passage, taken from the selection you have just read, has words omitted from it. Fill in each blank with the word that was omitted. Each blank filled correctly is worth two points. Ask your instructor if you may take credit for close synonyms. Enter your score in the box provided at the end of the selection. A list of the omitted words can be found on page 235.

If you were to begin a new job tomorrow, you would bring with you some basic strengths and weaknesses. Success or failure in your work would depend, to _____ great extent, on your ability to use your strengths
     1
_____ weaknesses to best advantage.
  2

Of utmost importance is your _____. A person who begins a job
       3
convinced that he _____ going to like it or sure that he is
        4
_____ to fail is exhibiting a weakness which can only
  5
_____ his success. On the other hand, a person who _____
  6   7
secure in his belief that he is probably as _____ of doing the work as
         8
anyone else and who _____ willing to make a cheerful attempt at
      9
it possesses _____ certain strength of purpose. Chances are he will
       10
do _____.
  11

Having the prerequisite skills for a particular job is _____ strength.
            12
Lacking those skills is obviously a weakness. A _____ who can't add
       13
or a carpenter who can't cut _____ straight line with a saw are hope-
      14
less cases.

This _____ has been designed to help you capitalize on the
     15
_____ and overcome the weaknesses that you bring to the
  16
_____ of learning. But in order to measure your development,
  17
_____ must first take stock of where you stand now.
  18
_____ we get further along in the book, we'll be _____ in
  19   20
some detail with specific processes for developing and _____ learning
          21
skills. However, as a beginning, you should pause _____ examine your
       22
present strengths and weaknesses in three areas _____ are critical to
       23
your success or failure in school: _____ attitude, your reading and
      24
communication skills, and your study _____.
      25

ATTITUDE

In his book *Why College Students Fail*, Dr. Robert Pitcher has defined under-achieving as *underbelieving* in oneself.

COMPREHENSION TEST 1-B

Directions: This is another passage from the selection, again with words omitted. Proceed as before, giving yourself two points for each blank filled correctly. Add this score to the one from Test A and enter your total score in the box at the end of the selection. Use the conversion table on page 254 to convert your *total* score to a comprehension percentage, and record that grade in the box also. A list of omitted words can be found on page 235.

STUDY SKILLS

Some students have an intuitive feeling for doing the right things when they study. Other students stumble into correct methods through trial and _____1_____. Unfortunately, the vast majority of students just don't know _____2_____ to study efficiently and they suffer needlessly because of _____3_____. The problem? Usually no one has bothered to tell _____4_____ the "tricks of the trade."

Use the study skills _____5_____ following this selection to find out what you know _____6_____ studying in general and about your own study habits _____7_____ particular. Many of the selections in this book deal _____8_____ specific study skills; you're told very explicitly *how* to _____9_____, and exercises are provided to help you get on _____10_____ right track. But after that you are on your _____11_____; what you do with the suggestions is up to _____12_____.

We spoke earlier of attitudes. As you progress in _____13_____ school and go from high school to college, you _____14_____ find yourself with new freedoms and new responsibilities that _____15_____ must cope with. Consequently, the sooner that childhood attitudes _____16_____ way to the demands of adulthood, the better off _____17_____ will be. You are expected to shift your attitude _____18_____ short-range to long-range goals and to understand _____19_____ need for studying. You are suddenly in a serious _____20_____, and your attitude must become more serious accordingly. In _____21_____, you are expected to mature.

If you mean to _____22_____ in school, you must begin to consider why you _____23_____ in school and for whose benefit. If you are _____24_____ school only because you have to be there, because _____25_____ fashionable in your group, or because your parents insist on it, chances are you won't last long and you won't do very well. You won't have the motivation to study or the will to put up with the work it entails.

READING INVENTORY

Directions: Rate yourself on the following reading habits and abilities. Put an X in the box which you feel best describes your usual performance. Scores below average indicate areas which need to be improved. (1 — Superior; 2 — Above Average; 3 — Average; 4 — Below Average; 5 — Poor)

	1	2	3	4	5
How would you rate your ability					
1. to read?	☐	☐	☐	☐	☐
2. to enjoy reading?	☐	☐	☐	☐	☐
3. to read fast?	☐	☐	☐	☐	☐
4. to understand material the first time you read it?	☐	☐	☐	☐	☐
5. to maintain a good vocabulary?	☐	☐	☐	☐	☐
6. to accurately summarize material you have just read?	☐	☐	☐	☐	☐
7. to read without moving your lips or pronouncing every word to yourself?	☐	☐	☐	☐	☐
8. to remember what you have read?	☐	☐	☐	☐	☐
9. to concentrate while you read?	☐	☐	☐	☐	☐
10. to use context (surrounding words) to help you understand new words?	☐	☐	☐	☐	☐
11. to recognize the main idea of what you are reading?	☐	☐	☐	☐	☐
12. to refer to a dictionary to check new or unfamiliar words as an integral part of your reading process?	☐	☐	☐	☐	☐
13. to use graphs and tables in a book?	☐	☐	☐	☐	☐
14. to skim certain materials rapidly when necessary?	☐	☐	☐	☐	☐
15. to understand and follow directions?	☐	☐	☐	☐	☐
16. to preview a chapter or lesson before you read it?	☐	☐	☐	☐	☐
17. to read actively, questioning passages and marking important points?	☐	☐	☐	☐	☐
18. to adjust your reading speed to suit the materials being read?	☐	☐	☐	☐	☐

STUDY HABITS INVENTORY

Directions: Consider each of the following questions carefully, and answer each with a *yes* or *no*. Those answers which fall in the *no* column indicate areas which need to be improved.

	Yes	No
1. Are you able to study for a sustained period (at least twenty minutes)?	☐	☐
2. Are you in the habit of getting right down to serious work at study time?	☐	☐
3. Do you arrange your study time and area so that distractions and interruptions are minimized?	☐	☐
4. Are you in the habit of reviewing each subject regularly during the term?	☐	☐
5. Do you prepare for examinations without cramming?	☐	☐
6. When preparing for exams, do you outline your course work?	☐	☐
7. Are you able to anticipate important topics that might be covered on exams?	☐	☐
8. Do you make it a habit to prepare possible answers to essay questions in advance?	☐	☐
9. Do you study regularly at a regular study time?	☐	☐
10. Do you schedule your time intelligently to cover all subjects?	☐	☐
11. Do you schedule social activities so that they won't interfere with studying?	☐	☐
12. Do you rest properly so that fatigue does not reduce efficiency?	☐	☐
13. Do you recognize the need to devote extra time to overlearn certain subjects?	☐	☐
14. Are you able to concentrate in class?	☐	☐
15. Are you able to listen while taking notes?	☐	☐
16. Do you use the library regularly?	☐	☐
17. Are you able to isolate and learn definitions?	☐	☐
18. Do you make it a habit to review daily for each class?	☐	☐

VISION CHECKLIST

Directions: Put an X in the box which best indicates how often you experience the difficulty asked about: 1 — Rarely; 2 — Occasionally; 3 — Frequently. Enlist the services of a friend to appraise those difficulties or symptoms which must be observed by others.

The more often you answer *frequently* (column 3), the more likely it is that you have a visual problem, and a complete examination would be prudent. Seek out the services of an eye specialist for a complete visual screening. These services are readily available today, even for those who cannot afford to pay. When in doubt, make it a point to talk to the doctor, nurse or other person in charge of health problems in your school.

	1	2	3
1. Do you hold your body rigid while viewing distant objects?	☐	☐	☐
2. Do you thrust your head forward or backward while viewing distant objects?	☐	☐	☐
3. Do you avoid work that requires close-up viewing?	☐	☐	☐
4. Are you unable to maintain attention?	☐	☐	☐
5. Does your mind tend to wander; do you daydream frequently?	☐	☐	☐
6. Do you tend to use only one eye at times?	☐	☐	☐
7. Do you habitually tilt your head to one side?	☐	☐	☐
8. Are you obliged to keep your head very close to your book or desk when reading or writing?	☐	☐	☐
9. Do you frown or scowl when reading or writing?	☐	☐	☐
10. Do your eyes blink uncontrollably?	☐	☐	☐
11. Do you rub your eyes?	☐	☐	☐
12. Do you tend to close one eye?	☐	☐	☐
13. Do you find yourself avoiding visually oriented tasks?	☐	☐	☐
14. Do you become nervous or irritable after periods of visual concentration?	☐	☐	☐
15. Do you become tired after reading?	☐	☐	☐
16. Do you lose your place while reading?	☐	☐	☐
17. Do you use your finger to keep your place while reading?	☐	☐	☐
18. Do you move your head back and forth (instead of your eyes) while reading?	☐	☐	☐
19. Do you forget what you have just read?	☐	☐	☐
20. Do you re-read lines just read?	☐	☐	☐
21. Do you return to the beginning of a line you have just read instead of to the next line?	☐	☐	☐
22. Do your eyes burn or itch while reading?	☐	☐	☐
23. Do you have blurred or double vision?	☐	☐	☐
24. Do you get headaches or dizzy spells during or after reading?	☐	☐	☐
25. Do you see rainbows around lights?	☐	☐	☐

ATTITUDE CHECKLIST

Directions: Consider each of the following questions carefully, and try to answer with an honest *yes* or *no*. If after careful consideration you can't make up your mind, mark that question *not sure*.

If you have more than just a few answers in the *yes* column, or many *not sure* answers, it would be a good idea for you to review your general attitude toward school. You should probably review your feelings and outlook with a school counselor or other professional, your parents, or a trusted confidant.

	Yes	No	Not Sure
1. Are you in school only because you have to be?	☐	☐	☐
2. Do you dislike more of your courses than you like?	☐	☐	☐
3. Do you dislike more of your teachers than you like?	☐	☐	☐
4. Do you arrive late or cut classes frequently?	☐	☐	☐
5. Are you certain there are some courses you will fail?	☐	☐	☐
6. Are you convinced you are frequently picked on or treated unfairly?	☐	☐	☐
7. Do you believe school is a waste of time?	☐	☐	☐
8. Are most of your classes boring?	☐	☐	☐
9. Does studying or homework upset you?	☐	☐	☐
10. Are you unable to bring yourself to study or do assignments?	☐	☐	☐
11. Are school and studying less important than most of the things you have to do?	☐	☐	☐
12. Are you grouchy, argumentative, belligerent, or difficult to get along with in school?	☐	☐	☐
13. Are you withdrawn or fearful in class?	☐	☐	☐
14. Do you arrive at midterm or final exams with massive amounts of work undone?	☐	☐	☐
15. Do you regularly miss assignment deadlines?	☐	☐	☐
16. Are you secretly pleased or relieved when others do poorly?	☐	☐	☐
17. Do you panic at exam time?	☐	☐	☐
18. Are you frequently absent with minor ailments or because you are tired?	☐	☐	☐
19. Do you rely on others for completing assignments?	☐	☐	☐
20. Do you actively seek excuses to miss class?	☐	☐	☐
21. Generally speaking, do you consider yourself a failure in school?	☐	☐	☐
22. Do you feel you are not as bright as most other students?	☐	☐	☐
23. Are you frequently "in trouble" at school?	☐	☐	☐
24. Do you feel that no one in school likes you?	☐	☐	☐
25. Do you snear at or make fun of students who do well?	☐	☐	☐

Reading Skills

Reading is a combination of several processes — physical, mechanical and mental — that you probably are not even conscious of. Eye movement, your eye-voice span and your sight vocabulary all contribute to how fast and how well you read. Knowing how these elements interact can help you develop better reading skills.

What Reading Is

Reading begins with the eyes. Before the mind can comprehend, the eyes must first apprehend. In other words, the net result of seeing words and understanding them is *reading*. In order to get the most benefit from a program of reading and study improvement, you should understand a little bit about how you see and recognize words when you read.

WHAT THE EYES SEE

1. **Eye Fixations.** The eyes do not move smoothly across a printed line, although it may seem as if they do for a good reader. The eyes move in jerks, making stop-and-go movements along the lines of print. The stops are called fixations, and only during these stops do you actually read. Your eyes move too quickly between fixations for any clear vision; they must stop, or fixate, in order to read words.

When you read, 90 to 95 percent of your time is spent fixating. The movement from one stop to the next is extremely rapid, taking less than 1/40 of a second in normal reading. This happens so quickly that you are usually unaware of anything but a smooth movement of your eyes across the page.

2. **Return Sweep.** At the end of each line, your eyes make a return sweep to the beginning of the next line. This motion is also rapid, usually taking less than 1/20 of a second, and must be done accurately for efficient reading. Inaccurate return sweeps occur when the eyes return to the beginning of the same line, when they skip a line, or when they miss the beginning of the next line.

3. **Regressions.** Sometimes your eyes move back for a second look at something you've already read. These movements are called regressions. Your eyes tend to regress when a word is missed the first time or when the meaning of a word or phrase is not clear.

In comparison studies of good and poor readers, the records consistently show that good readers make fewer fixations per line, since they see more words during each fixation, and make fewer regressions.

Eye movements, then, reveal certain characteristics of a reader's skill. It is possible for you to obtain a rough, informal measure of your own eye movements with the help of a friend.

Place a book flat on the table and position a mirror beside it. Sit beside each other facing the book. Have your friend observe your eye movements in the mirror as you read aloud. Read at least twenty lines so that an average count of fixations, regressions and return sweeps can be made.

One study has shown that fairly good student readers average six fixations a line and one regression every two lines and that 1/4 of a second is the average duration of each fixation. Compare your performance with these averages.

Since the eye movements of good readers are known and are recognized as indications of reading proficiency, visual training is often incorporated in reading improvement instruction. Its purpose is to teach students to enlarge the span of their fixations and improve the efficiency of eye movements.

However, the eyes will take in only as much as the mind can understand; so it is more accurate to think in terms of comprehension span. Just as important as pressing for shorter fixations and taking in greater gulps of words is the need for developing techniques which encourage reading for meaning. One way of doing this is to see words in thought groups by combining words meaningfully when reading. Exercises follow this selection which will give you practice in this kind of reading.

4. Eye-Voice Span. When you read aloud, your eyes normally read ahead of your voice. The number of words between a word being spoken and the word farthest along that can be seen at the same time makes up what is called the eye-voice span.

Good readers display a wide eye-voice span of about five words. Poor readers, on the other hand, possess a narrow span (one or two words) because they are reading word by word with little sense of what is coming next. To see how important this concept is to efficient reading, listen to a child read and notice how difficult it is to understand.

To measure your eye-voice span, have someone turn off the lights as you are reading orally. The number of words you can continue to say constitutes your eye-voice span. Studies have shown that individuals who display efficient eye movements in oral reading also tend to use efficient eye movements when reading silently.

Thus, the skills you develop in oral reading help you to read better silently. Practice in increasing eye-voice span is practice in seeing word groups intelligently and using context as an aid to meaning.

RECOGNIZING WORDS

Once you have seen the words, you must recognize or identify them before any comprehension can take place. This involves association, which, in fact, is the way you first learned to read. We have to be taught to associate our response to a spoken word with that same word when it is written. Reading is a controlled form of talking, with print substituted for spoken words:

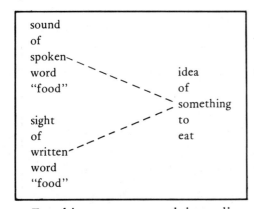

For this process to work in reading, the spoken word must mean something to us. A brand new word, or one that we don't recognize, won't mean anything to us written or spoken.

1. Phonics. When we are first taught to read, we learn to sound out words, to pronounce them. Once we say the word, we then recognize it as a word we know. It is the discovery of the pronunciation of words which makes reading possible. Simply defined, phonics are the sounds given to words by their letters.

By the time you finish high school, you probably can recognize more than 50,000 words when you hear them. Using your knowledge of phonics, you can identify a printed word as one of these.

Your knowledge of phonics begins with the sounds made by the vowels and consonants. Vowels give words their distinctive sounds, but they are not as important to word recognition as the consonants. Try reading the following sentences with the consonants left out and then with the vowels left out.

Consonants omitted:

I— i— —o— —a—— —o —ea— —o——— —i—e ——i—.

Vowels omitted:

—t —s n—t h—rd t— r——d w—rds l—k— th—s.

Even as a beginning reader, you cannot long escape some of the more complex problems of phonics. You must recognize short versus long vowels: *can* versus *cane*. You must learn the sounds produced by combinations of vowels: *round, fear, field, moon, rain.* You must learn that certain letter combinations produce their own sounds: *th*ing, *th*at, *ch*ance, *sh*ape, *ph*one. You must struggle with the peculiarities of the English language: *write, wright, right; through, enough; weather, whether.*

Following this selection, you will find an exercise which will check your skill with phonics. Any difficulty in completing the exercise quickly and accurately would suggest a phonics difficulty which needs to be corrected. If you suspect that you are weak in phonics, seek the advice of your instructor or a reading specialist. There are materials available that can help strengthen your skill.

2. Sight Vocabulary. The more they read, the more good readers build their sight vocabularies — words that can be recognized at a glance without sounding them out. In fact, it would be pure drudgery to read if every word had to be sounded out every time.

School children today are encouraged to learn lists of sight words. But some students, perhaps you are one, have never mastered the basic sight words. This causes stumbling and loss of meaning of some of the easiest words. Anyone with this problem obviously can't enjoy reading and faces real trouble in subjects with a heavy reading load.

A list of the 200 most common words in English follows this selection. Test yourself on them. If you discover a weakness, you must correct it; you will never enjoy reading if you don't. If necessary, build a set of flash cards from the list and practice with them until you can confidently and instantaneously recognize every word.

Naturally, the more words you can recognize on sight, the fewer you will have to sound out while you are reading.

Your reading, then, is a complex combination of physical, mechanical and mental processes. Strengthening your reading requires an awareness of each process and practice where you are weak. Serious problems in any one area can cause serious reading difficulties that you should take steps to correct at once.

_____: Reading Time

_____: Reading Rate

_____: Score, Test A

_____: Score, Test B

_____: Total Score

_____%: Comprehension

COMPREHENSION TEST 2-A

Directions: The following passage, taken from the selection you have just read, has words omitted from it. Fill in each blank with the word that was omitted. Each blank filled correctly is worth two points. Ask your instructor if you may take credit for close synonyms. Enter your score in the box provided at the end of the selection. A list of the omitted words can be found on page 235.

Reading begins with the eyes. Before the mind can comprehend, the eyes must first _____ . In other words, the net result of seeing words
1
_____ understanding them is *reading*. In order to get the
2
_____ benefit from a program of reading and study improvement,
3
_____ should understand a little bit about how you see
4
_____ recognize words when you read.
5

WHAT THE EYES SEE

1. _____ Fixations. The eyes do not move smoothly across a
6
_____ line, although it may seem as if they do _____ a
7   8
good reader. The eyes move in jerks, making _____-and-go movements
9
along the lines of print. The _____ are called fixations, and only
10
during these stops do _____ actually read. Your eyes move too
11
quickly between fixations _____ any clear vision; they must stop, or
12
fixate, in _____ to read words.
13

When you read, 90 to 95 _____ of your time is spent fixating. The
14
movement from _____ stop to the next is extremely rapid, taking
15
less _____ 1/40 of a second in normal reading. This happens
16
_____ quickly that you are usually unaware of anything but
17
_____ smooth movement of your eyes across the page.
18

2. **Return** _____ . At the end of each line, your eyes make
19
_____ return sweep to the beginning of the next line.
20
_____ motion is also rapid, usually taking less than 1/20
21
_____ a second, and must be done accurately for efficient
22
_____ . Inaccurate return sweeps occur when the eyes return to
23
_____ beginning of the same line, when they skip a _____ ,
24   25
or when they miss the beginning of the next line.

3. **Regressions.** Sometimes your eyes move back for a second look at something you've already read.

COMPREHENSION TEST 2-B

Directions: This is another passage from the selection, again with words omitted. Proceed as before, giving yourself two points for each blank filled correctly. Add this score to the one from Test A and enter your total score in the box at the end of the selection. Use the conversion table on page 254 to convert your *total* score to a comprehension percentage, and record that grade in the box also. A list of omitted words can be found on page 235.

Even as a beginning reader, you cannot long escape some of the more complex problems of phonics. You must recognize short versus long vowels: *can* vs. _____1_____. You must learn the sounds produced by combinations of _____2_____: *round, fear, field, moon, rain.* You must learn that _____3_____ letter combinations produce their own sounds: *th*ing, *th*at, *ch*ance, _____4_____, *ph*one. You must struggle with the peculiarities of the _____5_____ language: *write, wright, right; through, enough; weather, whether.*

Following _____6_____ selection, you will find an exercise which will check _____7_____ skill with phonics. Any difficulty in completing the exercise _____8_____ and accurately would suggest a phonics difficulty which needs _____9_____ be corrected. If you suspect that you are weak _____10_____ phonics, seek the advice of your instructor or a _____11_____ specialist. There are materials available that can help strengthen _____12_____ skill.

2. Sight Vocabulary. The more they read, the more _____13_____ readers build their sight vocabularies — words that can be _____14_____ at a glance without sounding them out. In fact, _____15_____ would be pure drudgery to read if every word _____16_____ to be sounded out every time.

School children today _____17_____ encouraged to learn lists of sight words. But some _____18_____, perhaps you are one, have never mastered the basic _____19_____ words. This causes stumbling and loss of meaning of _____20_____ of the easiest words. Anyone with this problem obviously _____21_____ enjoy reading and faces real trouble in subjects with _____22_____ heavy reading load.

A list of the 200 most _____23_____ words in English follows this selection. Test yourself on _____24_____. If you discover a weakness, you must correct it; _____25_____ will never enjoy reading if you don't. If necessary, build a set of flash cards from the list and practice with them until you can confidently and instantaneously recognize every word.

CHECKING YOUR PHONICS SKILL

Directions: Following is a list of just over 250 words that contain many of the sounds and letter combinations of the English language. The words range from hard to easy. It is not important to know what all the words mean, but you should be able to pronounce even the difficult words by "sounding them out."

Read all the words aloud to someone who you know is an expert reader. Read steadily at the rate of about one word per second. Have your listener count each time you stumble badly or make a mistake in pronunciation. If you have a strong regional dialect, try to get someone to listen to you who is familiar with the dialect. If you get more than 20 words wrong, you should consider checking your phonics skill with your instructor or a reading specialist.

Accomplice, acquittal, advisable, aerial, assault, batten, bearish, beckon, befriend, beguile, blight, blithe, bluish, bodkin, breath, breathe, bronchitis, Bronx, chasten, chastise.

Choctaw, choir, conception, concise, conspiracy, deal, dealt, debauch, deceit, diagnose, dichromatic, digitate, dreadnought, eaglet, eagre, ectoplasm, eczema, embarkation, encourage, endomorphism.

Epithet, espouse, exuberant, fiend, friend, fiery, flamboyant, flammable, forswear, frizzle, furor, fuse, gallivant, gambrel, gauze, gelatin, genteel, gentile, gentle, geyser.

Ghastly, gossamer, graphite, habituate, haughty, heliograph, hierarchy, honorific, hound, hourly, hypochondria, hypocrisy, ichthyology, idiot, idol, impartial, incest, incision, indigent, infectious.

Instantaneous, instinct, irate, irrational, itinerary, jactation, jigger, jocular, Jonah, Jonathan, jonquil, kindle, kindliness, kinky, knapsack, knave, lactation, Lancelot, league, legislate.

Liquefy, localize, lustily, macabre, magnetite, manageable, mercerize, meridian, militaristic, mobilize, modulation, monstrous, morphine, million, mullion, multiplicity, narcotic, nestle, neurologist, neutral.

Nomenclature, notorious, numerator, observant, obsolete, occident, oceanographic, officiate, omnifarious, Omsk, optimistic, orangutan, ostensible, ouster, oyster, pacify, penumbra, phone, phoneme, phosphorous.

Piquant, plasma, platitude, pleasant, please, plethora, polyphonic, potential, poultry, precept, percept, precipitous, prestige, privilege, profuse, pudgy, pueblo, pyrex, quagmire, qualm.

Quibble, quinine, quit, quite, quittance, quotidian, rabid, rabies, raillery, rancor, rankle, ravine, reciprocal, reciprocity, recoup, redouble, regency, regurgitation, reinsure, represent.

Resonant, riddance, rifle, righteous, ritual, robust, rookery, rooty, roust, rudimentary, rummage, rustler, sacrosanct, satire, savior, scarlet, scholar, scintillate, secession, shambles.

Shrubby, skirmish, slattern, sleuth, smirk, snaggletoothed, solicitous, spectroscope, squelch, stagger, stalwart, strategic, strontium, surgeon, swerve, sword, synchronize, tactic, tactician, talkative.

Taut, technique, temple, Teutonic, thatch, thence, thermocouple, thrombus, tract, tranquil, tubercular, tweak, twinkle, tyrant, ultimate, unassuming, unique, universal, unusual, uranium.

Vague, valvular, vellum, velocipede, vicar, vulcanize, wag, wager, waggery, wayward, weigh, whelp, wherewithal, whether, whither, wrestle, wretch, wrought, xylophone, yawl, youthful, zephyr, zither, Zurich, zygote.

CHECKING EYE-VOICE SPAN

Directions: In order to read the following sentences aloud and have them make sense, you have to be looking ahead of the words being spoken. Certain ambiguous words will cause you to misread if you do not have a sense of the rest of the sentence.

Do not study the sentences before you read them; simply read them out loud in their most meaningful way.

1. Make a bow to the audience when you finish.
2. Make a bow to shoot the arrows.
3. Make a bow out of pretty ribbon to wrap the package.
4. Read aloud, stories are more enjoyable for most people.
5. Read aloud for greater enjoyment of most stories.
6. John, said his mother, is at the library.
7. John said his mother is in the kitchen preparing dinner.
8. Proceed to the nearest exit in the event of fire.
9. Proceeds all go to charity.
10. The merchants were forced to close down following the hurricane.
11. Close by the river stood an old shack.
12. His conduct left much to be desired.
13. To conduct an orchestra requires much study and musical competence.
14. A duplicate key can be made by any locksmith in a few minutes.
15. To duplicate that feat is impossible for most people.
16. Perfect timing is essential for participating in many sports.
17. Perfect the model before you go into production.
18. A contest will determine the winner.
19. Do you plan to contest the decision of the judges?
20. A live-and-let-live attitude prevailed among the inhabitants of the area.
21. A live wire can give a nasty shock.
22. Lead the parade down Main Street past the reviewing stand.
23. Lead paint, which is harmful if swallowed, has been taken off the market.
24. Lead time for new product development is at least six months.
25. The road winds up the side of the mountain.
26. Summer winds blow across the lake in the evening.
27. Wind the watch each morning before putting it on your wrist.
28. The mayor was present at the ceremony.
29. We are proud to present this award to you.
30. Mouth and lip exercises improve diction.
31. Mouth and speak each syllable clearly.
32. Do you object to the many interruptions that occur?
33. Put the object down on the table and stand back.
34. Separate ways are sometimes better.
35. Separate and meet back here in one hour.

READING IN THOUGHT GROUPS

Directions: Good readers, as you have learned, read several words during each fixation. Instead of reading word by word, they group words into meaningful phrases. You can develop the same skill. Practice reading aloud the material below. It has been segmented into meaning or thought groups for you. As you read, try to visualize each group as a unit. Strive to apply the same technique to all your reading.

Cramming has been called "the much-practiced educational crime" along with other nasty names. I cannot say that I am wholly in favor of it. But I do think that a certain type of person should cultivate the cramming habit. A debater frequently needs to work up a subject quickly. A lawyer is often called upon to prepare a brief in a hurry. A student who hasn't studied all year must pass a final examination. When the pressure is on, these people have to produce. What better way is there to do it than by brief periods of intensive study?

Obviously, all this work must be done quickly, and after the performance on the rostrum, in court, or in examination, the knowledge so quickly gained can be more quickly forgotten. Cramming fits the need in each case. Moreover, it reveals a person's cleverness and shows what he can accomplish when his back is to the wall and it is a question of "do or die," flunk or pass.

Cramming benefits the lazy student, but it is of even greater value to the industrious student. He has been studying the matter regularly. Cramming, for him, becomes another review. He has studied the subject until he understands it. Now he is going over it again so that he will not forget it. This is important. If you wish to retain material for any length of time, you should not only learn, but overlearn; that is, learn it over and above the amount necessary for mastery. Just as you tie a rope with an extra knot and drive a nail with an extra clout to prevent loosening, so also you should intensively review material until it is firmly fixed in the mind.

On the other hand, the disadvantages of cramming, when it is made a substitute for previous work, are evident. First of all, I am convinced that the average student who has neglected study during the year cannot possibly pass final examinations by cramming. If he does pass, it is either by accident or because of the teacher's generosity. In the case of the more talented student, cramming before examinations without previous study does get results if just passing is the result desired. But it also clogs the mental processes, causes intellectual constipation, and tells us something about the character of the student.

Again, cramming is a system of rapid memorization. As such, it cannot be a sound method of studying. It violates many sound processes, such as thinking reflectively, maintaining a critical attitude, relating new material to old, and working in a thorough, painstaking way. It substitutes haste for care, superficiality for thoroughness, and rote memory for reasoning.

BASIC SIGHT WORDS

Directions: The following list contains the 200 most frequently used words in the English language, ranked according to their frequency of occurrence.[1]

Using a card, briefly expose each word on the list in turn. You should be able to recognize each word with just a brief glance at it. Check and study those words where recognition was doubtful or in error. Every word on the list should become part of your permanent sight vocabulary.

1. the	41. there	81. my	121. name	161. such
2. of	42. use	82. than	122. good	162. because
3. and	43. an	83. first	123. sentence	163. turned
4. a	44. each	84. water	124. man	164. here
5. to	45. which	85. been	125. think	165. why
6. in	46. she	86. called	126. say	166. asked
7. is	47. do	87. who	127. great	167. went
8. you	48. how	88. oil	128. where	168. men
9. that	49. their	89. its	129. help	169. read
10. it	50. if	90. now	130. through	170. need
11. he	51. will	91. find	131. much	171. land
12. was	52. up	92. long	132. before	172. different
13. for	53. other	93. down	133. line	173. home
14. on	54. about	94. day	134. right	174. us
15. are	55. out	95. did	135. too	175. move
16. as	56. many	96. get	136. means	176. try
17. with	57. then	97. come	137. old	177. kind
18. his	58. them	98. made	138. any	178. hand
19. they	59. these	99. may	139. same	179. picture
20. I	60. so	100. part	140. tell	180. again
21. at	61. some	101. over	141. boy	181. change
22. be	62. her	102. new	142. following	182. off
23. this	63. would	103. sound	143. came	183. play
24. have	64. make	104. take	144. want	184. spell
25. from	65. like	105. only	145. show	185. air
26. or	66. him	106. little	146. also	186. away
27. one	67. into	107. work	147. around	187. animals
28. had	68. time	108. know	148. form	188. house
29. by	69. has	109. place	149. three	189. point
30. words	70. look	110. years	150. small	190. page
31. but	71. two	111. live	151. set	191. letters
32. not	72. more	112. me	152. put	192. mother
33. what	73. write	113. back	153. end	193. answer
34. all	74. go	114. give	154. does	194. found
35. were	75. see	115. most	155. another	195. study
36. we	76. number	116. very	156. well	196. still
37. when	77. no	117. after	157. large	197. learn
38. your	78. way	118. things	158. must	198. should
39. can	79. could	119. our	159. big	199. American
40. said	80. people	120. just	160. even	200. world

[1]The 3,000 most frequently used words are listed in *3,000 Instant Words* by E. Sakiey and E. Fry (Jamestown Publishers).

> Good readers preview everything; they become familiar with the content and know what to expect before beginning to read. Previewing is one of the most important reading techniques you can learn.

How to Preview when Reading

This is the era of the shortcut, the day of the easy way. Practically anything you want to do or learn is explained in a how-to-do-it guide. Everywhere you look, you discover manuals with inviting titles letting you in on secret techniques for easy accomplishment. Check any bookstore and you'll see them: *Spelling Made Easy, Chess in Ten Easy Lessons, How to Make a Million in the Stock Market,* and so on.

You are not likely to be taken in by such titles because you have probably learned over the years that shortcuts to learning don't really exist. What we have achieved, we have gained through hard work.

Therefore, you will be skeptical when I suggest that there is a single, easily-learned technique which can make you a more effective reader immediately. It's true, however, and this selection will discuss it and encourage you to adopt it. It is the Preview.

You've heard of the Preview (or the Survey, as it is also called) if you've ever enrolled in a reading course because it is a part of every successful program. That this is so attests to its value as a reading tool.

WHAT IS THE PREVIEW?

The Preview is a visual survey of a chapter, article, selection or, in some cases, book prior to reading. Its purpose is to acquaint a reader with the content of the material to be read so that he knows what to expect.

In some respects, previewing is like consulting a road map before taking a trip. You know that it's not essential to use a map to get where you're going. You can start out, follow the signs, take the roads as they come, and you will reach your destination. But, checking the map first eliminates uncertainty and doubt concerning the route; you proceed more confidently knowing what to expect. Previewing accomplishes the same end: you can read an article without previewing, but previewing gives you a chance to anticipate what is coming. Thus, you proceed down the road to comprehension with greater confidence.

You perform better at any job when you have some advance knowledge of what it is you will have to do and what you may expect to encounter along the way. Even digging a hole in the ground can be done more efficiently if you know in advance whether the soil is sandy, muddy or rocky and you are prepared for it.

When a coach briefs his team in advance about the strengths, weaknesses and style of the opposition, the team plays better knowing what to expect. A new tennis player will learn the game faster and better after watching expert players and gaining some advance idea of what the game is all about.

From your own experience you are aware that you read better, faster, and with greater comprehension when you are reading about something that is familiar. When something is familiar, you approach it comfortably and with greater confidence. The confidence comes from preliminary knowledge and understanding. Things unknown and totally unfamiliar are frightening and intimidating.

So when we read something new and unfamiliar without taking the time to become acquainted with the nature of the material, we often say that it is dull and uninteresting when what we really mean is that we are lost in a strange place and are a little frightened.

Much of what you have to read in school is hard, slow reading. Comprehension comes with effort, and retention is at a minimum all because study reading deals with new and unfamiliar subjects. The Preview, therefore, is especially valuable to you as a student because it gives you some background in a new field, serves to put you on somewhat familiar ground and takes much of the uncertainty out of what you have to do.

You are certainly aware by now that your textbooks have not been thrown together without plan or organization. Material that is going to be published and presented to students has to be carefully researched, outlined, written, edited and rewritten if it is to do its job — communicate clearly to the reader. With the proper kind of survey, you can discover the author's organization and, as a result, organize your reading plan.

All of this should suggest to you the reason for the popularity and effectiveness of previewing. When properly applied, you will find that it is the single most important reading tool that you can acquire.

HOW TO PREVIEW

1. **See the Big Picture.** The purpose of previewing is to gain an overall impression of the reading selection. You are not interested in details or specifics at this time. Think of a jigsaw puzzle. Previewing is like looking at a picture of the assembled puzzle. You keep the picture in mind so that you can fit the pieces together intelligently.

2. **Read the Title.** You probably do this anyway before reading, but as a step to previewing, be alert for what you can learn from the title. Frequently you can learn not only the writer's subject, but also how he feels about it.

Lester David once wrote an article entitled "The Natural Inferiority of Women." From this it should be easy to infer what his position might be regarding women's rights. You have learned something about the author's feelings about his subject. Consequently, you would expect this article to present arguments supporting his position and illustrations reinforcing his case. Having seen just the title prepares you to approach the selection intelligently.

Another article, written by Mark Clifton, bore the title "The Dread Tomato Addiction." A moment's deliberation would suggest to the reader that humor would be a recurring aspect of the account.

3. Read the Subhead. In textbooks, especially, and in popular magazines as well, subheads are presented following the title to provide a little advance information about the subject. In texts, the subhead is frequently a brief digest of the chapter, stating what the lesson is all about. In magazines, subheads are used as teasers to entice the reader and arouse his curiosity.

4. Read Illustrations. When a picture or illustration accompanies an article, don't just admire it, *read* it. Study it to learn what you can about the content of the lesson. Many preschool children are quite adept at "reading" the pictures in their storybooks. They've learned that good illustrations are much more than pretty pictures.

When maps, charts or graphs are given, stop for a moment and interpret them. These visual aids are used to portray several facts and, at the same time, to show a relationship among them. Complex, interrelated facts and ideas, sometimes requiring hundreds of words to describe verbally, can be clearly and more efficiently taught through a chart or diagram. The Chinese have said that a picture is worth ten thousand words. The wise reader gives visual aids the attention they deserve.

5. Read the First Paragraph. The first paragraph is the author's opening, his first opportunity to address the reader. This is called the introductory paragraph because it is exactly that: an introduction to the subject by the author. Opening paragraphs are

used in various ways. Some authors announce what they plan to present in the paragraphs to follow. Others tell why they have written this article or chapter; what their purpose is; why this is important to the reader; what they hope to accomplish. Still other writers will do what speakers do: start off with a story or anecdote to set the stage. This provides the setting or mood they need to present their material.

6. Read the Closing Paragraph. The next step in previewing is to skip to the final paragraph and read it. If the author has any final remarks or closing thoughts to leave with the reader, here is where they'll come. If the writer wishes to reemphasize or restate his main point, he will do it here. Because this is the concluding paragraph, you'll often find a short summary of what has gone before.

7. Skim Through. To complete your preview, skim quickly through the chapter to see what else you can learn. Be on the watch for headings and numbers indicating important divisions in the presentation. You may learn, for example, that the selection will discuss five major aspects of the subject. Knowing this will help you as you read. Find out whatever else you can about the structure and organization of the selection.

Starting now, make it a firm rule: preview everything before you read. It will be hard at first to bring yourself to take the two or three minutes that previewing requires. The old habit of starting to read with the first word has been with you for years. But without doubt the Preview is the most important reading technique available to you. As a good previewer, you will find that you can learn more from an assignment in five minutes of active previewing than a non-previewer who takes an hour to plod through every word without the least idea of what he is trying to learn or what it is he is seeking to understand.

_____: Reading Time

_____: Reading Rate

_____: Score, Test A

_____: Score, Test B

_____: Total Score

_____%: Comprehension

COMPREHENSION TEST 3-A

Directions: The following passage, taken from the selection you have just read, has words omitted from it. Fill in each blank with the word that was omitted. Each blank filled correctly is worth two points. Ask your instructor if you may take credit for close synonyms. Enter your score in the box provided at the end of the selection. A list of the omitted words can be found on page 235.

WHAT IS THE PREVIEW?

The Preview is a visual survey of a chapter, article, selection or, in some cases, book prior to reading. Its purpose is to acquaint a reader with the _____(1)_____ of the material to be read so that he _____(2)_____ what to expect.

In some respects, previewing is like _____(3)_____ a road map before taking a trip. You know _____(4)_____ it's not essential to use a map to get _____(5)_____ you're going. You can start out, follow the signs, _____(6)_____ the roads as they come, and you will reach _____(7)_____ destination. But, checking the map first eliminates uncertainty and _____(8)_____ concerning the route; you proceed more confidently knowing what _____(9)_____ expect. Previewing accomplishes the same end: you can read _____(10)_____ article without previewing, but previewing gives you a chance _____(11)_____ anticipate what is coming. Thus, you proceed down the _____(12)_____ to comprehension with greater confidence.

You perform better at _____(13)_____ job when you have some advance knowledge of what _____(14)_____ is you will have to do and what you _____(15)_____ expect to encounter along the way. Even digging a _____(16)_____ in the ground can be done more efficiently if _____(17)_____ know in advance whether the soil is sandy, muddy _____(18)_____ rocky and you are prepared for it.

When a _____(19)_____ briefs his team in advance about the strengths, weaknesses _____(20)_____ style of the opposition, the team plays better knowing _____(21)_____ to expect. A new tennis player will learn the _____(22)_____ faster and better after watching expert players and gaining _____(23)_____ advance idea of what the game is all about.

_____(24)_____ your own experience you are aware that you read _____(25)_____, faster, and with greater comprehension when you are reading about something that is familiar. When something is familiar, you approach it comfortably and with greater confidence.

COMPREHENSION TEST 3-B

Directions: This is another passage from the selection, again with words omitted. Proceed as before, giving yourself two points for each blank filled correctly. Add this score to the one from Test A and enter your total score in the box at the end of the selection. Use the conversion table on page 254 to convert your *total* score to a comprehension percentage, and record that grade in the box also. A list of omitted words can be found on page 236.

5. Read the First Paragraph. The first paragraph is the author's opening, his first opportunity to address the reader. This is called the introductory paragraph because it is _____1_____ that: an introduction to the subject by the author. _____2_____ paragraphs are used in various ways. Some authors announce _____3_____ they plan to present in the paragraphs to follow. _____4_____ tell why they have written this article or chapter; _____5_____ their purpose is; why this is important to the _____6_____; what they hope to accomplish. Still other writers will _____7_____ what speakers do: start off with a story or _____8_____ to set the stage. This provides the setting or _____9_____ they need to present their material.

6. Read the Closing _____10_____. The next step in previewing is to skip to _____11_____ final paragraph and read it. If the author has _____12_____ final remarks or closing thoughts to leave with the _____13_____, here is where they'll come. If the writer wishes _____14_____ reemphasize or restate his main point, he will do _____15_____ here. Because this is the concluding paragraph, you'll often _____16_____ a short summary of what has gone before.

7. Skim _____17_____. To complete your preview, skim quickly through the chapter _____18_____ see what else you can learn. Be on the _____19_____ for headings and numbers indicating important divisions in the _____20_____. You may learn, for example, that the selection will _____21_____ five major aspects of the subject. Knowing this will _____22_____ you as you read. Find out whatever else you _____23_____ about the structure and organization of the selection.

Starting _____24_____, make it a firm rule: preview everything before you _____25_____. It will be hard at first to bring yourself to take the two or three minutes that previewing requires.

STEPS TO PREVIEWING

Directions: From now on we want you to preview everything before you read. Previewing is the single most important technique you can adopt to improve your reading ability. The steps to previewing are summarized below. Study and learn them. Apply them to all your reading and study matter.

Step 1. Read the Title. Discover what the subject will be and how it will be presented. Try to see how the writer feels toward his subject, what special views he proposes.	**Step 4. Read First Paragraph.** An author's opening is his first opportunity to address the reader. See what insights he offers, what assistance and advice he gives his reader.
Step 2. Read the Subhead. Subheads are included to give the reader a brief digest of the chapter. Most often used in textbooks, they are an important aid to organization.	**Step 5. Read Last Paragraph.** The final paragraph is the author's last chance to reach his reader. Whatever final advice or information he has to give will appear here. Look for it.
Step 3. Study Illustrations. Maps, charts, tables, graphs, diagrams and pictures all help the reader visualize some of the important elements of the chapter or lesson. Study them.	**Step 6. Skim Through.** As a final preparation for reading, skim the entire chapter. Look for keys to organization; see how the presentation is structured and arranged.

PRACTICE PREVIEWING

Practice Exercise 1

Directions: The titles listed below are from Daniel J. Boorstin's famous historical trilogy. Answer the following questions about each title.

a. What subject matter do you think is included under each title?
b. Think of at least three facts that you know about the subject.
c. What does the author imply in each title?
d. What would you expect to learn from the subject matter?

1. Volume Title: *The Americans: The Colonial Experience*
2. Book One: *The Vision and the Reality*
3. Part Four: "Transplanters: The Virginians"
4. Chapter 17:   "English Gentlemen, American Style"
5. Chapter 19:   "Government by Gentry"
6. Chapter 23:   "Citizens of Virginia"

Practice Exercise 2

Directions: Examine several pictures in any textbook and read the captions. Then answer the following questions about each picture:

a. What are at least three facts conveyed by the picture?
b. What are at least two facts conveyed by the caption?
c. What do you expect to learn from the subject matter that is related to the picture?

Practice Exercise 3

Directions: Read each of the following opening and closing statements. After reading each statement, answer these questions:

a. What is the article about?
b. What do you already know about the subject?
c. What do you hope to learn about the subject from the article?

1. "The number of calories used by the body each day to maintain present weight is called the daily caloric need."
2. "The key to fighting forest fires successfully lies in speed of attack."
3. "The American colonies might not have had the needed strength to implement the Declaration of Independence without the aid of France."
4. "The winter of 1886 was the bitterest in memory. Thousands of cattle starved and froze to death on the plains. The cattle bonanza was over."
5. ". . . during the years between 1940 and 1945. The final verdict, however, would have to wait until the postwar period, when the soldiers came home . . . and the country attempted to decide where women belonged in a normal social order."

> Because verbal ability and knowledge of word meanings are identifying qualities of an educated person, students will want to acquire the specialized terminology of each subject. The rewards for such effort are higher grades and greater understanding of the subject. The use of contextual aids and familiarity with affixes and roots are two aids for promoting word growth.

Building Vocabulary

There is a vital connection between language and learning ability and between good grades and the ability to communicate your thoughts clearly and accurately.

An academic curriculum incorporates many subjects, each of which is characterized by its own vocabulary of specialized terms. These terms must be understood if the subject is to be mastered.

All teachers, when evaluating and grading students, reward those who can express their understanding of key concepts and fundamental facts clearly and concisely. Students display this kind of understanding through their use of appropriate terminology. Thus, familiarity with the vocabulary of a subject opens the avenues of communication between student and teacher.

This is not to say that random flaunting of specialized terms will deceive instructors, but it stands to reason that as you acquire the vocabulary of a subject, you will also be accumulating fundamental knowledge in that field. This becomes the base on which new learning is acquired and assimilated during your regular study.

It is a fact that familiar material is more easily read and understood than new material. This explains why we all tend to read articles in our field of interest with ease; we already have the necessary background of information. And this also explains why we sometimes find new subjects dull and uninteresting. Learning the basic vocabulary of a subject gives us a foundation to build on and assures that our study of that field will be profitable.

SPECIALIZED LISTS

The two prime sources of words for your specialized lists are your instructors and your textbooks.

Listen during class lectures for the words the speaker repeats and emphasizes. These are likely candidates. Identifying key words will present no problem because experienced lecturers understand the limitations of their listeners. They know that major points need the emphasis of repeated exposure. What would be in bold print in a textbook must be conveyed to students verbally. Be alert for unusual inflection and stress which may be given to certain words. These are considered important by the lecturer. Especially important terms are often written on the blackboard.

Listen to questions asked by the speaker. Oral quizzing is often used to draw greater attention to important points under discussion.

Another clue to identifying important words and ideas may be found in the length of time devoted to discussion of a single topic. Important points deserve more time.

When you discover that a major term is being presented, try to record the exact definition or explanation given. Being a specialist, your instructor will use precise terminology when defining a concept. Be sure to capture new words exactly as they are used. Indicate with an asterisk or star in your notes that here is a word for your specialized list.

Another source of specialized terms is your textbook. Alert readers soon discover that a chapter frequently hinges on only five or six major concepts. Often there are key words associated with these concepts; these are the words to collect and learn.

Such words are often highlighted in bold print or headlines. If you need additional assurance, refer to questions or other types of summaries that frequently appear at the end of the chapter. These summaries will emphasize major points, the ones the writer wants you to understand and remember.

When you have located the important terms for the unit you are studying, write them down with

accompanying definitions and explanations. As you read through the chapter, try to understand these new words and the concepts they represent as fully as you can. If you are not satisfied, following your first reading, that your understanding is complete, it may be necessary to re-read parts of the chapter.

Frequently, these same words will be the ones that are emphasized in class. When this is the case, the instructor will often explain the new terms in words different from those in the text. Be alert to catch these variances because they enrich the meaning of an idea, often increasing its significance for you and making it easier to understand.

A bonus aspect of having studied and learned a term *before* class is that the speaker's remarks now make more sense to you. You will also find that your mind will wander less because of the greater interest and understanding that advanced knowledge fosters.

USING SPECIALIZED LISTS

You will naturally want your lists of specialized terms to be readily accessible and easy to use when you need them. There are different ways to accomplish this.

Some students list each word on its own 3x5 card along with the definition and an explanation. The cards can be filed alphabetically or by unit. Words recorded in this fashion are easily sorted, located and reviewed.

Others prefer to use their notebooks. This arrangement allows new terms to be recorded close to the notes accompanying the lecture or chapter where the new terms were first used. Words catalogued this way make reviewing easier since you are able to use your knowledge of the terms as an aid to recall important concepts from the lecture or text.

Each night new terms should be studied during the review and memorization segment of your study period. The words will then be fresh in your mind for class the following day.

Periodically (before midterm examinations, for example) all specialized terms should be reviewed and studied. It is prudent at this time to attempt to write the definition of each term from memory. It is important to recall the exact wording since precise definitions are more useful to you both in understanding the subject matter and for demonstrating your understanding to your instructor.

OTHER WORD STUDY

Studying word lists is not the only (nor necessarily the best) method of developing vocabulary. Here are two other ways to study new words.

1. Contextual Aids. By seeing a word in context, we come to know it better and better with every exposure. At first, the word becomes part of our reading vocabulary. This means that we have seen it often enough to recognize it and remember its meaning. Many words remain just in our reading vocabulary. Other new words are repeated in print often enough for us to come to know them well; these words are then assimilated into our writing vocabulary. In effect, we are confident enough to use the word in our writing. When a word finally becomes totally familiar, it may join our speaking vocabulary.

When read in context, words often have different shades of meaning that are imperceptible when read cold from a list. A simple word like *root*, for example, has at least 22 different meanings. The word *perception* has very different meanings in law and in psychology. You can't even know how to pronounce *precedent*, let alone know its meaning, without seeing how it is being used. And the only way to avoid the confusion between words like *precept* and *percept* is to learn them in context.

Further, relating a word to the way it is used increases our understanding not only of the word, but also of the idea the word represents. Consequently, words learned through context are more permanent than those learned from lists.

2. Affixes and Roots. Still another kind of word study centers around prefixes, suffixes and roots. Because both prefixes and suffixes are added to words, they are collectively called affixes.

A prefix is added to the beginning of a word and it causes a change in the meaning of that word. For example, the prefix *un-*, when added to a word like *happy*, gives the word a completely opposite meaning.

Suffixes are added to the ends of words. Although they do not affect the basic meaning of a word, suffixes frequently alter its part of speech. For example, a verb, *hate*, can become an adjective, *hateful*, when a suffix is added.

Word roots are often Latin and Greek stems on which many of our English words are based. *Bio*, which means *life*, is a Greek root word. From it we get such English words as *biology, antibiotic*, etc.

Through the study of affixes and roots, you can get a better "feel" for the meaning of many new words. Understanding how a word has acquired its particular meaning makes it much more likely that the word will become a part of your vocabulary. Check each new word you encounter in a good dictionary. The origin of the root of the word is usually explained.

Following this lesson you will find lists of common affixes and roots and exercises designed to help make these word parts work for you. When you do the exercises, try to learn and remember the various affixes and roots being illustrated. As you become more familiar with words — their origins (etymology) and their formative parts — you will find that new and difficult words will be much less discouraging when you meet them.

Effective word use distinguishes the educated person. Throughout life, we are judged and evaluated on the basis of our ability to communicate. Since you have the opportunity now to develop your vocabulary, start at once by using the means suggested in this selection and make words the servants of your mind.

_____: Reading Time

_____: Reading Rate

_____: Score, Test A

_____: Score, Test B

_____: Total Score

_____%: Comprehension

COMPREHENSION TEST 4-A

Directions: The following passage, taken from the selection you have just read, has words omitted from it. Fill in each blank with the word that was omitted. Each blank filled correctly is worth two points. Ask your instructor if you may take credit for close synonyms. Enter your score in the box provided at the end of the selection. A list of the omitted words can be found on page 236.

There is a vital connection between language and learning ability and between good grades and the ability to communicate your thoughts clearly and accurately.

An academic curriculum incorporates many subjects, each of which _____ characterized by its own vocabulary of specialized terms. These

        1

_____ must be understood if the subject is to be _____.

        2   3

All teachers, when evaluating and grading students, reward those _____ can express their understanding of key concepts and

        4

fundamental _____ clearly and concisely. Students display this kind

        5

of understanding _____ their use of appropriate terminology. Thus,

        6

familiarity with the _____ of a subject opens the avenues of

        7

communication between _____ and teacher.

        8

This is not to say that random _____ of specialized terms will

        9

deceive instructors, but it stands _____ reason that as you acquire

        10

the vocabulary of a _____, you will also be accumulating fundamental

        11

knowledge in that _____. This becomes the base on which new

        12

learning is _____ and assimilated during your regular study.

        13

It is a _____ that familiar material is more easily read and

        14

understood _____ new material. This explains why we all tend to

        15

_____ articles in our field of interest with ease; we _____

        16   17

have the necessary background of information. And this also _____

        18

why we sometimes find new subjects dull and uninteresting. _____

        19

the basic vocabulary of a subject gives us a _____ to build on and

        20

assures that our study of _____ field will be profitable.

        21

SPECIALIZED LISTS

The two prime _____ of words for your specialized lists are your

        22

instructors _____ your textbooks.

        23

Listen during class lectures for the words _____ speaker repeats and

        24

emphasizes. These are likely candidates. Identifying _____ words will

        25

present no problem because experienced lecturers understand the limitations of their listeners. They know that major points need the emphasis of repeated exposure.

Directions: This is another passage from the selection, again with words omitted. Proceed as before, giving yourself two points for each blank filled correctly. Add this score to the one from Test A and enter your total score in the box at the end of the selection. Use the conversion table on page 254 to convert your *total* score to a comprehension percentage, and record that grade in the box also. A list of omitted words can be found on page 236.

2. **Affixes and Roots.** Still another kind of word study centers around prefixes, suffixes and roots. Because both prefixes and suffixes are added to words, _____ are collectively called affixes.
$$1$$

A prefix is added to _____ beginning of a word and it causes a change _____ the meaning of that word. For example, the prefix
$$2 \qquad 3$$
_____, when added to a word like *happy*, gives the _____
$$4 \qquad 5$$
a completely opposite meaning.

Suffixes are added to the _____ of words. Although they do not
$$6$$
affect the basic _____ of a word, suffixes frequently alter its part of
$$7$$
_____. For example, a verb, *hate*, can become an adjective,
$$8$$
_____, when a suffix is added.
$$9$$

Word roots are often _____ and Greek stems on which many of our
$$10$$
English _____ are based. *Bio*, which means *life*, is a Greek
$$11$$
_____ word. From it we get such English words as _____,
$$12 \qquad 13$$
antibiotic, etc.

Through the study of affixes and roots, _____ can get a better
$$14$$
"feel" for the meaning of _____ new words. Understanding how a
$$15$$
word has acquired its _____ meaning makes it much more likely that
$$16$$
the word _____ become a part of your vocabulary. Check each new
$$17$$
_____ you encounter in a good dictionary. The origin of
$$18$$
_____ root of the word is usually explained.
$$19$$

Following this _____ you will find lists of common affixes and
$$20$$
roots _____ exercises designed to help make these word parts work
$$21$$
_____ you. When you do the exercises, try to learn _____
$$22 \qquad 23$$
remember the various affixes and roots being illustrated. As _____
$$24$$
become more familiar with words — their origins (etymology) and
_____ formative parts — you will find that new and difficult words
$$25$$
will be much less discouraging when you meet them.

Effective word use distinguishes the educated person.

COMMON PREFIXES

	Prefix	Meaning	Examples
1.	ab-	away or from	abhor, absent
2.	ad-	to or toward	advance, adhere
3.	ante-	before	anteroom, antebellum
4.	anti-	against	antibiotic, antisocial
5.	bi-	two or twice	bicycle, bisect
6.	circum-	around	circumference, circumvent
7.	com-, con-	together or with	combine, connect
8.	contra-	against	contrary, contradict
9.	de-	down from	descend, degrade
10.	dia-	through or around	diameter, diagram
11.	dis-	apart	disconnect, discount
12.	ex-	out of	expel, extend
13.	il-	not	illogical, illegal
14.	in-	not	invisible, inert
15.	in-	in or into	invade, insert
16.	inter-	between or among	interrupt, interfere
17.	ir-	not	irregular, irreverent
18.	mono-	one	monopoly, monorail
19.	non-	not	nonsense, nonprofit
20.	ob-	against	obstruct, obstinate
21.	pan-	all	Pan-American, pantheist
22.	per-	through	pervade, peruse
23.	peri-	around	perimeter, periscope
24.	post-	after	postpone, postscript
25.	pre-	before	preamble, predestined
26.	pro-	for or forward	progress, promoter
27.	re-	back or again	return, reply
28.	retro-	backward	retroactive, retrospect
29.	se-	aside	select, segregate
30.	semi-	half	semicircle, semiannual
31.	sub-	under	submerge, subway
32.	super-	over or above	supervise, superior
33.	trans-	across	transport, transcontinental
34.	tri-	three	triangle, triple
35.	un-	not	unnatural, unless

COMMON SUFFIXES

	Suffix	Meaning	Examples
1.	-able	capable of being	readable, manageable
2.	-age	act or condition	wastage, postage
3.	-al	like or suitable for	comical, theatrical
4.	-an	person who	musician, American
5.	-ance	state of being	circumstance, resemblance
6.	-ant (noun)	person who	occupant, accountant
7.	-ant (adjective)	state of being	defiant, vacant
8.	-ar	relating to	muscular, lunar
9.	-ary	place where	library, dictionary
10.	-ate	to make	create, formulate
11.	-ee	person who is	nominee, employee
12.	-en	made of	golden, wooden
13.	-ence	state or quality	permanence, excellence
14.	-ent	person who	student, superintendent
15.	-fic	causing or producing	scientific, prolific
16.	-fy	to make	simplify, glorify
17.	-hood	state or condition	childhood, neighborhood
18.	-ible	capable of being	legible, divisible
19.	-ic	of or characteristic of	angelic, symphonic
20.	-ice	condition or quality	justice, malice
21.	-id	state or condition	fluid, squalid
22.	-ile	relating to	servile, infantile
23.	-ion	state of being	condition, confusion
24.	-ist	person who	chemist, moralist
25.	-ive	relating to	massive, inventive
26.	-ize	to make	Americanize, sterilize
27.	-less	without	helpless, motionless
28.	-ment	state of being	improvement, fulfillment
29.	-or	person who	conductor, inventor
30.	-ory	place for	directory, dormitory
31.	-ous	abounding in	famous, pious
32.	-some	tending to	lonesome, troublesome
33.	-tude	condition	gratitude, attitude
34.	-ty	state or condition	liberty, sanity
35.	-ward	direction or course	backward, eastward

COMMON ROOTS

	Root	Meaning	Examples
1.	aqua	water	aqualung, aquarium
2.	audio	hear	audience, audition
3.	auto	self	automatic, autonomy
4.	bene	well	benefit, beneficiary
5.	bio	life	autobiography, biology
6.	cor, cord	heart	core, cordial
7.	corp	body	corpse, incorporate
8.	cred	belief	incredible, credit
9.	ego	self	egocentric, egotist
10.	fact	make	factory, manufacture
11.	frater	brother	fraternal, fraternize
12.	geo	earth	geography, geology
13.	graph	write	autograph, graphic
14.	loc	place	location, local
15.	log	speech or science	logic, dialogue
16.	micro	small	microscope, micrometer
17.	mit, mis	send	transmit, missile
18.	mort	death	immortal, mortuary
19.	omni	all	omnibus, omnipotent
20.	pater	father	paternal, paternity
21.	ped	foot	pedal, pedestrian
22.	philo	love	bibliophile, philosophy
23.	phob	fear	phobia, claustrophobia
24.	phon	sound	phonics, symphony
25.	poly	many	polygon, polytechnic
26.	pos	place	position, impose
27.	pot	strength or ability	impotent, potential
28.	pseud	false	pseudonym, pseudoclassic
29.	psych	soul or mind	psychology, psychic
30.	script	write	scripture, subscription
31.	sol	alone	solo, solitude
32.	soph	wise	philosopher, sophomore
33.	tele	far	telephone, telepathy
34.	vert	turn	convertible, invert
35.	vid, vis	see	invisible, vision, video

PRACTICE WITH WORD ELEMENTS

If you know the meanings of the common prefixes, suffixes and roots, you are better able to work out the meanings of words. One writer has estimated that a knowledge of only 14 basic Latin and Greek roots can help us recognize more than 14,000 English words. Here are some exercises to help you get a feeling for how words are put together and how they may be deciphered from their parts.

Practice Exercise 1

Directions: Separate the following words into their basic parts. Using the meaning of each part of a word, provide a *literal* definition for the word. Use the lists of word parts in this unit to help you. The first one has been done for you. When you finish, compare your answers with those suggested on page 247.

Words	Word Elements and Their Meanings		Literal Meaning
1. biography	bio = life	graph = write	write about life
2. postscript	_____	_____	_____
3. supervise	_____	_____	_____
4. revert	_____	_____	_____
5. credible	_____	_____	_____
6. mortuary	_____	_____	_____
7. transmit	_____	_____	_____
8. paternal	_____	_____	_____
9. solitude	_____	_____	_____
10. biped	_____	_____	_____

Practice Exercise 2

Directions: A knowledge of word elements can enable you to determine the meaning of unfamiliar words in your reading. In the first column is a list of words which may be unfamiliar to you. Using your knowledge of word elements, match the word with the proper definition without looking the words up in a dictionary. Use the lists of word parts in this unit to help you. The first one has been done for you. (Answer Key Page 247)

Words	Meaning	Word Defined
triarchy	1. knowing all things	1. omniscient
antecede	2. of many colors	2. _____
omniscient	3. knowledge of actions or events before they occur	3. _____
polychromatic	4. of, relating to, or resembling water	4. _____
acrophobia	5. the development of life from preexisting life	5. _____
corporeal	6. of or relating to the period after death	6. _____
abduce	7. to draw a line around	7. _____
biogenesis	8. government by three persons	8. _____
retrogress	9. to agree with; to act together to a common end	9. _____
interstellar	10. relating to a physical material body	10. _____
circumscribe	11. to move backward	11. _____
prescience	12. located or taking place among the stars	12. _____
postmortem	13. to go before in time or place	13. _____
concur	14. abnormal fear of high places	14. _____
aqueous	15. to draw away from the original position	15. _____

> Good readers use the context, the surrounding words, to help them recognize and understand new words or meanings. The ways in which the context works to help the reader are called contextual aids. Intelligent use of context is the reader's most important tool for sound vocabulary development.

How to Use Context

During political campaigns in election years, we invariably hear one candidate accuse his opponent of quoting him "out of context." The danger in taking a speaker's words out of context is that a sentence by itself may imply a meaning entirely different from the meaning it had conveyed when surrounded by other thoughts.

This suggests an important aspect of word usage: a word's true meaning depends upon how it is used. This is readily apparent in the case of ambiguous words, like *bow* or *sink*. Context tells the reader when a *bow tied with ribbon* is meant rather than a *bow to the audience*. Similarly, without the context the reader does not know whether the writer is referring to *sink* as in *water* or *sink* as in *kitchen*.

Not so apparent is the effect of context on words generally thought to have consistent and unchanging meanings. The word *conventional* in one context may suggest all that is stable, reliable and in the most time-honored tradition. In another context *conventional* could imply staleness, the refusal to change or adapt to modern ways.

Beginning as youngsters, we add to our understanding of a word's meaning every time we hear it or use it. For example, the first few times you heard the word *school*, you may have understood it to mean a place where older brothers and sisters spend most of the day. Later, *school* came to mean a place where things are learned. Today, your understanding of the word encompasses several comprehensive ideas.

This same growth pattern occurs with other words. As a student, you will come across new words, or words you only vaguely understand. Being aware of the way words function in context helps you to understand these words and make them part of your vocabulary. Each time you hear an unfamiliar word, the context it is being used in will add to your understanding. With repeated exposure, you will come to understand all that the word implies, and eventually you will be able to use it comfortably in your writing and speaking.

Context, then, helps us in a way no dictionary can. Various shades and richness of meaning cannot be gained from dictionary definitions alone; we must see the word used to grasp its full meaning.

CONTEXTUAL AIDS

Studies of good readers show that they are aware of the different contexts in which words are set. These are commonly referred to as contextual aids. Using contextual aids intelligently is the reader's most important vocabulary tool. And it is a reading skill which can be mastered and developed.

1. Common Expressions. Words can be recognized as part of a common phrase or idiomatic expression. Certain phrases and expressions are used regularly and become well known to the reader. A word omitted can readily be supplied because of its familiarity.

In the old saying *His bark is worse than his* _____, the reader can easily fill in the missing word, *bite*. If you came across this expression in your reading, you could automatically supply any missing elements of this familiar saying.

2. Modifying Phrases. Words can be understood and recognized through the use of phrases which modify the unknown word. Frequently a word is accompanied by a prepositional phrase which modifies it, giving the reader valuable clues to understanding and recognition. For example, if you were to read the sentence _____ *by the finest artists of our century were displayed at the exhibit,* you could easily guess that the missing word is *paintings*. The phrase *by the*

finest artists is the contextual aid which acts as the clue.

3. **Accompanying Description.** An unknown word can often be understood because it has been defined or described in the context. This kind of contextual aid, naturally enough, is commonly used in textbooks. Authors frequently provide a description or definition to assist their readers. In the sentence *Students should use _____; these are books containing definitions of words*, the reader would know that the missing word is *dictionaries* because of the accompanying description.

4. **Parts of a Series.** Whenever items appear in a list or series, the items themselves give clues to the reader. If one of them were omitted from the list, the reader could probably supply it. This is possible because the parts of a series are related; they share some feature in common. An additional clue is provided by the connector *and*; this tells the reader that the items are alike in some way. For example, if you see the sentence *The theatre was packed with men, women and _____*, you can confidently fill in the blank with the missing word, *children*, the next word in the series. Notice how the *and* in the series leads you to expect another related item.

5. **Comparison and Contrast.** Unknown or unfamiliar words become meaningful when compared or contrasted with known words. We know that when parallels are being drawn, like things are being examined. In the case of contrast, we are dealing with things that are opposite. The reader's ability to recognize that a comparison or contrast is being made permits him to exploit this type of contextual aid. Take this sentence: *The two brothers were as different as day and _____.* It is simple for the reader to complete the comparison with the word *night*.

6. **Synonyms.** Words can be understood through synonyms provided in the context. A synonym, as you recall, is a word with the same or nearly the same meaning as another word. The reader's task is to discover that a synonym is being given. With this knowledge, he can properly use the contextual aid. For example, a student reading the sentence *It was his custom never to be on time; he made a _____ of tardiness* must recognize that the missing word is a synonym for *custom.* The word *habit* instantly comes to mind, completing the sentence perfectly. This contextual aid, too, is often found in textbook writing.

7. **Setting and Mood.** The setting or mood created by the context can suggest to the reader the meaning of an unfamiliar word. In the sentence *It was a lovely _____ scene, with snow blanketing the fields and trees*, the setting is obviously *winter*. This would appear to be the word indicated by the context. Using setting and mood effectively requires imagery comprehension on the part of the reader; he must get the feeling or tone. Highly descriptive writing and poetry abound with this type of contextual aid.

8. **Association.** Certain words can arouse associations in the mind of the reader. These, in turn, serve as aids to recognizing an unfamiliar word. The student reading the sentence *Tuning their instruments, the _____ awaited the appearance of the conductor* can see that the missing word is probably *musicians, band* or *orchestra*. The words *tuning, instruments* and *conductor* trigger the correct associations. The context of much of what we read provides opportunities for making associations like these.

9. **Adjective Clauses.** New words can be understood when accompanied by adjective clauses. Frequently an unknown word modified by an adjective clause can be understood by the information contained in the clause. In the sentence *The _____ which*

shine in the sky at night have always fascinated man, the missing word is modified by an adjective clause. The same clause acts as a contextual aid, telling the reader that the missing word is *stars*.

10. **Appositives.** Words can be recognized and understood through another word used in apposition to it. A word in apposition is placed beside another word, further explaining it. Appositives give the reader a clue to the meaning of the unknown word. In the sentence _____, *policemen in plain clothes, joined the investigation*, the reader is informed by the appositive *policemen* that the missing word is probably *detectives*. Appositives are always placed next to the word they explain. For this reason they are relatively easy to recognize and exploit as contextual aids.

11. **Cause and Effect.** Words can be understood through a cause and effect relationship between the unknown word and other words in the sentence. The reader's understanding of the cause-effect pattern offers a clue to the meaning of the unknown word. In the sentence *Because they ate a hearty lunch just before swimming, many of the bathers suffered* _____, anyone who understands the effects of eating just before swimming knows that the missing word is *cramps*.

When it comes to deciphering the meaning of a word, a dictionary is a very useful tool. However, words acquire a precise meaning only when used in context. Using context clues, in fact, is the way lexicographers prepare definitions for dictionaries.

Discovering word meaning through context clues is not new to you; you have been using context intuitively all your life. However, as you encounter more and more difficult words with subtle or complex meanings, you will come to realize that the use of context clues is one of your most powerful learning tools.

_____: Reading Time

_____: Reading Rate

_____: Score, Test A

_____: Score, Test B

_____: Total Score

_____%: Comprehension

COMPREHENSION TEST 5-A

Directions: The following passage, taken from the selection you have just read, has words omitted from it. Fill in each blank with the word that was omitted. Each blank filled correctly is worth two points. Ask your instructor if you may take credit for close synonyms. Enter your score in the box provided at the end of the selection. A list of the omitted words can be found on page 236.

During political campaigns in election years, we invariably hear one candidate accuse his opponent of quoting him "out of context." The danger in taking a speaker's words out of _____1_____ is that a sentence by itself may imply a _____2_____ entirely different from the meaning it had conveyed when _____3_____ by other thoughts.

This suggests an important aspect of _____4_____ usage: a word's true meaning depends upon how it _____5_____ used. This is readily apparent in the case of _____6_____ words, like *bow* or *sink*. Context tells the reader _____7_____ a *bow tied with ribbon* is meant rather than _____8_____ *bow to the audience.* Similarly, without the context the _____9_____ does not know whether the writer is referring to _____10_____ as in *water* or *sink* as in *kitchen*.

Not _____11_____ apparent is the effect of context on words generally _____12_____ to have consistent and unchanging meanings. The word *conventional* _____13_____ one context may suggest all that is stable, reliable _____14_____ in the most time-honored tradition. In another context _____15_____ could imply staleness, the refusal to change or adapt _____16_____ modern ways.

Beginning as youngsters, we add to our _____17_____ of a word's meaning every time we hear it _____18_____ use it. For example, the first few times you _____19_____ the word *school*, you may have understood it to _____20_____ a place where older brothers and sisters spend most _____21_____ the day. Later, *school* came to mean a place _____22_____ things are learned. Today, your understanding of the word _____23_____ several comprehensive ideas.

This same growth pattern occurs with _____24_____ words. As a student, you will come across new _____25_____, or words you only vaguely understand. Being aware of the way words function in context helps you to understand these words and make them part of your vocabulary.

COMPREHENSION TEST 5-B

Directions: This is another passage from the selection, again with words omitted. Proceed as before, giving yourself two points for each blank filled correctly. Add this score to the one from Test A and enter your total score in the box at the end of the selection. Use the conversion table on page 254 to convert your *total* score to a comprehension percentage, and record that grade in the box also. A list of omitted words can be found on page 236.

8. **Association.** Certain words can arouse associations in the mind of the reader. These, in turn, serve as aids to recognizing an _____ word. The
1
student reading the sentence *Tuning their instruments,* _____ ---
2
awaited the appearance of the conductor can see that _____ missing
3
word is probably *musicians, band* or *orchestra*. The _____ *tuning,*
4
instruments and *conductor* trigger the correct associations. The _____
5
of much of what we read provides opportunities for _____
6
associations like these.

9. **Adjective Clauses.** New words can be _____ when accompanied
7
by adjective clauses. Frequently an unknown word _____ by an
8
adjective clause can be understood by the _____ contained in the
9
clause. In the sentence *The --- which* _____ *in the sky at night*
10
have always fascinated man, _____ missing word is modified by an
11
adjective clause. The _____ clause acts as a contextual aid, telling
12
the reader _____ the missing word is *stars*.
13

10. **Appositives.** Words can be _____ and understood through
14
another word used in apposition to _____. A word in apposition is
15
placed beside another word, _____ explaining it. Appositives give the
16
reader a clue to _____ meaning of the unknown word. In the sentence
17
---, policemen _____ *plain clothes, joined the investigation,* the
18
reader is informed _____ the appositive *policemen* that the missing
19
word is probably _____. Appositives are always placed next to the
20
word they _____. For this reason they are relatively easy to recognize
21
_____ exploit as contextual aids.
22

11. **Cause and Effect.** Words can _____ understood through a cause
23
and effect relationship between the _____ word and other words in
24
the sentence. The reader's _____ of the cause-effect pattern offers a
25
clue to the meaning of the unknown word. In the sentence *Because they ate a hearty lunch just before swimming, many of the bathers suffered ---,* anyone who understands the effects of eating just before swimming knows that the missing word is *cramps*.

PRACTICE IN USING CONTEXTUAL AIDS

Practice Exercise 1

Directions: Using contextual aids discussed in the selection, fill in the missing word in each sentence. There may be more than one suitable word choice; try to supply the word that usually appears in the context presented. After making your word choice, tell *why* you chose the word you did. When you finish, compare your answers with those suggested on page 247.

1. The product is available in two sizes, large and _____.

2. It's impossible to fit a square peg in a _____ hole.

3. _____, a mixture of hydrogen and oxygen, is essential for life.

4. Cover your head if you're going out in the pouring _____.

5. The _____, weeks and months seemed to fly by.

6. An expert is one who knows more and more about _____ and less.

7. If you can't stand the _____, get out of the kitchen.

8. Hire a _____, someone who knows how to fix broken pipes.

9. The difference is as great as night and _____.

10. The question facing us is not war or peace, it is life or _____.

11. When five o'clock comes, many workers leave the city for the _____.

12. A famous surgeon was called in to perform the _____.

13. Without a _____, you are not allowed to drive a car.

14. Voters lined up at the _____ on election day.

15. Auto exhaust contributes heavily to air _____.

16. Start the day with a nutritious _____.

17. To get the full story, you must read between the _____.

18. Although he took several aspirin, his _____ remained.

19. Don't tell a soul; it's supposed to be a _____.

20. The police have questioned several _____.

PRACTICE IN USING CONTEXTUAL AIDS

Practice Exercise 2

Directions: For each of the following sentences, write a brief definition of the italicized word using clues from the sentence itself. Compare your definitions with those in a dictionary and explain how you arrived at your definition. When you finish, compare your answers with those suggested on page 247.

1. The politician was attacked by a *barrage* of criticism for his stand on abortion.

2. A fight broke out between the two teams when one side made *disparaging* remarks about the other players.

3. The *guileless* youth lost all his money to the scheming swindlers.

4. The worker disapproved of his employer's unethical business practices, but he didn't have the *gumption* to say anything about it.

5. The convict was declared *incorrigible* after all attempts to reform him had failed.

6. The woman didn't get as much as she expected for her car because its value had *depreciated* since she bought it.

7. Feeling he had reached his *nadir*, the depressed patient decided there was nowhere to go but up.

8. The large woman's gaudy clothes and loud voice made her an *ostentatious* figure at the funeral.

9. The *inclement* weather kept everyone indoors.

10. The *pusillanimous* lion hoped that the Wizard would give him some courage.

11. The miser had no *scruples* when it came to making money.

12. The *opportunist* sold lumber at exorbitant prices to the families who had lost their homes in the great fire.

13. The millionaire's dime was a *paltry* contribution to the fund-raising drive.

14. The gossipy old lady *prated* on harmlessly about her neighbors' comings and goings.

15. Knowing her guest's *predilection* for solving mysteries, she told him of an unusual crime which had taken place in the house some years ago.

16. The gambler tried to *recoup* his losses at the race track by investing in the stock market.

17. The reformed alcoholic suffered a *relapse* and went on a drinking binge.

18. Her coarse manners *belied* her fine clothes.

19. He was such a *voluble* talker that no one else could get a word in edgewise.

20. The politician *straddled* the controversial issue by saying that it had its good points and its bad points.

Textbooks contain signs and signals to guide readers. Numbers, letters, special typographic devices, words and phrases are all used to direct your attention to those things that will enable you to get the most from your text. Alert readers let these signs work for them toward greater understanding of study material.

Using the Author's Signs and Signals

To help students along, authors supply many signs and signals. Like directions to travelers, they help keep readers on the track and save them from needless and time-consuming delays. Once you become accustomed to using them, signs and signals not only speed your reading along and help you to read with greater comprehension, but they also make your reviewing easier later on by helping you to identify important points.

NUMBER AND LETTER SIGNS

Authors often use numbers and letters to indicate the relative importance or sequence of ideas. The most obvious signs are the numbers *1, 2, 3* . . . and, of course, the Roman numerals *I, II, III* . . . . Frequently, numbered sequences are introduced by a verbal signal: "There are *three* major causes." The reader, seeing the verbal clue, knows to look for the numbers *1, 2, 3.*

Letters may also be used. *A, B, C* . . . or *a, b, c* . . . appear in textbooks with the same purpose as numbers: to help readers organize and follow the author's thought sequence in their own minds. Many students make it a standard practice to circle such signs in their texts.

Sometimes authors prefer to use words in place of numbers or letters. We are used to seeing the words *one, two, three* or *first, second, third*. These should have the same significance as numbers for you even though they are not as prominent on a printed page. If you own the book, it is a good idea to circle or number such word signs so that they stand out from the rest of the copy.

Still other word signs are contained in phrases like *in the first place, for one thing,* and similar expressions. These alert you to the fact that a list is coming, and it is a good place for a circle or other mark in case you want to find the list easily later on.

Signs of this kind occur throughout textbooks, but they are more likely to turn up at the beginning of a chapter to enumerate the sections to follow or the main points that will be discussed. At the end of a chapter, number and letter signs may be used in a summary listing of the important elements covered.

TYPOGRAPHIC SIGNS

When an author wants you to take special notice of something, he will often ask the publisher to emphasize it in the design of the book or in a change of typeface. The use of **boldface** or *italics* is one of the most common ways to make certain words stand out. Boldface is frequently used for headings and subheadings. When used skillfully, such headings virtually provide you with a ready-made study outline at review time.

Boldface or italic type is often used to make definitions stand out from the rest of the text. Italic type is also used for long quotations. Once you become familiar with your text and your instructor's requirements, you will know if such quotations are important for the work you are doing. If so, italic type becomes a sign to stop and take another careful look.

Boxes, small print, large print, special or fancy typefaces, indentations of margins and color changes are all used to alert you to special features of a text. Moreover, these devices are usually used consistently by the publisher, so that once you have become familiar with your text in your preview of it, you know how these special signs can help you whenever you encounter them.

FORWARD SIGNALS

Signals are another kind of guide for the reader. They can be just as useful as signs although they are not so readily identifiable.

Commonly used forward signals are *and, more, moreover, more than that, furthermore, also* and *likewise.*

Naturally, of this group, the most frequently used signal is *and*. It tells you that another item of equal importance is following or that this is the last of a series.

The signals *more, moreover, more than that* and *furthermore* all indicate that new and perhaps stronger thoughts in the same vein are coming, as in the example: "He's clever, all right; *more than that*, he's a genius." Notice how the signal reinforces the preceding point while adding to it.

The signal *also* means *all in the same manner*. Its appearance suggests that what is coming is related to what has gone before: "Along with signals, authors *also* use signs." The word *likewise* is also used this way.

Signs, as you recall, stand out in the text. Most of them are easy to find; in fact, they are almost impossible to overlook. Signals, however, appear with the context; they are not set apart from the rest of the copy.

COUNTER SIGNALS

Counter signals tell a reader that the author is about to present an idea opposed to one just offered and that the reader should be alert for it. Commonly used counter signals include *but, yet, nevertheless, otherwise, although, despite, in spite of, not, on the contrary* and *however*. These all introduce an idea that is different from what has gone before, and they lead the reader in a new direction.

By far, the most common of these adversative words is *but*. In the words of the English poet Samuel Daniels: "Oh, now comes that bitter word — *but*, which makes all nothing that was said before . . . ."

Most of us have learned from experience the power of the word *but*. It's a little word, but it's loaded. Don't pass it over lightly in your

reading; check to see how it influences the thought of the passage.

When you meet any of the counter signals, prepare to change direction. The thought is not going forward any longer; it has turned and an opposing idea is coming.

SUMMARY SIGNALS

Another group of signals that urge the reader forward is called summary signals. These include such words as *thus, therefore, consequently*, and *accordingly*. Not only do these words signal that a thought is continuing, but they also signal a new idea — one of summary, result or consequence.

Summary signals tell the reader that the author is continuing along the same line, but now he has a more weighty idea to introduce, an idea that summarizes what has gone before

or an idea revealing the result of previous ideas. This is what the author has been leading up to. Now he is going to pause and summarize his thoughts or show the result they have been building up to.

Examine the following sentence: "*Thus* it was that after years of trial and error, experimentation and failure, frustration and despair, he and his laboratory colleagues had isolated the virus." The word *thus* tells the reader that much had occurred to bring about a particular result. This is not simply more of the same; this is a thought carrying greater meaning for the reader.

In textbooks, summary signals introduce important ideas and concepts. They are used in statements that summarize the writer's presentation. Pay close attention to these signals; in study-type reading their value is enormous.

TERMINAL SIGNALS

We have discussed two types of signals which carry the reader ahead — forward signals, which indicate the continuance of similar or related thoughts, and summary signals, which announce a more weighty or important thought, one brought about as a result of preceding ideas.

Still another type of forward signal performs an even more critical function. This is the terminal signal.

As the name suggests, terminal signals indicate to the reader that the end is near; the author is now concluding his remarks. The signals announce that the writer has developed all of the ideas in his presentation and is now about to sum up or draw an appropriate conclusion.

Some common terminal signals are *as a result, finally* and *in conclusion*. These all signal that a last or final thought is being presented.

A major distinction between summary and terminal signals is this finality. Summary signals indicate a pause in the forward trend while the writer gathers his thoughts and tells the reader where he stands. But there is more to come. The author has reached a summary point, not the conclusion.

Often a terminal signal comes in the author's tone; there's a noticeable winding down from the momentum generated earlier in the presentation. There is an air of finality.

For example, after talking about the historic development of national parks, an author said: "*Today* American society is mature in an economic sense . . . ." The word *today* changes the historic tone, giving a sense of finality to a discussion of things past.

Condition yourself to become aware of signs and signals in your texts. To be a flexible and efficient reader, you cannot afford to be without their valuable assistance.

_____: Reading Time

_____: Reading Rate

_____: Score, Test A

_____: Score, Test B

_____: Total Score

_____%: Comprehension

COMPREHENSION TEST 6-A

Directions: The following passage, taken from the selection you have just read, has words omitted from it. Fill in each blank with the word that was omitted. Each blank filled correctly is worth two points. Ask your instructor if you may take credit for close synonyms. Enter your score in the box provided at the end of the selection. A list of the omitted words can be found on page 237.

NUMBER AND LETTER SIGNS

Authors often use numbers and letters to indicate the relative importance or sequence of ideas. The most obvious signs are the numbers *1, 2,* _____
1
. . . and, of course, the Roman numerals *I, II, III* . . . . _____ ,
2
numbered sequences are introduced by a verbal signal: "There _____
3
three major causes." The reader, seeing the verbal clue, _____ to look
4
for the numbers *1, 2, 3.*

Letters _____ also be used. *A, B, C* . . . or *a, b,* _____
5   6
. . . appear in textbooks with the same purpose as numbers: _____
7
help readers organize and follow the author's thought sequence _____
8
their own minds. Many students make it a standard _____ to circle
9
such signs in their texts.

Sometimes authors _____ to use words in place of numbers or
10
letters. _____ are used to seeing the words *one, two, three*
11
_____ *first, second, third.* These should have the same significance
12
_____ numbers for you even though they are not as _____
13   14
on a printed page. If you own the book, _____ is a good idea to circle
15
or number such _____ signs so that they stand out from the rest
16
_____ the copy.
17
Still other word signs are contained in _____ like *in the first*
18
place, for one thing, and _____ expressions. These alert you to the
19
fact that a _____ is coming, and it is a good place for
20
_____ circle or other mark in case you want to _____
21   22
the list easily later on.

Signs of this kind _____ throughout textbooks, but they are more
23
likely to turn _____ at the beginning of a chapter to enumerate the
24
_____ to follow or the main points that will be discussed. At the end
25
of a chapter, number and letter signs may be used in a summary listing of the important elements covered.

USING THE AUTHOR'S SIGNS AND SIGNALS

COMPREHENSION TEST 6-B

Directions: This is another passage from the selection, again with words omitted. Proceed as before, giving yourself two points for each blank filled correctly. Add this score to the one from Test A and enter your total score in the box at the end of the selection. Use the conversion table on page 254 to convert your *total* score to a comprehension percentage, and record that grade in the box also. A list of omitted words can be found on page 237.

In textbooks, summary signals introduce important ideas and concepts. They are used in statements that summarize the writer's _____. Pay close

                        1
attention to these signals; in study-type _____ their value is enormous.

      2

TERMINAL SIGNALS

We have discussed _____ types of signals which carry the reader

                  3
ahead — forward _____, which indicate the continuance of similar

          4
or related thoughts, _____ summary signals, which announce a more

        5
weighty or important _____, one brought about as a result of

        6
preceding ideas.

_____ another type of forward signal performs an even more

    7
_____ function. This is the terminal signal.

    8

As the name _____, terminal signals indicate to the reader that the

        9
end _____ near; the author is now concluding his remarks. The

    10
_____ announce that the writer has developed all of the

    11
_____ in his presentation and is now about to sum _____

    12   13
or draw an appropriate conclusion.

Some common terminal signals _____ *as a result, finally* and *in con-*

              14
clusion. These all _____ that a last or final thought is being presented.

      15
_____ major distinction between summary and terminal signals

    16
is this _____. Summary signals indicate a pause in the forward trend

    17
_____ the writer gathers his thoughts and tells the reader

    18
_____ he stands. But there is more to come. The _____

    19   20
has reached a summary point, not the conclusion.

Often _____ terminal signal comes in the author's tone; there's

      21
a _____ winding down from the momentum generated earlier in the

    22
_____. There is an air of finality.

    23

For example, after _____ about the historic development of

        24
national parks, an author _____: "*Today* American society is mature

        25
in an economic sense . . . ." The word *today* changes the historic tone, giving a sense of finality to a discussion of things past.

PRACTICE FINDING SIGNS AND SIGNALS

Directions: The paragraphs below contain signs and signals, some of which were mentioned in the selection you have just read and some which were not mentioned. Find and underline them. It is not necessary for you to label or identify each kind of signal, so long as you can find them all. When you finish, compare your answers with those suggested on page 248.

1. There are many other reasons for joining in conversation. The braggart talks to bolster his ego. The idler chats to pass time and to escape work. The emotionally agitated person talks to let off steam. The frustrated individual talks to ease tension and to make an unhappy situation more tolerable. The windbag speaks because of some compulsion.

2. Finally, the practical problem of "having to pass" remains unmet and unsolved. The cheater erroneously believes that the only solution to the problem of passing a course centers around a single alternative—cheating or not cheating—when the problem might be more efficiently, more safely and more successfully solved by many other possible alternatives. For instance, he could ask for suggestions regarding improvement, do extra work, develop better study habits, seek further instruction and suggestions from the instructor. All these methods are certainly better alternatives to cheating—and they allow a student to maintain his dignity, integrity and self-respect.

3. Everyone who attends or has attended college harbors his own ideas about college loyalty. Since none of these notions is the last word on the subject, let me join voice to the chorus by offering a few thoughts. Loyalty to Alma Mater rests, I believe, upon three pillars of college life: (1) a sense of community, (2) affection, and (3) identification of self with college interests.

4. There are two attitudes, however, that sabotage the best efforts to encourage reading. One denies the value of reading by charging that books are divorced from life. The bookworm has always been an object of contempt. The other attitude contends that reading is thinking with someone else's head instead of one's own. And in these days of a "thinking man's cigarette," no one likes to admit that he cannot use his own mind.

5. To recognize and relate ideas as they are presented in speech, which flows and never stands, is doubly difficult. Yet there are certain characteristics of a classroom lecture which should aid the student in this task.

First of all, the instructor usually announces by word, and sometimes by blackboard diagram, the plan of his lecture. Make that the heading of your notes. Then, during the period, it is a customary professorial practice to cover about a dozen points, more or less. This may be represented by any combination, from one or two major points with several important subpoints to a series of equal ideas. You may well become suspicious—either of your notes or of the lecture—when you jot down an eighteenth major point. You have "missed the boat" or the "prof" has run amuck mentally.

Again, the teacher ordinarily marks off in some way the main divisions of his lecture. Sometimes these are enumerated in advance; sometimes in conclusion. When in the course of his presentation he says: "Second," "third" and "finally," latch on to it. It is usually important.

6. The freedom of the college campus, therefore, implies a recognition by college authorities of your sense of responsibility in regard to the main obligation of study. Let not the newly-won independence dazzle you, nor let it give occasion for a swagger or a strut, but may it deepen your resolution to use that liberty to the best advantage. Malapertness and maturity mix like oil and water on the college campus.

7. Concentration, then, narrows your consciousness to some object and heightens your awareness of that object. There are a thousand things that might enter consciousness if you let them. The fact is you allow only a few things into your consciousness at any one time. Those things, moreover, are in some way bound up with your wants, needs, hopes, interests and purposes. Thus, concentration functions something like a spotlight. It highlights things that are of significance to you so that they stand out in sharp relief. At the same time, it throws into shadow (that is, to the background of consciousness) items of experience that are not of particular interest or importance at the moment.

8. When a person cheats, he discloses two facets of his personality. First, in turning to his neighbor for academic salvation, he asserts that another, perhaps any other, is proficient, competent and able in comparison to himself who is ignorant, inept and inefficient. The cheater perceives himself as ignorant while all others are knowledgeable. Second, the cheater betrays a perfectionist tendency because he says in action, if not in words, that he feels himself measured against standards which are, at best, unrealistic and overstrict, even though his classmates are measured by the same standards.

9. This type of transfer is frequently subsconscious. For example, if you dislike a man because he has harmed you, and many years later you come across another man who resembles your old enemy in features or in tone of voice, you will instantly dislike him. So also if you hate a particular course, your distaste for that course may spread to other related subjects. Similarly, if you dislike a professor, you may transfer that aversion to the subject he teaches. As a result, when the course is finished, you will never look at another book that reminds you of your previous unpleasant experience.

10. The juvenile attitude towards study looks upon it as a chore to be ducked as soon as possible. At best it is an unpleasant duty. It is begun under constraint, continued under duress and escaped whenever it is possible to do so. The mark of truly adult learning, on the other hand, is that it is done with no thought of labor or work at all, with no sense of being forced. It is entirely voluntary and performed with a keen sense of enjoyment.

11. One last word: Do not be discouraged if you fail to see all the implications, applications and associations of what you now learn. The ability to unify knowledge and to recognize the interrelationship of the various sciences is the product of ripened mentality, an enriched experience and prolonged study. Some college graduates fail to perceive the relation of their undergraduate studies to the world in which they live because they have either ceased to study after commencement or, when in college, they relied too heavily on rote memory and intellectual verbalism. In either case, they defeated the very purpose of a liberal education.

In textbooks, paragraphs perform very specific functions. They serve to introduce, define, and illustrate subject matter. They provide further information, prepare you for a transition, and present concluding thoughts. Identifying these types of paragraphs can help you organize the chapter in your mind and find the information you're after more efficiently.

How to Use Paragraphs when Reading

Books are a medium of communication, and in order to be useful to you they must communicate their message as clearly as possible. To accomplish this end, writers take great pains to construct the books they write in an organized way. Experienced authors virtually take you by the hand and guide you from a deliberately planned beginning of their book, through a carefully constructed middle, to a clearly wrought ending; and they accomplish this chiefly through an expert use of one of the basic units of organization — the paragraph.

There is no fat, no padding, in a well-written book. Every paragraph is included for a reason, and every paragraph has a purpose. In most textbooks and other expository or instructional writing, paragraphs usually function in one of six major roles: introduction, definition, illustration, information, transition and conclusion. When dealing with study or research-type reading, whether you are plowing through an entire text or extracting a single bit of information, you will find it pays to be aware of how authors use these different kinds of paragraphs to make things easier for you.

INTRODUCTION

A good introductory paragraph does two things for you: it captures your interest, preparing you for the reading ahead; and it tells you in a general way what you may expect to find in the paragraphs that follow.

When previewing assigned reading material, you can use key introductory paragraphs to give you the broadest possible picture of the subject matter at a glance. If you are skimming to find out if a particular book, article or chapter is worth reading more thoroughly, introductory paragraphs are your best guideposts to tell you if the information you are looking for might be found nearby.

Don't make the mistake of looking for introductory paragraphs only at the beginning of a chapter. Chapters are often constructed like a series of related essays, and every time a major subdivision or new concept is begun, there will be an introduction.

DEFINITION

Paragraphs of definition appear frequently in textbooks, and they are usually essential to understanding large blocks of information that precede and follow. Definitions are key bits of information and are favorite choices among teachers to be included on examinations.

As the name implies, paragraphs of definition are used to define words or ideas that are important in the development of the author's theme. To spot them, watch for a variety of familiar words or expressions: *this means; this might suggest that; this signifies; it is defined as; may be described as; denotes; indicates; is called;*

it is used in this sense. Once found and read with care, paragraphs of definition should be marked in your book so that they can be found easily when you review for examinations.

TRANSITION

Paragraphs of transition can sometimes be recognized by their brevity. These paragraphs are used by an author to progress from one aspect of his subject to another.

Because transitional paragraphs are used to move on to new material, they sometimes function like an introductory paragraph, offering a brief preview of the material next in line for discussion. At the same time, by taking you out of the preceding subject matter, they may also function like a concluding paragraph.

Transitions clearly announce themselves, however, by directing or shifting your attention in a very obvious manner from one idea to another. The author makes it very plain when he has finished with one thing and is about to move on to the next. Usually,

the better the author, the clearer the transition will be. But if you are looking for signal words, watch for the simple connectors like *and, but, or, now, also, moreover, for*.

Shifts in thought or contrasting ideas may be introduced by: *however, on the other hand, nevertheless, on the contrary, another point to consider*, and similar expressions.

Transitions are important in making ideas hang together. And just as an author uses them to organize his presentation, you can use them to help organize your reading.

INFORMATION

Passing along information to the reader is another role assigned to the paragraph. Paragraphs of information may contain names, dates, details, facts and explanations. It is here that you can expect to find the meat of the subject under discussion.

In presenting information, an author will probably do one or more of the following: state an opinion with supporting reasons; pose a problem and offer a solution; draw a conclusion and present proof; present steps in an argument; make comparisons; present facts and data.

There is usually so much to deal with in paragraphs of information that you must learn to be both discerning and discriminating in selecting what is most important. It is here that you should read most actively — questioning and evaluating everything that is being said and marking those arguments or ideas most useful to you in understanding the subject.

ILLUSTRATION

Paragraphs of illustration present examples, personal experiences, case studies, anecdotes, and so on. They are used to illustrate, clarify, reinforce or amplify the author's ideas.

Often a paragraph of illustration is easy to recognize because of certain phrases such as: *for example, an illustration of this, take the case of, when I was*, and similar expressions.

Authors use many paragraphs of illustration to help their readers understand the subject. Half of a chapter or article may be paragraphs of this sort. Unlike a lecturer who is face-to-face with his audience, an author is confined to print. He cannot see his readers; he cannot tell how effectively ideas are coming across for individual readers of varying abilities and experience. He must, therefore, use many illustrations. He must make sure that everyone will understand.

Furthermore, a writer cannot be questioned by his audience. So most authors rely heavily on illustrations in the hope that at least one of the examples will trigger a positive response in the mind of a reader. Knowing this enables you to dispose of some paragraphs of illustration expeditiously. After all, if you understand the point being illustrated, it is not necessary to linger over additional paragraphs illustrating the same thing. You can move on to something new.

CONCLUSION

The role of a concluding paragraph is obvious: to give the author's concluding remarks or final thoughts on the subject. The author may do this in several ways.

First, although it is rather unusual, an author may draw a conclusion based on all of the material presented in an entire chapter or lesson. Authors are reluctant to do this, however, because conclusions based on an entire chapter are much too important to be mentioned just once at the end. We can expect to find conclusions given earlier in the lesson along with supporting facts and arguments. You may expect to find concluding or wrap-up statements at the end of every major and many minor chapter divisions. It is likely, though, that an important conclusion will be repeated or restated in a final paragraph even if it has been dealt with before.

Second, the author may use a concluding paragraph to summarize. This is an opportunity to give readers the facts again for the last time. These summarizing remarks are most valuable to use both when previewing and when reviewing.

Finally, authors use paragraphs of conclusion to leave readers with a final thought: the central, all-inclusive idea around which the entire chapter was developed. In effect the writer is saying: "Above all, remember this."

MULTIPURPOSE ROLES

Once you become aware of the roles paragraphs play in good writing, you will soon notice that a paragraph often serves more than one purpose.

It was mentioned earlier, for example, that a transitional paragraph can contain elements of both introduction and conclusion. Similarly, an author might choose to use an illustration to introduce his subject or to weave definitions in with general information. Writing is a creative process that often refuses to be governed too strictly by formulas. But no matter how an author organizes his work, his paragraphs will fulfill one or more of the roles we have discussed.

By being able to identify the roles that paragraphs play, you quickly become aware of how an author has organized his book, and you are able to approach the book more analytically and use it more efficiently.

Following this selection you will have an opportunity to put to use what you have learned about paragraph roles. Try to become proficient in recognizing and utilizing the various types of paragraphs. Before long you will realize how valuable they can be in helping you to organize your reading and studying.

_____: Reading Time

_____: Reading Rate

_____: Score, Test A

_____: Score, Test B

_____: Total Score

_____%: Comprehension

COMPREHENSION TEST 7-A

Directions: The following passage, taken from the selection you have just read, has words omitted from it. Fill in each blank with the word that was omitted. Each blank filled correctly is worth two points. Ask your instructor if you may take credit for close synonyms. Enter your score in the box provided at the end of the selection. A list of the omitted words can be found on page 237.

Books are a medium of communication, and in order to be useful to you they must communicate their message as clearly as possible. To accomplish this end, writers take great pains to _____ the books they write in an organized way. Experienced _____ virtually take you by the hand and guide you _____ a deliberately planned beginning of their book, through a _____ constructed middle, to a clearly wrought ending; and they _____ this chiefly through an expert use of one of _____ basic units of organization — the paragraph.

There is no _____, no padding, in a well-written book. Every paragraph _____ included for a reason, and every paragraph has a _____. In most textbooks and other expository or instructional writing, _____ usually function in one of six major roles: introduction, _____, illustration, information, transition and conclusion. When dealing with study _____ research-type reading, whether you are plowing through an _____ text or extracting a single bit of information, you _____ find it pays to be aware of how authors _____ these different kinds of paragraphs to make things easier _____ you.

INTRODUCTION

A good introductory paragraph does two things _____ you: it captures your interest, preparing you for the _____ ahead; and it tells you in a general way _____ you may expect to find in the paragraphs that _____.

When previewing assigned reading material, you can use key _____ paragraphs to give you the broadest possible picture of _____ subject matter at a glance. If you are skimming _____ find out if a particular book, article or chapter _____ worth reading more thoroughly, introductory paragraphs are your best _____ to tell you if the information you are looking for might be found nearby.

Don't make the mistake of looking for introductory paragraphs only at the beginning of a chapter.

COMPREHENSION TEST 7-B

Directions: This is another passage from the selection, again with words omitted. Proceed as before, giving yourself two points for each blank filled correctly. Add this score to the one from Test A and enter your total score in the box at the end of the selection. Use the conversion table on page 254 to convert your *total* score to a comprehension percentage, and record that grade in the box also. A list of omitted words can be found on page 237.

The role of a concluding paragraph is obvious: to give the author's concluding remarks or final thoughts on the subject. The author may do this in several ways.

First, _____ it is rather unusual, an author may draw a
     1
_____ based on all of the material presented in an _____
     2   3
chapter or lesson. Authors are reluctant to do this, _____, because
     4
conclusions based on an entire chapter are much _____ important to
     5
be mentioned just once at the end. _____ can expect to find
     6
conclusions given earlier in the _____ along with supporting facts and
     7
arguments. You may expect _____ find concluding or wrap-up
     8
statements at the end of _____ major and many minor chapter
     9
divisions. It is likely, _____, that an important conclusion will be
     10
repeated or restated _____ a final paragraph even if it has been
     11
dealt _____ before.
     12

Second, the author may use a concluding paragraph _____
     13
summarize. This is an opportunity to give readers the _____ again for
     14
the last time. These summarizing remarks are _____ valuable to use
     15
both when previewing and when reviewing.

_____, authors use paragraphs of conclusion to leave readers with
     16
_____ final thought: the central, all-inclusive idea around which
     17
_____ entire chapter was developed. In effect the writer is
     18
_____: "Above all, remember this."
     19

MULTIPURPOSE ROLES

Once you become _____ of the roles paragraphs play in good
     20
writing, you _____ soon notice that a paragraph often serves more
     21
than _____ purpose.
     22

It was mentioned earlier, for example, that a _____ paragraph can
     23
contain elements of both introduction and conclusion. _____, an
     24
author might choose to use an illustration to _____ his subject or to
     25
weave definitions in with general information. Writing is a creative process that often refuses to be governed too strictly by formulas.

IDENTIFYING PARAGRAPH ROLES

Directions: The following excerpts are from a memorandum to the F.B.I. written by J. Edgar Hoover and part of a treatise on the 1970s recession by the noted economist Harrison Westfield.

Each of the numbered paragraphs plays a specific role in the work in which it is included. As you read, identify the role of each paragraph as *introduction, definition, transition, information, illustration* or *conclusion*. If you think a paragraph plays more than one role, identify both roles.

Next, identify the word, phrase, sentence or tone that caused you to designate the paragraph role as you have. When you finish, compare your answers with those suggested on page 248.

The following paragraphs are from a memorandum from J. Edgar Hoover to the F.B.I.

(1) The question of capital punishment has sent a storm of controversy thundering across our nation — millions of spoken and written words seek to examine the question so that decisions may be reached which befit our civilization.

(2) The struggle for answers concerning the taking of men's lives is one to which every American should lend his voice, for the problem in a democracy such as ours is not one for a handful of men to solve alone.

(3) As a representative of law enforcement, it is my belief that a great many of the most vociferous cries for abolition of capital punishment emanate from those areas of our society which have been insulated against the horrors man can and does perpetrate against his fellow beings.

(4) At the same time, nothing is so precious in our country as the life of a human being, whether he is a criminal or not, and on the other side of the scales must be placed all of the legal safeguards which our society demands.

(5) Experience has clearly demonstrated, however, that the time-proven deterrents to a crime are sure detection, swift apprehension and proper punishment.

(6)   Who, in all good conscience, can say that Julius and Ethel Rosenberg, the spies who delivered the atomic bomb into the hands of the Soviets, should have been spared when their treachery caused the shadow of annihilation to fall upon all the world's peoples? . . . What would have been the chances of rehabilitating Jack Gilbert Graham, who placed a bomb in his own mother's luggage and blasted her and forty-three other innocent victims into oblivion as they rode an airliner across a peaceful sky?

(7)   A judge once said, "The death penalty is a warning, just like a light-house throwing its beams out to sea. We hear about shipwrecks, but we do not hear about the ships the lighthouse guides safely on their way."

(8)   We must never allow misguided compassion to erase our concern for the hundreds of unfortunate, innocent victims of bestial criminals.

The following paragraphs on economics were taken from the work of the well-known economist Harrison Westfield.

(9)   Inflation — recession — depression. What do these words mean, simply stated, in economic terms and in broader human terms? And how do these conditions come about in the first place?

(10)   In simpler days, Americans spoke of *good times* and *hard times*. It was good times when you had a job; it was hard times when you didn't. When securities markets and banks crumbled under the heavy hands of speculators, taking tens of thousands of investors to their ruin, it was called — descriptively and candidly — a *panic*.

(11)   Panics happened with dependable regularity from the beginning of the Republic until 1929 and were invariably followed by hard times for millions of wage earners and farmers. With the advent of the New Deal, however, hard times were no longer fashionable and the nightmare of joblessness became known as a *depression*. When, in 1937, the economy took a fresh downturn in defiance of government assurances that the depression was over, the word *recession* was used to salvage what was left of the reputations of government advisers.

> Because the textbook is the student's primary learning tool, time should be spent becoming familiar with it. The structure and organization of the text give the student valuable clues to its exploitation and efficient use.

Getting the Most from Textbooks

It is unnecessary to point out the value of textbooks. As a student, you will probably spend more time studying your texts than you will devote to all your other college activities. In the words of Francis Bacon: "Some books are to be tasted, others to be swallowed, and some few to be chewed and digested." Textbooks are ones to be chewed and digested; they are the student's learning tools. How well you learn depends in good measure on how well you use your texts.

ORGANIZATION OF THE TEXT

A textbook is not a novel, and it should not be treated like one. It is not like, nor meant to be like, books you find lying around the house. Your texts have been carefully designed for their special educational purpose.

To understand all that goes into it, let us examine the textbook from a manufacturing or publishing point of view.

Production costs today are substantial. What you have to pay for your books reflects this expense. Starting with the salaries of the editors on the publisher's staff and considering the cost of setting type for every page, producing photographs, diagrams and illustrations, purchasing the paper, printing, binding, warehousing, marketing and distributing, the completed text in the student's hand represents a sizable investment.

What does all this mean to you? It means that if the publisher expects to recover his investment, his text must last and be used. Accordingly, every step of book production is carefully controlled to ensure that the finished product will be current, concise and comprehensive.

The first step involves the manuscript. Textbook authors must be experts and specialists in their fields, usually professors who have taught the subject for many years. No one would publish a text by a newcomer to the field. Today, we commonly find multiple authors of a single book, assuring the student, in this case, that two heads are better than one.

The completed manuscript next undergoes editing. Two things are considered. The book must be accurate and comprehensive in its treatment of the subject, and it must be well organized and readable. Other authorities in the field do the initial editing. They pass judgment and suggest changes and improvements. They make sure that the information is accurate; there must be no errors in the content. Next, they check to be sure that the work is up to date. The instruction must be current if the book is to sell. Finally, they consider how thoroughly the subject has been treated. Has anything been left out?

The publisher's staff goes to work next. Their job is to help organize and structure the work. Is the writing clear? Are there enough charts, tables and illustrations? Will students be able to read and understand the text?

Book designers select a readable typeface of a suitable size. They specify the grade and quality of paper to be used. Pages are laid out and color introduced for a pleasing and inviting appearance. Finally, a cover is designed. Every effort is expended to make the book appeal to students.

Because all this thought and planning have gone into the text, it lends itself readily to analysis. The wise student, therefore, will spend a half hour or so examining the features of his new text. He will learn whatever he can about his learning tool to help him master the subject.

EXAMINING THE TEXT

1. **The Author.** Whenever you purchase a new text, your first step should be to evaluate the author or authors. Of course, he knows more about the subject than you; you cannot evaluate him on that basis. But you can try to discover his background and experience. Is he a lecturer, a professor? Where does he teach? Is he a practitioner; that is, does he work in the field as well as teach? These answers may indicate his approach to the subject: practical or theoretical. The level at which he teaches may tell you how specialized or how broad his discussion will be.

2. **Copyright Date.** Check to see how current the text is. The copyright date is normally found on the back of the title page. The sciences, especially, accumulate new knowledge daily, and up-to-date texts are essential. Look for a listing of earlier copyrights. A series of such dates indicates that this is a standard text in the field. Its value and worth have been proven over the years.

3. **Preface/Introduction.** Read the

author's preface and introduction. Try to learn his approach to the subject. Does he consider his text to be an intensive examination or a broad survey? Does he plan to include examples gained from his own experience in the field? Most important, discover his reason for writing. What does he expect you to gain from his book? Why does he consider this subject important for you to learn?

The introduction is his first opportunity to address the reader. Anything he wants you to keep in mind as you use the text will be covered here. His opening remarks are designed to get you off to a good start. Don't gloss over this important part of the text.

4. Table of Contents. The contents page not only discloses the material to be covered, it also reveals how it will be organized. Is the subject presented

historically? If so, you know that current thought will appear near the back of the book. You might also expect the early part of the text to present biographical information on early contributors to the field.

The author's approach might be analytical. He may proceed from the simple to the complex. If so, the fundamental or basic concepts will be discussed early in the text. You will need to know and understand these to grasp material presented later.

Even though you may not know much about the subject, you can still discover how it will be presented. Preview a section which interests you and see how the author reveals his information. This will contribute to your background in the subject and help you later in your studying.

5. Bibliography. A bibliography is a list of books. At the end of most texts, authors tell the reader which books they have referred to or obtained information from in presenting their subject. Check to see if he has referred to other textbooks, if he has consulted original materials, or if he has done his own research. Examine the level of his sources. Are they wide-ranging, or do they appear to be highly specialized?

6. Index. Another valuable feature of the text is the index in the back of the book. Almost every textbook contains a subject index. This index lists alphabetically the various topics which are discussed in the body of the text. The appropriate page numbers accompany each listing.

There may be other indexes, too. For example, an authors index may be included so that you can look up by name those authorities mentioned throughout the text. Also listed will be their writings and works.

7. Appendix. Many of your textbooks will also contain an appendix at the back of the book. The appendix is a sort of all-purpose catch-all of useful material that the author wants

you to have at your fingertips. For example, the appendix in your American history text might contain a variety of information: lists of the states of the Union and pertinent facts about their statehood; presidential elections and their vital statistics; the Declaration of Independence, the Constitution, the Monroe Doctrine and other key speeches; inaugural addresses and policy-making documents. The information offered in the appendix is likely to prove a valuable reference source throughout your course work.

8. **Glossary**. You will often find a glossary at the back of the book. Science texts, or any subject that has a special vocabulary all its own, will list significant words alphabetically, along with their special meanings as they pertain to the subject matter. Check to see which of your textbooks include glossaries and use them — it's more convenient than reaching for the dictionary, and you can be sure that you're reading the right definition for the word as it is used in context.

In addition to your assigned text, it is always a good idea to have one or two supplementary texts on hand for easy reference. You may want to refer to these for a more detailed discussion of the subject. Or, you may wish to view another approach to the material to increase your understanding and to reinforce what you have learned. A supplementary text by an authority other than the author of your textbook may provide an opposing point of view or present controversial issues related to the material in your text. Such a reference book will broaden your knowledge and perhaps increase your interest in the subject.

Keep in mind that textbooks are the tools of your trade. Become skilled in the use of them. Examining your textbooks first will heighten your appreciation of them and help you get the most out of these essential learning tools.

_____: Reading Time

_____: Reading Rate

_____: Score, Test A

_____: Score, Test B

_____: Total Score

_____%: Comprehension

Directions: The following passage, taken from the selection you have just read, has words omitted from it. Fill in each blank with the word that was omitted. Each blank filled correctly is worth two points. Ask your instructor if you may take credit for close synonyms. Enter your score in the box provided at the end of the selection. A list of the omitted words can be found on page 237.

ORGANIZATION OF THE TEXT

A textbook is not a novel, and it should not be treated like one. It is not like, nor meant to be like, _____ you find lying around the house. Your
1
texts have _____ carefully designed for their special educational
2
purpose.

To understand _____ that goes into it, let us examine the textbook
3
_____ a manufacturing or publishing point of view.
4

Production costs _____ are substantial. What you have to pay for
5
your _____ reflects this expense. Starting with the salaries of the
6
_____ on the publisher's staff and considering the cost of
7
_____ type for every page, producing photographs, diagrams and
8
illustrations, _____ the paper, printing, binding, warehousing,
9
marketing and distributing, the _____ text in the student's hand
10
represents a sizable investment.

_____ does all this mean to you? It means that _____
11   12
the publisher expects to recover his investment, his text _____ last
13
and be used. Accordingly, every step of book _____ is carefully
14
controlled to ensure that the finished product _____ be current,
15
concise and comprehensive.

The first step involves _____ manuscript. Textbook authors must
16
be experts and specialists in _____ fields, usually professors who have
17
taught the subject for _____ years. No one would publish a text by a
18
_____ to the field. Today, we commonly find multiple authors
19
_____ a single book, assuring the student, in this case,
20
_____ two heads are better than one.
21
The completed manuscript _____ undergoes editing. Two things
22
are considered. The book must _____ accurate and comprehensive
23
in its treatment of the subject, _____ it must be well organized and
24
readable. Other authorities _____ the field do the initial editing.
25
They pass judgment and suggest changes and improvements.

COMPREHENSION TEST 8-B

Directions: This is another passage from the selection, again with words omitted. Proceed as before, giving yourself two points for each blank filled correctly. Add this score to the one from Test A and enter your total score in the box at the end of the selection. Use the conversion table on page 254 to convert your *total* score to a comprehension percentage, and record that grade in the box also. A list of omitted words can be found on page 238.

There may be other indexes, too. For example, an authors index may be included so _____1_____ you can look up by name those authorities mentioned _____2_____ the text. Also listed will be their writings and _____3_____.

7. Appendix. Many of your textbooks will also contain an _____4_____ at the back of the book. The appendix is _____5_____ sort of all-purpose catch-all of useful material _____6_____ the author wants you to have at your fingertips. _____7_____ example, the appendix in your American history text might _____8_____ a variety of information: lists of the states of _____9_____ Union and pertinent facts about their statehood; presidential elections _____10_____ their vital statistics; the Declaration of Independence, the Constitution, _____11_____ Monroe Doctrine and other key speeches; inaugural addresses and _____12_____-making documents. The information offered in the appendix is _____13_____ to prove a valuable reference source throughout your course _____14_____.

8. Glossary. You will often find a glossary at the _____15_____ of the book. Science texts, or any subject that _____16_____ a special vocabulary all its own, will list significant _____17_____ alphabetically, along with their special meanings as they pertain _____18_____ the subject matter. Check to see which of your _____19_____ include glossaries and use them — it's more convenient than _____20_____ for the dictionary, and you can be sure that _____21_____ reading the right definition for the word as it _____22_____ used in context.

In addition to your assigned text, _____23_____ is always a good idea to have one or _____24_____ supplementary texts on hand for easy reference. You may _____25_____ to refer to these for a more detailed discussion of the subject. Or, you may wish to view another approach to the material to increase your understanding and to reinforce what you have learned.

THINKING ABOUT YOUR TEXTBOOKS

Practice Exercise 1

Directions: Select a textbook that you are using this semester in one of your major courses. Using this textbook, answer the following questions or discuss them in class.

1. What are the author's credentials; that is, why might he be qualified to write the book?

2. What sources did the author use? Did anyone or any organizations help with the book? If so, how?

3. Who published the book? When? Have there been reprints or revisions made since the book was first published? What does this have to do with the value of the book you are looking at?

4. What do you think of the design of the book? Does the appearance make you want to use it? Does it appear easy or difficult to read? Does the design of the text clearly indicate the major points being covered? What is your opinion of the illustrations and graphics used with the text?

5. What special or unusual features does the book have that might prove useful to you?

6. Read the preface of your textbook. If your book contains an introduction, read that also. Point out at least three interesting or useful bits of information that you find there.

7. Is the table of contents simply a listing of chapter titles? How can you use the table of contents for study or review?

8. Examine the system of footnoting in your book carefully. Also examine the bibliography. These two items are found in different places in different books. How are they handled in your book? How can you use footnotes and bibliography? How might other people find these features useful — researchers or teachers, for example?

9. Does your text have an appendix? If so, what kinds of information can be found there?

THINKING ABOUT YOUR TEXTBOOKS

Practice Exercise 2

Directions: Consider yourself in the following hypothetical situation. On the first day of class in a new course, you arrive with a brand new, unopened, 800-page textbook under your arm. The instructor says: "When we meet tomorrow we will have a one-hour essay exam with exactly one question: What is your book about?" How would you prepare for the exam?

Practice Exercise 3

Directions: Having selected a book from the library shelf, you want to find out if it will help you with a term paper you are writing for American history. Some of the requirements for the paper are listed below. How would you find out if the book will help with your paper and if it meets the requirements?

a. The general subject is the Civil War.

b. The specific subject is the Battle of Vicksburg.

c. General Grant's role in the battle must be explained in detail.

d. Your information must reflect recent opinion and research that is no more than five years old.

e. The author of your source material must be a specialist in the Civil War period.

f. You need to find other books dealing with specific aspects of the battle.

g. You have to know something about the approach that the author is taking toward the subject and why he is writing the book.

Practice Exercise 4

Directions: The table of contents can offer important clues to the overall organization of a textbook. Knowing the author's approach to the subject gives you a head start at understanding because it enables you to relate each chapter that you read to the whole.

Using one of your major texts, analyze the table of contents to discover the author's approach to the material. Does the author begin with fundamentals and move on to general concepts and theories? Is the text organized chronologically, with the most recent events coming toward the end, or geographically, by region or country?

> The most efficient textbook reading is done with a pencil. Students who mark their texts are thinking, and thinking is essential for effective studying. Specific kinds of marks help you designate items of special importance.

Marking Your Text

In the words of Thoreau, "Books must be read as deliberately and reservedly as they were written." In other words, this means that novels can be read lightly; textbooks must be studied. Students realize this, of course; they know that academic success depends upon how well they read and study their textbooks.

Many students read with a pencil. They mark the text as they read to help them understand the material now and make review easier later. This is a good practice; intelligent marking can significantly improve your comprehension and retention.

WHY MARK?

Why is the most efficient reading done with a pencil? First, marking improves your concentration and attention because it focuses more of your faculties on the task at hand. While you are writing, you are probably speaking and listening to yourself as you compose your thoughts, thus using three other senses in addition to vision. With so much conscious activity directed to the task, daydreaming and mind-wandering are much less likely to occur. Comprehension is also heightened under these conditions.

Second, thinking precedes writing. In order for you to make a mark or underline a sentence or write a marginal note, you must first evaluate and decide. In short, marking makes you think. Good reading, reading that results in learning, always involves thinking. Reading with a pencil is an excellent way of motivating yourself to think as you read.

Third, marking the text helps you remember. This is the principal reason for marking a text. Because, as we have seen, marking causes you to concentrate and think, remembering is vastly improved. On the other hand, retention is much more difficult for students who have only read through the material in their usual fashion.

Finally, if you have marked well and meaningfully, you will not only recall ideas later, you'll also be able to locate key points when reviewing.

Some students are reluctant to write in their textbooks. Their regard for books is such that it goes against their grain to write in them; in a sense they feel that they are defacing valuable property. This is understandable; we all own books that we value highly. But textbooks are tools; they are the means to an end. As such, they should be exploited in the most efficient manner possible.

Naturally, you shouldn't mark in books that don't belong to you. If the textbook you're using belongs to a friend or is borrowed from the library, take notes on the material. The selection in this book titled "How to Take Notes" reviews the best methods of note-taking. You may want to combine your textbook notes with your lecture notes on that topic, so that all your review material is in one handy place.

The difference between textbooks and other books is that textbooks are not meant to be read casually; they need to be studied.

Study-type reading is different from reading for other purposes. A detective novel can be read rapidly for enjoyment; you can stop in the middle of a chapter and take it up again later. Textbooks, on the other hand, must be read carefully and understood thoroughly. This kind of reading and studying is best done with pencil in hand.

Don't make the mistake of most students when they first start to mark. In their zeal to underline everything of importance, they underline everything. Check the book of a student with this problem. You'll find the excessive underscores so distracting that the eye tends to seek out the unmarked lines to read.

You must learn to mark selectively. Students who underline everything do

so because they are unable to distinguish between major points and supporting data. The selections in this text are designed to help you become selective — to help you learn to recognize and separate the main ideas from the rest of the matter. With this skill and the knowledge of how to mark a book wisely, you are well on your way to becoming a truly proficient student.

HOW TO MARK

1. **Summarize Graphic Data.** If you see a table, graph, map or diagram, stop and study it. When you feel that you understand what is being illustrated, make a brief note in the margin. Graphs and charts are used to show how two or more factors are related. To ensure that you grasp the relationship and to help you reinterpret the visual aid later during review, write a brief summary of it in the margin. In the case of maps, state what the map shows the reader.

You are asked to do this with graphic information because only very important matter is shown this way. In textbook production, visuals cost extra. Only essentials deserve the expense.

2. **Underline Major Points.** In any textbook chapter, only five or six major points can be properly presented and explained. Find these and underline them.

Clues point to the main ideas. You will find numbers in the margin or bold headlines whenever a new point is presented. A statement usually follows. Locate the statement which gives the important facts and underline it. Underlining helps you give the matter the attention it deserves now and helps you find it again when reviewing.

Don't over-underline. Reserve this mark for one purpose only: to emphasize the major points.

3. **Bracket Key Passages.** Use a bracket — [ ] — to mark off important sections. Such passages might be introductory or summary statements. An introductory statement, of course, appears early in the chapter announcing what is to be discussed, or why this material is important, or something else of significance. A summary statement comes at or near the end. The writer uses it to restate what has been covered or to summarize the major points presented. Or he may leave you with a final thought which he considers important.

The content of these passages is of a different value from that contained in the sentences you have underlined. Normally, introductory and summary passages do not tell the reader *about* the main points; they merely list them or indicate what they are.

Items to be bracketed may appear in the middle of a chapter, too. They may serve to summarize what has been presented so far and announce what is to follow next.

4. **Star Important Facts.** In addition to the major points which you underline, there are other important facts which should be singled out. Put an asterisk or star in the margin beside them.

Facts to be starred will be found throughout the chapter. They will follow the main points and present information relating to them. Indicating these will help you fill in the gaps when you review.

5. **Enumerate Series.** Whenever a list appears, it is always wise to number the items in it. Circle the key word or phrase which introduces the series and number the items as they appear. The introductory phrases will be expressions like *several reasons, four causes, five steps, seven elements,* and so on. Make sure you find them all.

This type of marking can be a real aid, especially if the list is long. In addition to presenting the items on his list, the author usually has something to say about each one. This can extend the series over several pages, making it difficult for the reader to follow the sequence. The numbers keep you aware of the series and serve to connect the items.

6. **Use Abbreviations.** Write the abbreviation *def.* in the margin whenever a definition is given. Definitions are essential; comprehension of an entire lesson may depend on a key definition. Show that you know a definition has been given. This encourages you to give it the attention it deserves. Later, when reviewing, these are the things you will want to study for quizzes and exams.

Another paragraph you may wish to call attention to is one containing an illustration. Write *ill.* in the margin beside these. Not all illustrative paragraphs are important enough to be singled out, but occasionally your understanding of a particular point is reinforced by an example. Mark it. You will want to find it again later.

Other useful abbreviations are *intro.* to indicate a significant paragraph of introduction, and *conc.* to point out a conclusion. An obvious abbreviation you can use is *imp.*, meaning *important*. It tells you that here is a matter you want to learn and remember. You might use *imp.* in your text to mark information stressed in class.

7. **React.** Develop the habit of reacting as you read. This means agreeing, disagreeing, questioning or challenging. It is like carrying on a conversation with the author. From time to time, it is appropriate for you to comment. Do this in writing in the margins. Comments like "I think he's right" or "Can he prove this?" or "How can I use this information?" all serve to sharpen your attention and concentration as you read.

Use all of these devices for marking the text when you study. You'll find your concentration and retention considerably improved as a result.

_____: Reading Time

_____: Reading Rate

_____: Score, Test A

_____: Score, Test B

_____: Total Score

_____%: Comprehension

Directions: The following passage, taken from the selection you have just read, has words omitted from it. Fill in each blank with the word that was omitted. Each blank filled correctly is worth two points. Ask your instructor if you may take credit for close synonyms. Enter your score in the box provided at the end of the selection. A list of the omitted words can be found on page 238.

WHY MARK?

Why is the most efficient reading done with a pencil? First, marking improves your concentration and attention because it _____ more of your faculties on the task at hand. _____ you are writing, you are probably speaking and listening _____ yourself as you compose your thoughts, thus using three _____ senses in addition to vision. With so much conscious _____ directed to the task, daydreaming and mind-wandering are _____ less likely to occur. Comprehension is also heightened under _____ conditions.

Second, thinking precedes writing. In order for you _____ make a mark or underline a sentence or write _____ marginal note, you must first evaluate and decide. In _____, marking makes you think. Good reading, reading that results _____ learning, always involves thinking. Reading with a pencil is _____ excellent way of motivating yourself to think as you _____.

Third, marking the text helps you remember. This is _____ principal reason for marking a text. Because, as we _____ seen, marking causes you to concentrate and think, remembering _____ vastly improved. On the other hand, retention is much _____ difficult for students who have only read through the _____ in their usual fashion.

Finally, if you have marked _____ and meaningfully, you will not only recall ideas later, _____ also be able to locate key points when reviewing.

_____ students are reluctant to write in their textbooks. Their _____ for books is such that it goes against their _____ to write in them; in a sense they feel _____ they are defacing valuable property. This is understandable; we _____ own books that we value highly. But textbooks are tools; they are the means to an end.

COMPREHENSION TEST 9-B

Directions: This is another passage from the selection, again with words omitted. Proceed as before, giving yourself two points for each blank filled correctly. Add this score to the one from Test A and enter your total score in the box at the end of the selection. Use the conversion table on page 254 to convert your *total* score to a comprehension percentage, and record that grade in the box also. A list of omitted words can be found on page 238.

5. Enumerate Series. Whenever a list appears, it is always wise to number the items in it. Circle the key word or phrase which introduces the _____ 1 and number the items as they appear. The introductory _____ 2 will be expressions like *several reasons, four causes, five* _____ 3 , *seven elements,* and so on. Make sure you find _____ 4 all.

This type of marking can be a real _____ 5 , especially if the list is long. In addition to _____ 6 the items on his list, the author usually has _____ 7 to say about each one. This can extend the _____ 8 over several pages, making it difficult for the reader _____ 9 follow the sequence. The numbers keep you aware of _____ 10 series and serve to connect the items.

6. Use Abbreviations. _____ 11 the abbreviation *def.* in the margin whenever a definition _____ 12 given. Definitions are essential; comprehension of an entire lesson _____ 13 depend on a key definition. Show that you know _____ 14 definition has been given. This encourages you to give _____ 15 the attention it deserves. Later, when reviewing, these are _____ 16 things you will want to study for quizzes and _____ 17 .

Another paragraph you may wish to call attention to _____ 18 one containing an illustration. Write *ill.* in the margin _____ 19 these. Not all illustrative paragraphs are important enough to _____ 20 singled out, but occasionally your understanding of a particular _____ 21 is reinforced by an example. Mark it. You will _____ 22 to find it again later.

Other useful abbreviations are _____ 23 to indicate a significant paragraph of introduction, and *conc.* _____ 24 point out a conclusion. An obvious abbreviation you can _____ 25 is *imp.,* meaning *important.* It tells you that here is a matter you want to learn and remember.

PRACTICE IN MARKING

Directions: This is an exercise designed to give you practice in marking. Your task is to apply the suggestions you have just read to the selections below. When you finish, check with others to see how they have marked. Discuss differences to determine how your marking can be improved.

UNLUCKY STRIKES

During the past forty years, cancer of the lung in the United States has shown the greatest increase of any cancer type. Compared to 3,000 deaths from lung cancer in 1930, the number of deaths is expected to rise to 84,000 in 1981. If the present trend continues, it is estimated that about one million persons who are now school children will die eventually of lung cancer.

Such an alarming increase assumes the proportions of an epidemic. At least 70 percent of the total increase can be attributed to cigarette smoking. An additional factor is air pollution caused by industrial wastes, automobile exhausts and household sources.

The first studies on the relationship of smoking to lung cancer were of patients with the disease who were asked about their smoking habits. Their answers were compared with those of noncancer patients. Almost all lung cancer patients replied that they had been long-term, heavy cigarette smokers.

The next studies were of large groups of men who were first identified by their smoking habits, then were followed for several years. Deaths from all causes increased among smokers according to the amount smoked. But the most striking proportional rise was in deaths from lung cancer.

While these clues were being obtained from population studies, scientists began to study the smoking and cancer relationship in the laboratory. Chemists isolated and identified at least a dozen carcinogenic chemicals of the hydrocarbon type in the tars from tobacco smoke. There is evidence that tobacco smoke contains yet further carcinogens.

The membranes lining the lungs absorb cancer-producing chemicals from tobacco smoke. The protective mechanisms by which the lungs rid themselves of impurities are first paralyzed and then destroyed by tobacco smoke. Prolonged exposure of animals to tobacco smoke produces changes in cells that resemble early stages of cancer development. These changes are also seen in the lungs of heavy smokers who die of causes other than lung cancer.

Health hazards of smoking are not limited to lung cancer. Bronchitis, emphysema and other crippling lung diseases are produced in even larger numbers. Deaths from heart disease are accelerated and increased. While cigarette smoking is a major cause of lung cancer, other uses of tobacco are associated with cancers of the oral cavity among cigar smokers and cancers of the lip among pipe smokers.

PRACTICE IN MARKING

MAJOR RISK FACTORS

More Americans die from heart disease than from any other disease. Every year a million people in this country have heart attacks or die suddenly from coronary heart disease. There are several manifestations of coronary heart disease, all related in part to atherosclerosis, a disease in which fatty materials accumulate in the walls of medium or large arteries.

Cigarette smoking is an important risk factor in the development of coronary heart disease and, by accelerating damage already present as a result of coronary heart disease, may contribute to sudden death. In the total male population, the death rate from coronary heart disease averages 70 percent higher for smokers than for nonsmokers. Men between the ages of 45 and 54 who are heavy smokers have coronary heart disease death rates three times higher than those of nonsmokers. Women smokers in the same age group have coronary heart disease death rates twice those of nonsmoking women.

In addition to cigarette smoking, a number of other biochemical, physiological, and environmental factors have been identified as contributing to the development of coronary heart disease. These risk factors include high blood pressure, high serum cholesterol, excess weight, lack of physical activity and a family history of coronary heart disease. The person who has one or a combination of these factors stands a good chance of developing coronary heart disease. However, high blood pressure, cholesterol and cigarette smoking are considered to be the major risk factors.

Cigarette smoking acts independently of these risk factors in relation to coronary heart disease, but it can also work jointly with the two major factors to greatly increase the risk of developing this disease. Thus smokers who have hypertension or high serum cholesterol, or both, have substantially higher rates of illness or sudden death from coronary heart disease, while those who are free of these three risk factors have lower rates.

Exactly how cigarette smoking affects the heart is being explored through experimental studies in animals and humans. Nicotine and carbon monoxide, both present in cigarette smoke, appear to be important factors in the mechanism that produces coronary heart disease. Nicotine increases the demand of the heart for oxygen and other nutrients while carbon monoxide decreases the ability of the blood to furnish needed oxygen.

> Far too many students fail to use the dictionary properly. Understanding the kinds of information given in a dictionary entry is essential. Certain skills can be developed to make using a dictionary easy and effective.

Using Your Dictionary

We will assume that you have a good, hard-cover, college-level, desk dictionary as a basic tool of your trade. Paperback or pocket-sized dictionaries and supermarket giveaways are just not complete enough to use for studying. However, if you are about to purchase your first dictionary, ask your instructor for a list of those most frequently recommended for school use.

It is generally taken for granted that everyone knows how to use a dictionary though, in reality, very few students can use one well or effectively.

While it is true that students can locate the entry (word) they are looking for, it is also true that most of them cannot translate the information they find into usable form. The result is that many students will take the first meaning given whether or not it makes sense in a particular context.

UNDERSTANDING DICTIONARIES

Take a few moments to become familiar with your dictionary. For each word entry, the order of items given here may vary slightly from one dictionary to the next, but the following information can usually be found.

1. **Entry Word.** The word you are looking up is shown in bold type, larger than the rest of the copy in the entry. In many dictionaries, the word overhangs or sticks out a little into the left margin to help you find it easily.

Words which are spelled alike but which are unrelated are listed separately. The word *bow*, for example, would be listed as three entries: (1) A *bow* to the audience, (2) A *bow* and arrow, and (3) the *bow* (front end) of a ship.

In addition to general words of the English language, most dictionaries include commonly used foreign words and expressions; the names of historical characters, artists, writers and other famous people; and many geographic locations. In special sections of your dictionary you can often find lists of colleges and universities; tables of weights and measures; lists of signs, symbols and abbreviations; and articles on grammar, usage and spelling. In this respect, a dictionary is like a small, concise encyclopedia.

2. **Syllabification.** How a word is divided into syllables is shown in the entry word. This shows you how to hyphenate that word (at the end of a line, for example) without looking further.

Dots are used to separate the syllables, and the word can be split at the end of a line only where dots are used. If a word does not show a dot, it cannot be divided, even though it may be pronounced as two syllables. *Rhythm* is such a word.

Dots are used instead of hyphens to indicate syllables because hyphens are needed for listing hyphenated words, such as *half-moon*. Naturally, hyphenated words can be divided at the hyphens.

3. **Pronunciation.** Immediately after the entry word, the pronunciation is shown in parentheses. When two pronunciations are used, the first one is the most common.

Symbols and special marks are used to show the correct pronunciation of words. Many of the marks are explained at the bottom of the page in a pronunciation key which uses sample, illustrative words. So don't be frustrated when you see unusual spellings and symbols; just refer to the notes at the bottom of the page and you will find a word you know to make the pronunciation clear to you.

Along with the pronunciation in parentheses, the syllables which should be stressed will be indicated. In multisyllable words, the syllable having the greatest stress will be designated with a primary stress mark (′); a secondary stress mark (′)

indicates a syllable receiving less stress; and a syllable having relatively weak stress will be unmarked.

4. **Parts of Speech.** Following the pronunciation, an abbreviation or letter in italics will be used to show the part of speech. In the case of *rhythm*, the letter *n.* tells the reader that the word is a noun. When a word can be used as more than one part of speech, a second italic abbreviation will appear later on in the entry before the definition is given for that usage. A bold dash (—) will appear before a second part-of-speech listing.

Many students err by selecting the first meaning or definition given for a word when the meaning they need is shown later on under a different part-of-speech label. When you look up a word, be sure you keep in mind the way the word is being used.

Part-of-speech abbreviations used in dictionaries are *adj.* (adjective), *adv.* (adverb), *n.* (noun), *pron.* (pronoun), *v.i.* (intransitive verb), *v.t.* (transitive verb), *interj.* (interjection), *prep.* (preposition) and *conj.* (conjunction).

5. **Inflected Forms.** Inflections are changes in spelling which occur in words because of plural form, verb tense, comparison of adjectives, and so on. Inflected forms come next in the entry. If a word forms a plural in an unusual way, like *mouse* and *mice*, the plural spelling is shown. Correct plural spellings for other words which cause confusion, such as *mothers-in-law* and *cupfuls*, are also given.

Inflected forms of adjectives are often given. Following *heavy*, the reader will find *heavier, heaviest*; after *good*, all dictionaries list *better, best*.

The past tense and past participles of verbs formed just by adding *-ed* (such as *add, added*) are usually not shown. These are the regular verbs. For irregular verbs, like *run*, the irregular forms (*ran, run,* and *running*) are given.

6. **Definitions.** The definitions for a word are numbered. While many

dictionaries list the most common or latest meaning for a word first, some dictionaries give definitions in historical order. This means that the *latest* definition for a word will appear last. You should find out which system your book uses. Idiomatic or slang uses of a word are sometimes given. Following the definitions for the word *sack*, for example, you may find the expressions *hit the sack* and *sack out* listed and defined.

Examine the definitions carefully to be sure you select exactly the right sense or meaning that suits the context of your reading.

7. Restrictive Labels. When a definition pertains to a certain subject field, an abbreviated label will show before it. In printing circles, the word *face* refers to a design or style of type. In the dictionary, this meaning is given along with the others, but it is preceded by the restrictive label, *Print*.

In England, a word may have a special meaning. The dictionary would show *Brit*. before it. Restrictive labels are also used to indicate *Slang* or *Informal* usages and definitions.

8. Etymologies. The history or derivation of a word is given. It may appear before the definitions or it may follow them. The etymology is shown in square brackets; it tells the reader the language a word comes from and also its spelling in that language. Useful information about the origins and meanings of the roots and affixes of a word can also be found with the etymology.

9. Run-on Entries. Near the end of the entry, derivative forms are listed. These forms are changes in words caused by the addition of suffixes. Accordingly, following *gradual*, you can expect to find *gradually* and *gradualness* listed.

10. Synonyms. For certain common words, dictionaries show synonyms, words with the same or nearly the same meaning as the entry word. Synonyms usually appear following the entry, at the left margin, preceded by the abbreviation *Syn*.

Antonyms, words with opposite meanings, may be given after the synonyms. These would also appear at the left margin and be preceded by the abbreviation *Ant*.

11. **Contextual Illustrations.** Every dictionary uses words in context to help make meanings clear. These appear as brief phrases, although occasionally complete sentences may be given. The usages indicate how the entry word can be used and how its meaning varies in context.

DICTIONARY SKILLS

1. **Locating Words in Alphabetical Order.** One way to speed up word location is to gain proficiency in locating words in alphabetical order. Dictionaries, as you know, list words alphabetically, so the faster you can find a word, the sooner you have the information you need.

2. **Using Guide Words.** To help you find words quickly, dictionaries print guide words at the top of each page. These tell you the first entry and the last entry for that page. Because entries are listed alphabetically, a glance at the guide words will tell you which words are on that page.

3. **Identifying Variant Spellings.** Some words can be correctly spelled in more than one way. For example, *practice* can also be spelled *practise*. Variant spellings preferred in England, such as *colour*, are labeled *Brit*. Your book might only list the more popular form.

4. **Using the Appropriate Meaning.** Most common words have several meanings. One dictionary shows forty-four definitions for the word *go*. You must be careful to choose exactly the right meaning that fits the sense of the material you are reading.

With just a little practice, you will be amazed to find that the simple act of using a dictionary regularly will make your school work easier and will markedly improve your grades.

_____: Reading Time

_____: Reading Rate

_____: Score, Test A

_____: Score, Test B

_____: Total Score

_____%: Comprehension

COMPREHENSION TEST 10-A

Directions: The following passage, taken from the selection you have just read, has words omitted from it. Fill in each blank with the word that was omitted. Each blank filled correctly is worth two points. Ask your instructor if you may take credit for close synonyms. Enter your score in the box provided at the end of the selection. A list of the omitted words can be found on page 238.

It is generally taken for granted that everyone knows how to use a dictionary though, in reality, very few students can use one well or effectively.

While it is true that students can locate the _____ (word) they are
                                                        1
looking for, it is also true _____ most of them cannot translate the
                                        2
information they find _____ usable form. The result is that many
                             3
students will _____ the first meaning given whether or not it makes
                    4
_____ in a particular context.
      5

UNDERSTANDING DICTIONARIES

Take a few _____ to become familiar with your dictionary. For
                      6
each word _____, the order of items given here may vary slightly
                   7
_____ one dictionary to the next, but the following information
      8
_____ usually be found.
      9

1. Entry Word. The word you are _____ up is shown in bold type,
                                              10
larger than the _____ of the copy in the entry. In many dictionaries,
                        11
_____ word overhangs or sticks out a little into the _____
      12   13
margin to help you find it easily.

Words which _____ spelled alike but which are unrelated are
                       14
listed separately. _____ word *bow*, for example, would be listed as
                            15
three _____: (1) A *bow* to the audience, (2) A *bow* and arrow,
              16
_____ (3) the *bow* (front end) of a ship.
      17

In addition _____ general words of the English language, most
                      18
dictionaries include _____ used foreign words and expressions; the
                              19
names of historical _____, artists, writers and other famous people;
                              20
and many geographic _____. In special sections of your dictionary
                               21
you can often _____ lists of colleges and universities; tables of weights
                      22
and _____; lists of signs, symbols and abbreviations; and articles on
        23
_____, usage and spelling. In this respect, a dictionary is
      24
_____ a small, concise encyclopedia.
      25

2. Syllabification. How a word is divided into syllables is shown in the entry word.

COMPREHENSION TEST 10-B

Directions: This is another passage from the selection, again with words omitted. Proceed as before, giving yourself two points for each blank filled correctly. Add this score to the one from Test A and enter your total score in the box at the end of the selection. Use the conversion table on page 254 to convert your *total* score to a comprehension percentage, and record that grade in the box also. A list of omitted words can be found on page 238.

8. Etymologies. The history or derivation of a word is given. It may appear before the definitions or it may _____ them. The etymology is shown

1
in square brackets; it _____ the reader the language a word comes

2
from and _____ its spelling in that language. Useful information

3
about the _____ and meanings of the roots and affixes of a

4
_____ can also be found with the etymology.

5

9. Run-on Entries. _____ the end of the entry, derivative forms are

6
listed. _____ forms are changes in words caused by the addition

7
_____ suffixes. Accordingly, following *gradual*, you can expect to

8
find _____ and *gradualness* listed.

9

10. Synonyms. For certain common words, dictionaries _____

10
synonyms, words with the same or nearly the same _____ as the entry

11
word. Synonyms usually appear following the _____, at the left

12
margin, preceded by the abbreviation *Syn.* _____, words with

13
opposite meanings, may be given after the _____. These would also

14
appear at the left margin and _____ preceded by the abbreviation *Ant.*

15

11. Contextual Illustrations. Every dictionary _____ words in

16
context to help make meanings clear. These _____ as brief phrases,

17
although occasionally complete sentences may be _____. The usages

18
indicate how the entry word can be _____ and how its meaning

19
varies in context.

DICTIONARY SKILLS

1. _____ **Words in Alphabetical Order.** One way to speed up

20
_____ location is to gain proficiency in locating words in

21
_____ order. Dictionaries, as you know, list words alphabetically,

22
so _____ faster you can find a word, the sooner you

23
_____ the information you need.

24

2. **Using Guide Words.** To help _____ find words quickly,

25
dictionaries print guide words at the top of each page. These tell you the first entry and the last entry for that page.

Practice Exercise 1

Alphabetizing. One way to speed up word location is to gain proficiency in placing words in alphabetical order. The words in Column A belong in Column B. Write them in alphabetically where they belong. (Answer Key Page 249)

Column A			Column B
effect	1.	affect _____	afraid
believe	2.	after _____	agent
frighten	3.	avenge _____	balance
cancel	4.	balcony _____	blotch
bait	5.	business _____	critical
afford	6.	cuticle _____	cystic
fissure	7.	dynamo _____	effusion
cycle	8.	embrace _____	enamel
emulate	9.	finesse _____	fistula
again	10.	fraction _____	frizzle

Practice Exercise 2

Using Guide Words. The words in Column A have been taken from the dictionary. Also given are the guide words from the pages where the words were found. In Column B, write the word which belongs with each set of guide words. (Answer Key Page 249)

Column A			Column B
recent	1.	pay — peach	_____
peace	2.	penstock — people	_____
security	3.	perfusion — periodic	_____
perhaps	4.	prospective — protein	_____
reversal	5.	rebut — receptacle	_____
redoubt	6.	reckless — recompense	_____
protection	7.	redeem — redound	_____
rural	8.	reverberant — review	_____
penurious	9.	runlet — rush	_____
recollect	10.	sectional — sedition	_____

DICTIONARY SKILLS

Practice Exercise 3

Variant Spellings. The following sentences all contain variant spellings and inflected forms of words. On the line following each sentence, write the base word that you would have to locate in a dictionary in order to find information about the word in italics. (Answer Key Page 249)

1. The *dining* hall was full.　　　　　　　　　　_____

2. He *busied* himself in politics.　　　　　　　　_____

3. Passengers were *ferried* across the river.　　　_____

4. His eyes were *fixt* on the bloody scene.　　　　_____

5. Several *curricula* were offered at the college.　_____

6. She wore *goloshes* in the snow.　　　　　　　_____

7. The victim appeared to have been *garrotted*.　_____

8. He wore the *gaudiest* tie he could find.　　　　_____

9. The *gage* recorded the air pressure in the tank.　_____

10. The *glamor* of Hollywood life appealed to her.　_____

Practice Exercise 4

Appropriate Meaning. The following sentences contain a word in italics. Following each sentence, four dictionary-correct definitions are listed for the italicized word. Circle the letter before the best meaning for the word as used. (Answer Key Page 249)

1. A *panel* of judges selected the winner from among the four contestants.
   a. Section of a wall　　　　　　c. Instrument board
   b. Group of persons　　　　　　d. Strip of dress material

2. Whenever he ate out, he ordered a *rare* steak.
   a. Of thin texture　　　　　　　c. Not completely cooked
   b. Uncommon, scarce　　　　　　d. Exceptionally fine

3. He was so angry he had to *compose* himself before continuing.
   a. Calm one's mind　　　　　　　c. Set type
   b. Make up, form　　　　　　　　d. Create

4. His mind was *torn* between conflicting desires.
   a. Pulled apart　　　　　　　　　c. Ripped out
   b. Separated into pieces　　　　　d. Divided with doubt

5. The *true* heirs to the fortune were never found.
   a. Faithful, loyal　　　　　　　　c. Reliable, certain
   b. Rightful, legitimate　　　　　　d. Truthful

PREFIXES, SUFFIXES AND ROOTS

Many English words were created from a root word to which prefixes and suffixes have been added. From the simple root word *bear*, we have *bearable, unbearable, bearing, bearably, bearer*. One writer estimated that at least eighty English words have arisen from the Latin root *ced* and its participle *cess* including *cede, recede, cessation, recess, recession* and others.

So you can see that familiarity with word parts can be a very powerful aid for learning, understanding and using words. That is why most dictionaries include common prefixes, suffixes and roots in alphabetical order just like any other word entry. If some variation of a word is not listed in the dictionary or if someone has coined a new word (*astronaut* was a new word in the 1960s), you are expected to look up the word parts and provide your own definition.

The following exercises are designed to make you more familiar with the way some words are constructed and how prefixes and suffixes can change root words.

Prefixes. A prefix, located at the beginning of a word, modifies the meaning of that word. For example, the prefix *dis-* added to *agree* reverses its meaning: *disagree*.

Below is a list of 10 prefixes. Form the words which correspond with the definitions in the first column by combining one prefix with each root or word given in the last column. Use each prefix only once. Use a dictionary to help you determine the meaning of each prefix. The first one has been done for you. (Answer Key Page 249)

Prefixes				
ante-	e-	pen(e)-	hemi-	circum-
ambi-	anti-	mal(e)-	non-	hyper-

	Definitions	Prefixes	Roots
1.	Half of a globe	hemi	-sphere
2.	Marked by excessive movement	_____	-kinetic
3.	Before the war	_____	-bellum
4.	An evildoer or criminal	_____	-factor
5.	Speaking around the topic; unnecessarily wordy speech	_____	-locution
6.	Tending to destroy the life of microorganisms	_____	-biotic
7.	Almost the last	_____	-ultimate
8.	Not poisonous	_____	-toxic
9.	Affecting both sides	_____	-lateral
10.	To send or give out	_____	-mit

PREFIXES, SUFFIXES AND ROOTS

Suffixes. A suffix added to the end of a word changes the part of speech of the word. For example, the suffix *-able* changes the verb *manage* to an adjective, *manageable*. Therefore, *-able* is considered an adjective suffix. The suffix *-ward* can change a noun, such as *front*, to an adverb, *frontward*; or a preposition, *in*, to an adverb, *inward*. Thus, *-ward* is considered an adverb suffix.

The suffix *-ance* is considered a noun suffix because it is used to form nouns: the noun form of the verb *disturb* is *disturbance*; the noun form of the adjective *brilliant* is *brilliance*. Another noun suffix is *-age*. It is used to change a verb, such as *marry*, to a noun, *marriage*. It is also used to change a noun like *ton* into another noun, *tonnage*, which has a different but related meaning.

Practice Exercise 1
Directions: For each verb listed below, (a) compose a sentence; (b) change the verb to an adjective by adding the suffix *-able*; and (c) compose a sentence using the adjective you have just created. The first one is done for you.

1. notice (v.)   I *notice* the climate is quite pleasant here.
   noticeable (adj.)   There is a *noticeable* difference in climate here.

| 1. notice | 2. believe | 3. present | 4. train | 5. allow |
| 6. use | 7. drink | 8. laugh | 9. read | 10. like |

Practice Exercise 2
Directions: For each noun and preposition listed below, (a) compose a sentence; (b) change the noun or preposition to an adverb by adding the suffix *ward*; and (c) compose a sentence using the adverb you have just created. Be sure the adverb modifies the verb in your sentence. The first one is done for you.

1. home (n.)   I went *home*.
   homeward (adv.)   I headed *homeward*.

| 1. home | 2. back | 3. heaven | 4. for | 5. out |
| 6. up | 7. down | 8. after | 9. wind | 10. sea |

Practice Exercise 3
Directions: For each verb listed below, (a) compose a sentence; (b) change the verb to a noun by adding the suffix *-ance*; and (c) compose a sentence using the noun you have just created. The first one is done for you.

1. appear (v.)   You will *appear* before the board tomorrow.
   appearance (n.)   Your *appearance* before the board is required.

| 1. appear | 2. admit | 3. resemble | 4. convey | 5. utter |
| 6. defy | 7. assist | 8. clear | 9. comply | 10. inherit |

PREFIXES, SUFFIXES AND ROOTS

Practice Exercise 4

Directions: For each verb and noun listed below, (a) compose a sentence; (b) change the verb or noun to a new noun by adding the suffix *-age*; and (c) compose a sentence using the noun you have just created. The first one is done for you.

1. cover (v.)   My insurance *covers* many items.
   coverage (n.)   I have ample insurance *coverage* on my home.

1. cover	2. pilfer	3. lever	4. post	5. waste
6. break	7. acre	8. bond	9. spill	10. pass

Practice Exercise 5

Directions: Below is a list of suffixes, their meanings, and the part of speech each forms when added to a word. Using this list, match a suffix to each group of words numbered below and write your answer in the first column. In the second column, tell what part of speech the words would become if the suffix were added to them. The first one has been done for you. (Answer Key Page 249)

Suffix	Meaning	Part of Speech
-ly	in a certain manner	adverb
-ment	the action or process of	noun
-fy	to make or to cause to be	verb
-ist	one who is associated with	noun
-some	tending to	adjective
-en	to make or to cause to be	verb
-ize	to make or to cause to be	verb
-ward	indicates direction	adverb
-able	capable of being	adjective
-ful	full of or characterized by	adjective

	Word Groups	Part of Speech	Suffix	Part of Speech
1.	notice, present, use	verb	-able	adjective
2.	recruit, develop, adjourn	verb		
3.	sterile, final, public	adjective		
4.	bashful, perfect, simultaneous	adjective		
5.	after, down, up	preposition		
6.	burden, awe, quarrel	verb		
7.	weak, red, sweet	adjective		
8.	beauty, liquid, deity	noun		
9.	novel, geology, botany	noun		
10.	harm, event, peace	noun		

PREFIXES, SUFFIXES AND ROOTS

Roots. The English language is a composite of a variety of languages: Latin, Greek, Old English, French, Spanish and others. Latin and Greek have been especially important influences in our language. As noted earlier, it has been estimated that knowledge of only 14 basic Latin and Greek roots can help you to recognize and understand as many as 14,000 English words.

The following exercise will help you to become familiar with some basic roots. For more practice, refer to the list of common roots on page 51.

Write down at least three words that contain each of the following roots. Use a dictionary to help if you can't think of enough words. Be sure that the words you choose have the meaning of the root as part of their definitions. The first one has been done for you. When you finish, compare your answers with those suggested on page 249.

Root	Words Derived from the Root		
1. anthropo (man)	anthropoid	anthropology	misanthrope
2. astro (star)			
3. bene (well)			
4. chrono (time)			
5. circum (around)			
6. cogni (know)			
7. cosmo (world)			
8. dict (say)			
9. duct (lead)			
10. gen, gener (birth, race, beget)			
11. gram, graph (write)			
12. helio (sun)			
13. phon (sound)			
14. posit (place)			
15. rupt (break)			
16. scrib, script (write)			
17. sept (seven)			
18. spect (look)			
19. tain (hold)			
20. terra (earth)			

Libraries contain all the facts, information and literature that you require both as a student and as an individual. The vast amount of materials under the library's roof are cataloged so that you can put your hands on them quickly and easily. A great variety of reference books keeps isolated facts at your fingertips. Knowing how to get the most out of the library is one of the most valuable skills you can learn.

How to Use the Library

It has been observed that the world could blow itself to bits, but if enough of the great libraries survived, man could eventually pick up the pieces and reestablish the machinery, the buildings, the schools and the culture. This would be accomplished first by those men or nations knowing most about how to locate and use the right library materials because only libraries contain the records, formulas, blueprints, theories and information that sustain and inspire mankind.

Despite the staggering amount of materials contained within their walls, libraries are among the most orderly places on earth. Once you've learned some basic rules for using a library, you'll be able to walk into any library and feel comfortable and confident.

THE CARD CATALOG

The card catalog is your key to the library's collection of books, reference works and other materials. These are listed in three ways — by author, title and subject — with a separate catalog card for each entry. So if you know only the title or only the author of a particular book, you could look it up either way to find out if it is included in the library collection. Similarly, if you were interested in learning what the library has on a particular subject, you would consult the subject catalog. The entries are filed alphabetically, and all the drawers are labeled on the outside to tell you which parts of the alphabet they contain.

A catalog card usually includes the following information: the call number of the book, the author's name (last name first) followed by the dates of his birth and death, the title, publisher, place and date of publication, the number of pages, whether there are maps or illustrations, the contents of the book when this supplies important information to the reader, and other card entries for this book.

THE CALL NUMBER

Once you have identified a book that is of interest to you, you'll want to know how to put your hands on it.

In the upper left-hand corner of each catalog card is the "call number" for that book, indicating where you'll find that volume on the library shelves. The call number is also marked on the spine of the book.

The call number is the library's way of classifying that book. There are two popular systems in use by libraries today for classifying material — the Dewey Decimal system and the Library of Congress system — and most libraries use one or the other.

1. The Dewey Decimal System. The Dewey Decimal system was devised by Melvil Dewey in 1873 and is still used by libraries all over the world. Briefly, Dewey divided the field of knowledge into a series of tables based on the decimal system. There are ten large divisions which can be subdivided into smaller divisions:

000	General Works	500	Science
100	Philosophy	600	Useful Arts
200	Religion	700	Fine Arts
300	Sociology	800	Literature
400	Linguistics	900	History

Thus, a science book would have a number between 500 and 600. In addition, there will be another set of numbers directly below, preceded by the first letter of the author's last name. So 590.6/M284 might be the Dewey Decimal number for a book about science written by a person named Morris.

2. The Library of Congress System. The Library of Congress, the national library in Washington, D.C., has its own system of classification which has been adopted by many other libraries. The L.C. plan classifies subjects by letters of the alphabet. *A* represents General Works; *B*, Philosophy; *C* and *D*, History; *E* and *F*, America; and so

on. Subdivisions are made by different combinations of letters. Thus an almanac, which is regarded as a general work and would therefore come under *A*, might have a Library of Congress number that looks like this: AY67.N5W7. Find out which system your library uses.

If the library you're using has "open stacks," you can go directly to the shelves and find the book you want. Look around for a chart telling you where the call number you are looking for is located. Often, a simple diagram of the library directs you to the appropriate section.

If the library's shelves are "closed," you must fill out a *call slip* telling the librarian which books you want. You'll find quantities of these three-by-five-inch slips of paper near the card catalogs. Copy the call number, author and title of the book carefully on the slip. Include the volume number if there is one. Use a separate call slip for each book and turn them in at the proper desk.

USING REFERENCE BOOKS

Before you head for the book stacks, consider whether the information you're seeking can be found more readily in a reference book.

Reference books are collections of information arranged so that any one piece of information can be found as easily as possible. The reference books most people think of first are encyclopedias, and while these offer an excellent starting point in the investigation of almost any subject, remember that there are other reference books — both general and specific — that might be geared more directly to your inquiry. Among them are:

1. Specialized Encyclopedias. These encyclopedias list information about a certain field of knowledge or from a special point of view. Thus, you will find Catholic encyclopedias, Jewish encyclopedias and also encyclopedias

devoted to music or the social sciences. Such reference books should be consulted for special interpretations or for specialized information not found in a general encyclopedia.

2. **Dictionaries.** When you don't know where to start your research, start with a good dictionary. Suppose you had to write about Herodotus and you weren't sure if it were a man or a fish. The dictionary would quickly clue you in on the essentials — that Herodotus was a fifth century Greek historian — and you would then be able to go to the subject catalog under ancient Greek history for books by and about him.

3. **Yearbooks.** Yearbooks are the annual publications which supplement the encyclopedias. They bring our knowledge of old subjects up to date and introduce new ones.

Almanacs are among the most commonly used yearbooks. It is well worth your time to examine an almanac closely to get an idea of the range of information it contains. The almanac gives up-to-date miscellaneous and statistical information on government, business, population, sports, education, religion and almost everything else. In addition, each volume also repeats certain information which is always handy to have, such as the Constitution of the United States, the Declaration of Independence, a list of societies and associations with their addresses, and much more. Never assume it's not in the almanac until you've looked — carefully.

4. **Atlases.** Atlases are another trove of information, offering much more than just simple maps. A good atlas will tell you about agriculture, industry, natural resources, population distribution, topography, land use, languages, religion, monetary units, and much more. When your research involves current events, an atlas will give you a succinct, thumbnail sketch of a particular country's situation.

5. **Indexes.** Any index is simply a list of materials available and where they are. There are almost as many indexes as there are areas of interest.

One index you'll find especially useful lists magazine articles by author, title and subject. Called *The Readers' Guide to Periodical Literature*, this index is essential for tracing popular thought, social trends and public opinion in general. *The New York Times Index* is a subject index of newspaper articles from the daily and Sunday editions of *The New York Times* newspaper. *Who's Who* gives concise information about prominent people in the news.

Specialized indexes catalog narrow fields of interest, such as book reviews, art, education, engineering, music, and so on. Ask your reference librarian whether the topic you're investigating is covered in a specialized index.

One specialized index students shouldn't overlook is the index to United States Government publications. The government of the United States is one of the largest publishers in the world. If you are investigating problems of labor, education, housing, agriculture, social security, youth, law, consumer affairs, etc., government publications are an invaluable authority. You may find some of these works under the heading "United States Government" in the subject card catalog, but the indexes issued by the U. S. Superintendent of Documents will give the most complete list of available government publications.

OTHER SERVICES

Don't forget about the little extras that most libraries offer: picture collections, record collections, 16mm movies and audio-visual aids offer a nice change of pace from the printed word.

And remember, reference librarians are specially trained to help you use the library to its best advantage. Why not give them the chance to put this knowledge to work for you?

As a student, you'll be depending on libraries more and more. The skills you learn now will serve you in good stead when you turn to the library in coming years for help in meeting, or temporarily escaping from, the problems of the day.

_____: Reading Time

_____: Reading Rate

_____: Score, Test A

_____: Score, Test B

_____: Total Score

_____%: Comprehension

COMPREHENSION TEST 11-A

Directions: The following passage, taken from the selection you have just read, has words omitted from it. Fill in each blank with the word that was omitted. Each blank filled correctly is worth two points. Ask your instructor if you may take credit for close synonyms. Enter your score in the box provided at the end of the selection. A list of the omitted words can be found on page 239.

The card catalog is your key to the library's collection of books, reference works and other materials. These are listed in three ways — by author, title
_____ subject — with a separate catalog card for each entry.
    1
_____ if you know only the title or only the _____ of
    2   3
a particular book, you could look it up _____ way to find out if it is
                                        4
included in _____ library collection. Similarly, if you were interested
            5
in learning _____ the library has on a particular subject, you would
            6
_____ the subject catalog. The entries are filed alphabetically, and
    7
_____ the drawers are labeled on the outside to tell _____
    8   9
which parts of the alphabet they contain.

A catalog _____ usually includes the following information: the
          10
call number of _____ book, the author's name (last name first)
               11
followed by _____ dates of his birth and death, the title, publisher,
            12
_____ and date of publication, the number of pages, whether
    13
_____ are maps or illustrations, the contents of the book
    14
_____ this supplies important information to the reader, and other
    15
_____ entries for this book.
    16

THE CALL NUMBER

Once you _____ identified a book that is of interest to you,
         17
_____ want to know how to put your hands on _____.
    18   19
In the upper left-hand corner of each catalog _____ is the "call
                                              20
number" for that book, indicating where _____ find that volume on
                                        21
the library shelves. The call _____ is also marked on the spine of the
                              22
book.

_____ call number is the library's way of classifying that
    23
_____. There are two popular systems in use by libraries
    24
_____ for classifying material — the Dewey Decimal system and the
    25
Library of Congress system — and most libraries use one or the other.

1. **The Dewey Decimal System.** The Dewey Decimal system was devised by Melvil Dewey in 1873 and is still used by libraries all over the world.

COMPREHENSION TEST 11-B

Directions: This is another passage from the selection, again with words omitted. Proceed as before, giving yourself two points for each blank filled correctly. Add this score to the one from Test A and enter your total score in the box at the end of the selection. Use the conversion table on page 254 to convert your *total* score to a comprehension percentage, and record that grade in the box also. A list of omitted words can be found on page 239.

5. Indexes. Any index is simply a list of materials available and where they are. There are almost as many indexes as there are _____ of interest.
1

One index you'll find especially useful lists _____ articles by
2
author, title and subject. Called *The Readers'* _____ *to Periodical*
3
Literature, this index is essential for tracing _____ thought, social
4
trends and public opinion in general. *The* _____ *York Times Index*
5
is a subject index of newspaper _____ from the daily and Sunday
6
editions of *The New* _____ *Times* newspaper. *Who's Who* gives
7
concise information about prominent _____ in the news.
8

Specialized indexes catalog narrow fields of _____, such as book
9
reviews, art, education, engineering, music, and _____ on. Ask your
10
reference librarian whether the topic you're _____ is covered in a
11
specialized index.

One specialized index _____ shouldn't overlook is the index to
12
United States Government _____. The government of the United
13
States is one of _____ largest publishers in the world. If you are
14
investigating _____ of labor, education, housing, agriculture, social
15
security, youth, law, _____ affairs, etc., government publications
16
are an invaluable authority. You _____ find some of these works
17
under the heading "United _____ Government" in the subject card
18
catalog, but the indexes _____ by the U.S. Superintendent of
19
Documents will give the _____ complete list of available government
20
publications.

OTHER SERVICES

Don't _____ about the little extras that most libraries offer:
21
picture _____, record collections, 16mm movies and audio-visual
22
aids offer a _____ change of pace from the printed word.
23

And remember, _____ librarians are specially trained to help you
24
use the _____ to its best advantage. Why not give them the chance to
25
put this knowledge to work for you?

World Almanac. A one-volume, yearly publication that presents statistics on business, education, industries, governments, populations, sports, foreign countries, etc. Also lists names and addresses of associations and societies, as well as important events of the past year. Contains a detailed index in the front of the book.

Information Please Almanac. In addition to statistical information, it features brief articles summarizing developments in various fields during the previous year.

Encyclopedia Americana. A useful, general encyclopedia that includes articles on American institutions, organizations and places. Well known for its history of World War I and its treatment of the different centuries. Its yearbook, *The Americana Annual*, keeps it up to date.

Encyclopedia Britannica. One of the most eminent and reputable encyclopedias, the *Britannica* contains scholarly articles and general information on just about everything. Updated by the *Britannica Book of the Year*.

Columbia Encyclopedia. A one-volume, comprehensive encyclopedia designed to give the largest possible amount of information in all fields of interest in the smallest number of words.

Compton's Pictured Encyclopedia and Fact Index. This profusely illustrated children's encyclopedia is also helpful for anyone desiring a simple explanation of technical subjects.

World Book Encyclopedia. Generally considered a young people's reference, it gives good general coverage of subjects usually studied in school.

The Reader's Encyclopedia. Presents an assortment of information on many subjects, including authors, books, fictitious characters, music, works of art, etc.

Book Review Digest. Contains quotations from various reviews of the most important English and American books. Arranged alphabetically by author of the book, this digest also acts as an index to book reviews.

Guide to the Best Fiction, English and American. As complete a list as possible of the most notable prose fiction in English.

Oxford Companion to American Literature. Includes short biographies and bibliographies, summaries of important works and literary movements, etc. Similar to the *Oxford Companion to English Literature*.

Bartlett's Familiar Quotations. Quotations arranged chronologically by author, with author and subject indexes. Has special sections for: Anonymous, Translated, Biblical, Epitaphs, the Koran.

Oxford Dictionary of Quotations. Frequently quoted quotations and familiar sayings are arranged alphabetically by author with a complete index.

Secretary's Handbook. Manual for correct English usage; also gives examples of various types of letters for business, social and official occasions.

Funk and Wagnall's New Standard Dictionary; Webster's New International Dictionary; and *The Oxford English Dictionary.* These are among the most notable, comprehensive dictionaries that act as authorities on word meaning, spelling, pronunciation, syllabication, derivation and usage.

Who's Who; Current Biography. These biographical dictionaries give brief facts about notable men and women, past and present, in the news. Various versions concentrate on regional, national, international and historical personages.

Rand McNally Commercial Atlas and *Rand McNally International World Atlas.* Both feature large, clear maps that give detailed treatment of states and countries.

The United States Geological Survey publishes topographical quadrangle maps showing buildings, brooks, streams, roads and contours.

Historical atlases give factual information on exploration, settlements, population changes, early plans of cities, boundaries, distribution of schools, churches, political parties and more.

Atlas of the World's Resources. Gives overall view of geographical distribution of mineral and agricultural products.

Atlas of Economic Development and the *Oxford Economic Atlas of the World.* Both treat world production and cultural, economic and social patterns by country and region.

Statesman's Yearbook. An excellent source of information about the countries of the world — their governments, constitutions, defense, agriculture, commerce, education, etc.

Facts on File. A weekly 8 to 10 page news digest that gives unbiased coverage of significant news events of each day. Indexed so you can find information readily.

Congressional Record. Contains all speeches, debates and actions of Congress and its committees. Useful for tracing the progress of pending legislation.

Official Congressional Directory. Gives detailed information on the federal government, how it is organized and the people who run it.

U.S. Government Organization Manual. Gives information on government agencies, their history, current activities and principal officials.

Statistical Abstract of the U.S. Compiled by the U.S. Census Bureau, this yearly publication contains data on commerce, finance, immigration, population, transportation and more.

A GUIDE TO INDEXES

Readers' Guide to Periodical Literature. Indexes articles from more than 130 popular, general magazines by author, title and subject. Indexed monthly and yearly for more than seventy-five years.

Nineteenth Century Readers' Guide to Periodical Literature. A valuable guide to magazine articles published during the 19th century.

The New York Times Index. A twice-monthly index of newspaper articles appearing in *The New York Times.* Articles are indexed according to their subject matter. The brief summaries of each indexed article can be as helpful as consulting the actual story. Also useful for ascertaining dates of various events.

Book Review Digest. Contains quotations from various reviews of the most important English and American publications of the year. Arranged alphabetically by author of the book reviewed, it includes bibliographical information on the reviews and the books themselves.

Vertical File Index. A monthly listing of booklets, leaflets and pamphlets currently available from a wide variety of sources.

Cumulative Book Index. A world list of books in the English language, indexed by author, title and subject.

The National Union Catalog. An index of books, pamphlets, maps, atlases, periodicals and other serials cataloged by the Library of Congress.

Essay and General Literature Index. An index to about 40,000 essays on various subjects.

Thomas' Register of American Manufacturers. A directory of American manufacturers with addresses, phone numbers, principal officers and products.

A Popular Guide to Government Publications. Indexes government publications of general appeal and usefulness.

Catholic Periodicals Index. Indexes over 200 Catholic bulletins, magazines and newspapers.

Applied Science and Technology Index. Lists articles from magazines devoted to aeronautics, automation, chemistry, construction, metallurgy, transportation and other related subjects.

Business Periodicals Index. Indexes more than 100 magazines in accounting, advertising, banking, business, insurance, labor and other related fields.

International Index. Indexes articles from magazines of many countries, particularly those publications devoted to the humanities and social sciences.

Biological and Agricultural Index. A guide to material on agriculture, forestry, biology, zoology and heredity.

Art Index. Covers museum periodicals and publications.

Education Index. Indexes material devoted to the teaching of fine arts.

DEWEY DECIMAL CLASSIFICATION SYSTEM

000 General Works
   010 Bibliographical Science and Technique
   020 Library Science
   030 General Encyclopedias
   040 General Collected Essays
   050 General Periodicals
   060 General Societies, Museums
   070 Journalism
   080 Collected Works
   090 Book Rarities

100 Philosophy, Esthetics
   110 Metaphysics
   120 Metaphysical Theories
   130 Fields of Psychology
   140 Philosophic Systems
   150 Psychology
   160 Logic
   170 Ethics
   180 Oriental and Ancient Philosophy
   190 Modern Philosophy

200 Religion
   210 Natural Religion
   220 Bible
   230 Systematic or Doctrinal Theology
   240 Devotional Theology
   250 Pastoral Theology
   260 Ecclesiastical Theology
   270 Christian Church History
   280 Christian Churches and Sects
   290 Non-Christian Religions

300 Social Sciences, Sociology
   310 Statistics
   320 Political Science
   330 Economics
   340 Law
   350 Public Administration
   360 Social Welfare
   370 Education
   380 Commerce
   390 Customs

400 Linguistics
   410 Comparative Linguistics
   420 English Language
   430 German, Germanic Languages
   440 French, Provençal
   450 Italian, Rumanian
   460 Spanish, Portuguese
   470 Latin, Other Italic
   480 Greek, Hellenic Group
   490 Other Languages

500 Pure Science
   510 Mathematics
   520 Astronomy
   530 Physics
   540 Chemistry; Mineralogy
   550 Earth Sciences
   560 Paleontology
   570 Biological Sciences
   580 Botany
   590 Zoology

600 Applied Sciences, Useful Arts
   610 Medical Sciences
   620 Engineering
   630 Agriculture
   640 Home Economics
   650 Business and Business Methods
   660 Chemical Technology
   670 Manufactures
   680 Mechanic Trades, Amateur Manuals
   690 Building Construction

700 Arts and Recreation
   710 Landscape Architecture
   720 Architecture
   730 Sculpture
   740 Drawing, Decorative Art
   750 Painting
   760 Prints and Print Making
   770 Photography
   780 Music
   790 Recreation

800 Literature
   810 American
   820 English
   830 German, Germanic
   840 French, Provençal, Catalan
   850 Italian, Rumanian, Romansch
   860 Spanish, Portuguese
   870 Latin, Other Italic
   880 Greek, Hellenic Group
   890 Other Languages

900 History
   910 Geography
   920 Biography
   930 Ancient World History
   940 European History
   950 History of Asia
   960 African History
   970 North American History
   980 South American History
   990 History of Oceania

LIBRARY OF CONGRESS CLASSIFICATION SYSTEM

Below is the Library of Congress classification system. The letters I, O, W, X and Y are not used and are left for expansion and development.

A General Works
   AE Encyclopedias (general)
   AI Indexes (general)
   AY Yearbooks (general)

B Philosophy, Religion
   B   Collection, History
   BC Logic
   BF Psychology
   BJ Ethics
   BP Christianity
   BS Bible and Exegesis
   BX Special Sects

C History, Auxiliary Sciences
   CB History of Civilization
   CC Antiquities, Archaeology
   CT Biography

D History and Topography (except America)
   D   General History
   DA Great Britain
   DK Russia
   DS Asia
   DT Africa

E–F   North and South America

G Geography, Anthropology
   G   Geography (general)
   GN Anthropology
   GV Sports and Amusements, Games

H Social Sciences
   H   Social Sciences (general)
   HA Statistics
   HB Economic Theory
   HF Commerce
   HQ Family, Marriage, Home
   HT Communities, Races
   HX Socialism, Communism

J Political Science
   JC Political Science
   JF Constitutional History

K Law

L Education
   LA History of Education
   LB Theory and Practice of Education
   LD Universities and Colleges

M Music
   M   Music
   ML Literature of Music
   MT Musical Instruction and Study

N Fine Arts
   NA Architecture
   ND Painting
   NK Art Applied to Industry

P Language and Literature
   PA Classical Languages and Literatures
   PB Modern European Languages
   PJ Oriental Languages and Literatures
   PN Literary History and Collections
   PR English Literature
   PS American Literature
   PZ Fiction and Juvenile Literature

Q Science
   Q   Science (general)
   QA Mathematics
   QC Physics
   QD Natural History, Biology
   QL Zoology

R Medicine
   RA Hygiene
   RT Nursing

S Agriculture, Plant and Animal Industry
   SD Forestry
   SK Hunting Sports

T Technology
   TA Engineering and Building Group
   TL Motor Vehicles, Aeronautics

U Military Science

V Naval Science

Z Bibliography

> Most readers are not flexible; they read everything in the same way. Light fiction and similar material can be skimmed. This is a rapid kind of reading suitable for many kinds of reading. It is another tool in the repertory of the skilled and flexible reader.

How to Skim

Superior readers are flexible. They have developed a variety of reading skills which they use to suit various reading tasks.

If the reading habits of most of today's adults were to be described, the single adjective *inflexible* would be the most appropriate description.

To illustrate what is meant by inflexible reading, take the situation in which most doctors find themselves. All of their school years and much of their adult lives have been spent studying vitally important material. Doctors *must* understand the content of textbooks and journals thoroughly. No dedicated medical practitioner is satisfied with less than 100 percent comprehension. Accordingly, medical students develop an appropriate reading skill — a thorough, slow and careful technique leading to mastery of many critically important details. The problem comes later, after medical school, when the doctor wants to settle down for an evening's enjoyment with a good novel. Most novels don't require the painstaking attention to detail that a medical text demands. But because of habits formed during years of study, the doctor has become an inflexible reader and plods intensively through whatever kind of reading material that comes to hand.

Medicine isn't the only profession displaying this syndrome. Even after college and law school days, lawyers continue to use a highly analytical, research-type reading technique. Successful lawyers have mastered the skill needed to study legal briefs, judicial opinions and trial transcripts, searching for the precedent applying to the case at hand. They, too, have become inflexible, reading newspapers, magazines, everything in this specialized way. It's easy to see how we're fast becoming a nation of inflexible readers.

Another factor leading to inflexibility can be found in the way we are first taught to read. Most of us were required to read aloud from our basal texts. By listening to us read, teachers could evaluate our progress and see how well we were learning to recognize, identify and understand words. Our parents, too, could tell how we were doing by listening to us read.

But as beginning readers, we often learn other things at the same time: we are taught to read slowly and to pronounce words carefully, we are taught not to skip words, and we are conditioned to read in this one acceptable fashion. So, as we learn to read, the habits which will later make us inflexible readers are being established.

CUE-REDUCTION

Faults which interfere with our becoming better readers are vocalization (lip reading) and subvocalization.

To understand how these become part of our reading pattern, let us see what happens whenever a new skill is acquired. All new learning is accompanied by excessive and waste motion. Beginning drivers oversteer and then pull the wheel wildly in the opposite direction. New swimmers splash ineffectively in the water. Watch a child dripping water all over the kitchen when washing dishes for the first time.

As a new skill is practiced, cue-reduction occurs. The extra and unnecessary motions are gradually discarded while necessary ones are retained. Thus, the accomplished and practiced swimmer moves smoothly through the water without a single wasted motion. New readers, as we mentioned above, read aloud at first. Later, they read silently, but still move their lips, forming the words silently. You may know readers who have never progressed past this stage. They are still lip reading or vocalizing. Check yourself as you read. Are you vocalizing?

Most readers progress from this step to the next, subvocalization. This describes the act of saying the words to yourself as you read, without moving your lips. Even though you are unaware of it, there is actual movement of the speech muscles. For the vast majority of adult readers, no further cue-reduction occurs; they subvocalize for the rest of their lives. It has been estimated that 80 percent of readers today fall into this category.

Saying every word to yourself is actually no more efficient than reading out loud: you will never read any faster than you can talk. Reading experts point out that even superior readers tend to subvocalize on certain difficult-to-understand materials, but most of us do it all the time.

To overcome the habit, you must read lots and lots of *very easy* material. Unfortunately, students cannot always do this; they are too busy studying difficult textbooks. Thus, in time, they become inflexible readers.

SKIMMING

Flexible readers choose the technique most appropriate for each reading occasion from a variety of skills. Skillful readers know that reading situations vary, and they try to develop skills for all of them.

Some materials demand a thorough analysis: textbooks, manuals, contracts and insurance policies are good examples. Light fiction, however, calls for a breezy, casual kind of reading at a fairly rapid rate. Other kinds of material permit readers to run their eyes down a column of print, snatching ideas on the run. This kind of reading is called skimming.

We regularly run across articles and stories which are only of passing interest to us. They probably contain little factual content and are usually written in simple language. Gossip columns, human interest stories and the Sunday comics are examples of this kind of reading. It would be a waste

of time to read these analytically. They need only be skimmed to be understood and appreciated.

Comprehension is another aspect of flexible reading. You should be aware that there are degrees or levels of understanding which are suitable for certain materials. For example, to follow directions we need total comprehension. Obviously we don't require total comprehension for the comics. Textbooks ask the reader to remember concepts and understand relationships. Simple articles of passing interest require only a temporary kind of comprehension, the kind that comes from skimming.

SKIMMING FOR FACTS

Textbooks, reference texts or journals can be skimmed when you wish to locate certain facts or extract specific data. Skimming to see if a particular topic is discussed is a research skill. Think of skimming for facts as an intensive kind of previewing.

1. **Read the Title.** This will tell you if the author's subject is one which might include the information you seek.

2. **Read the Subhead.** See if the author announces a category which might pertain to your topic.

3. **Read the Illustration.** Look for graphic information relating to what you are seeking.

4. **Read First Sentences.** Look for paragraphs which contain information and definitions. These are the ones most likely to contain factual data. Skim through these looking for your topic.

Introductory paragraphs may tell you that what you are seeking is coming next. Illustrative paragraphs will probably not contain much factual information and may be glossed over or skipped entirely. The concluding paragraph is not likely to help either.

Skimming for facts is a valuable reference skill and an asset to flexible readers.

DYNAMIC SKIMMING

We can label another type of skimming *dynamic* because of the impressive results it yields at high speeds. You may have seen demonstrations of this type of reading on television or have read about courses being offered in this technique. The fact that tuition fees for such courses approach $300 or more testifies to the value of this kind of reading. The steps to dynamic skimming are these:

1. **Preview.** As you have no doubt

begun to realize by now, previewing is a prerequisite to reading of almost any kind. In dynamic skimming it is more essential than ever. Before skimming, you must perform a thorough and comprehensive preview of the selection. Get as much advance information as you can before you start to skim. The steps to follow when previewing do not change, but more time is spent building a mental outline to use as a guide when skimming.

2. Skim. Now, let your eyes run down the page, snatching ideas on the run. Do not stop to read; do not pause to reflect. Strive to let the words trigger your mind as you race by.

This kind of skimming is difficult to learn because you've been in the habit of reading line by line. To overcome this natural tendency, use your finger as a pacer, forcing your eyes down the page. Begin by moving your finger back and forth across each line in zigzag fashion, encouraging the eyes to fixate (stop and read) just twice on each line. Gradually increase your speed by skipping lines until you are able to cover an entire page in a few seconds.

3. Review. This is done like previewing. Go back over the page and quickly pick up bits of information that fill in thought-gaps, add meaning to the passage, or furnish essential details. This last step is essential if skimming is to be productive.

Skimming is a highly specialized skill, especially appropriate where vast amounts of reading must be done quickly. It is a technique that works well with easy reading matter, with material that you consider relatively unimportant, or when you have to pick out particularly important passages from among a lot of miscellaneous details.

Practice skimming every opportunity you get since it is an essential skill to acquire on the road to becoming a thoroughly flexible reader.

_____: Reading Time

_____: Reading Rate

_____: Score, Test A

_____: Score, Test B

_____: Total Score

_____%: Comprehension

COMPREHENSION TEST 12-A

Directions: The following passage, taken from the selection you have just read, has words omitted from it. Fill in each blank with the word that was omitted. Each blank filled correctly is worth two points. Ask your instructor if you may take credit for close synonyms. Enter your score in the box provided at the end of the selection. A list of the omitted words can be found on page 239.

Superior readers are flexible. They have developed a variety of reading skills which _____ use to suit various reading tasks.
1

If the reading _____ of most of today's adults were to be described,
2

_____ single adjective *inflexible* would be the most appropriate
3

description.

_____ illustrate what is meant by inflexible reading, take the
4

_____ in which most doctors find themselves. All of their
5

_____ years and much of their adult lives have been _____
6   7

studying vitally important material. Doctors *must* understand the content

_____ textbooks and journals thoroughly. No dedicated medical
8

practitioner is _____ with less than 100 percent comprehension.
9

Accordingly, medical students _____ an appropriate reading skill
10

— a thorough, slow and careful _____ leading to mastery of many
11

critically important details. The _____ comes later, after medical
12

school, when the doctor wants _____ settle down for an evening's
13

enjoyment with a good _____. Most novels don't require the pains-
14

taking attention to detail _____ a medical text demands. But because
15

of habits formed _____ years of study, the doctor has become an
16

inflexible _____ and plods intensively through whatever kind of
17

reading material _____ comes to hand.
18

Medicine isn't the only profession displaying _____ syndrome.
19

Even after college and law school days, lawyers _____ to use a highly
20

analytical, research-type reading technique. _____ lawyers have
21

mastered the skill needed to study legal _____, judicial opinions and
22

trial transcripts, searching for the precedent _____ to the case at
23

hand. They, too, have become _____, reading newspapers, magazines,
24

everything in this specialized way. It's _____ to see how we're fast
25

becoming a nation of inflexible readers.

Another factor leading to inflexibility can be found in the way we are first taught to read.

COMPREHENSION TEST 12-B

Directions: This is another passage from the selection, again with words omitted. Proceed as before, giving yourself two points for each blank filled correctly. Add this score to the one from Test A and enter your total score in the box at the end of the selection. Use the conversion table on page 254 to convert your *total* score to a comprehension percentage, and record that grade in the box also. A list of omitted words can be found on page 239.

We can label another type of skimming *dynamic* because of the impressive results it yields at high speeds. You may have seen demonstrations of this type of _____1_____ on television or have read about courses being offered _____2_____ this technique. The fact that tuition fees for such _____3_____ approach $300 or more testifies to the value of _____4_____ kind of reading. The steps to dynamic skimming are _____5_____:

1. Preview. As you have no doubt begun to realize _____6_____ now, previewing is a prerequisite to reading of almost _____7_____ kind. In dynamic skimming it is more essential then _____8_____. Before skimming, you must perform a thorough and comprehensive _____9_____ of the selection. Get as much advance information as _____10_____ can before you start to skim. The steps to _____11_____ when previewing do not change, but more time is _____12_____ building a mental outline to use as a guide _____13_____ skimming.

2. Skim. Now, let your eyes run down the _____14_____, snatching ideas on the run. Do not stop to _____15_____; do not pause to reflect. Strive to let the _____16_____ trigger your mind as you race by.

This kind _____17_____ skimming is difficult to learn because you've been in _____18_____ habit of reading line by line. To overcome this _____19_____ tendency, use your finger as a pacer, forcing your _____20_____ down the page. Begin by moving your finger back _____21_____ forth across each line in zigzag fashion, encouraging the _____22_____ to fixate (stop and read) just twice on each _____23_____. Gradually increase your speed by skipping lines until you _____24_____ able to cover an entire page in a few _____25_____.

3. Review. This is done like previewing.

DYNAMIC SKIMMING

Directions: Find a *very easy* book to read. Even a children's book is suitable for beginning skimming. Select twenty pages and mark them off with paper clips. Your first skimming practice will be on just these pages. First, preview the pages thoroughly. Next, follow the steps below.

1. Skim through once, spending about 20 seconds on each page. Count to 20 as you move your finger back and forth (zigzag) under every other line, as shown.

2. Skim through the same pages again, this time on a count of 10. Move your finger back and forth 10 times, covering the whole page.

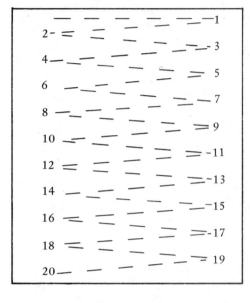

3. Skim the pages again on a count of 5. Keep your finger moving back and forth, just 5 times, covering the whole page.

4. On your last time through, skim on a count of 2. Strive to cover each page with just 2 sweeps.

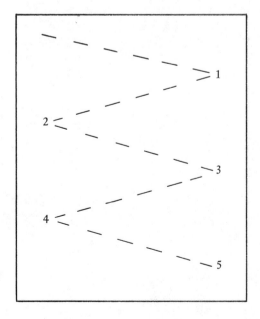

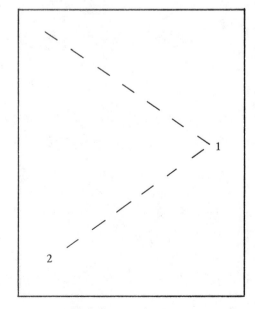

DYNAMIC SKIMMING

Directions: As you develop competence in skimming, you will adopt a count and motion of the hand which is most natural for you. Some suggested sweep motions are shown below.

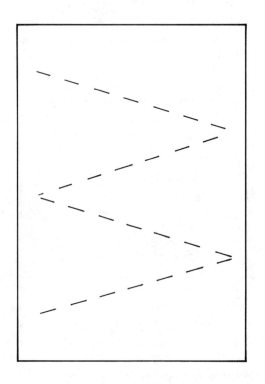

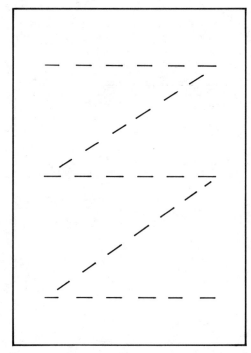

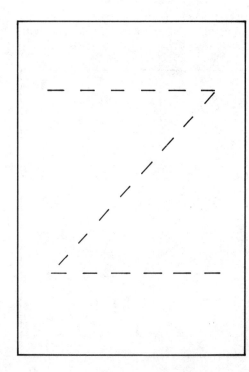

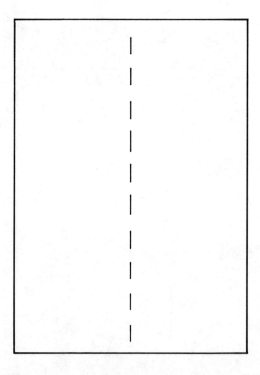

Study Skills

> For most students, study time is lost time because they are not organized for the task. Through organization, lost time becomes productive time. The first step is to plan and follow a carefully structured study schedule.

How to Study

In 1942 President Roosevelt remarked, "Never before have we had so little time to do so much." He did not have students in mind when he said it, but it seems to express how they feel. In today's fast-paced world the demands on study time are tremendous. Is there any hope then for busy students? Is there any way for them to study all that they must in the time that they have? Yes, there are methods and techniques which you can develop and use to keep up with all your assignments. In fact, once you become organized, you should be able to do your homework better and in less time.

To see how this is possible, consider what study is all about. The dictionary tells us that study is "the process of applying the mind in order to acquire knowledge." Notice the word *process*; study is not *one* activity but, rather, a *series* of activities. And whenever steps in a process are involved, organization is essential.

Most students are not organized; they have never learned efficient study procedures. Consequently, little is accomplished and valuable time is lost. This lost time can be converted to productive time through organization.

If you are a typical student, you have many responsibilities and many demands on your time. So, from a purely practical point of view, it pays to get your studying done in the shortest possible time. This selection will cover the techniques you need to accomplish this end.

1. Set Your Goal. Before you start any assignment, decide what your objective is and keep it clearly in mind. Industry has discovered the value of setting production goals for increasing productivity. No organized fund-raising campaign or advertising program ever gets off the ground until the goal or target has been defined. How can your study activities produce

results if you don't know exactly what results you are after?

When a student complains, "I do all my assignments and still get poor grades," chances are good that he is studying without clearly defined goals. When you sit down to study, your goal should be subject oriented; it must relate to the study matter itself. In biology, for example, your objective may be to understand the functions of the circulatory system; in history, to learn the causes of the Civil War. Whatever the subject, you must set your sights on *learning* some aspect of it.

Further, your objective should be specific. Too broad a goal, such as "learning this chapter" or "reading unit three" or "reading pages 21 through 27 by tomorrow" is self-defeating. General aims like these don't help you direct your efforts effectively.

You may argue, "How can I set a goal when I don't know anything about this subject?" One thing you can do is look over your classroom notes; find something stressed or some question raised by the instructor. Or read the subheads of the textbook chapter or the discussion questions following the unit. These will yield suitable themes and ideas around which to frame your goal.

2. Organize Your Approach. The saying goes that a mechanic is only as good as his tools. This might also apply to students. Your study will be productive only if you have the right tools — everything you need to do the assignment properly. When you sit down to study, have all of the things you'll need on hand: paper, ruler, notebook, pens, pencils, textbooks, dictionary, and so on. It's also a good idea to have with you the lecture notes you've taken in class. Don't begin until you have everything you need for each assignment.

As for where to study, there are differing points of view. It is traditionally held that absolute quiet creates the best atmosphere for studying.

On the other hand, research has shown that many workers are more productive against an unobtrusive musical background. No matter which type of worker you happen to be, one fact is certain: very loud and extreme noise will distract anyone. So don't expose yourself unnecessarily to distractions; find the study area best suited to you.

In many homes a quiet, lighted corner is just not available. Faced with these circumstances, you may have to make other, perhaps less ideal, arrangements. For instance, you may have to wait until smaller children have gone to bed before the noise level is sufficiently reduced for studying. In this case do your socializing and relaxing early; leave the later evening free for study. Perhaps an hour's homework can be disposed of by remaining at school longer, using the library or an empty classroom. If practical, do your most challenging subject then, the one requiring the most concentration. An alternative to a busy home may be to seek out less hectic surroundings. A friend or classmate's room or apartment may be available, or the local library may have a quiet room. Whatever your difficulty, a practical solution can be achieved with resourceful thinking. If you need help in finding an appropriate place to study, consult your teachers, counselors, advisors or librarian.

Your posture while studying is more important than you might think. If you are working, look alert and look like you are working. A relaxed position is good for one thing: relaxing. You cannot study for long sprawled in a chair, lying on a sofa, or lounging on the floor. Once you have all your materials together and have found a suitable study area, you must get right down to work. Sitting upright in a not-too-soft chair at a table or desk produces a slight muscular tension which is conducive to the concentration you need to study effectively.

3. **Schedule Your Time.** The president of a major corporation once paid a thousand dollars to learn a technique which would make him more productive. The secret? He was told to list on a small piece of paper the five most important things he had to do that day. Several times during the day he would refer to the list and complete the next item. This list was, in effect, a schedule, and the executive paid dearly for a tip which many people learn through experience: the value of planning.

Time is a limited resource. There are only twenty-four hours to do all the things we want to do in any one day. Therefore, it is very costly to study in an unplanned, unprogrammed way. To save you valuable time, we want you to devise a study schedule. Following this selection you will find a form to use and instructions for setting up a personal study schedule. The value of planning and following such a program cannot be overemphasized.

First, decide how much time you should spend studying each night. Depending on your course load, you may need to study an hour and a half each school night, two hours, three hours, or more.

Many high school courses will require no more than a half hour per night for you to stay current. College-level courses, on the other hand, often demand two hours of homework for every hour spent in class. Budget your time to match the difficulty of the course. If in doubt, ask your teacher for recommendations. More than likely you will have to revise your schedule as the school term progresses in order to devote more time to certain subjects.

It is generally recommended that no less than a full half hour of *productive* time be spent on any academic subject. This means that you should devote the full time to each subject each day that class meets. When, as occasionally happens, you are able to complete the day's assignment with time remaining, you have an opportunity to strengthen your knowledge by reviewing. Frequent reviewing of the subject could result in a higher grade, boosting your overall average. You may have need of such insurance should you falter in another subject.

Some students like to read ahead in the text for the remainder of the study time. This, they feel, gives them the jump on material to be covered in class lectures.

When assignments in different subjects call for different kinds of activities, like reading or writing, schedule them so that the same activities are not consecutive. For example, you may have two reading assignments and one writing assignment. Schedule the writing subject between the reading tasks.

Your final half hour (more or less) should be spent on memorization and review for classes the following day. Psychologists tell us that forgetting occurs when new learning displaces previous learning. Scheduling the things requiring memorization last reduces the risk of premature forgetting. Also, use this final half hour to review for upcoming quizzes.

Follow your study program faithfully until it becomes routine. Vary the routine only during examination periods, and break the routine only during school vacations. Man is a creature of habit; we derive enjoyment and satisfaction from a comfortable routine.

Lost time can be a thing of the past to students willing to follow the steps presented here conscientiously. Make your study time productive.

_____: Reading Time

_____: Reading Rate

_____: Score, Test A

_____: Score, Test B

_____: Total Score

_____%: Comprehension

COMPREHENSION TEST 13-A

Directions: The following passage, taken from the selection you have just read, has words omitted from it. Fill in each blank with the word that was omitted. Each blank filled correctly is worth two points. Ask your instructor if you may take credit for close synonyms. Enter your score in the box provided at the end of the selection. A list of the omitted words can be found on page 239.

If you are a typical student, you have many responsibilities and many demands on your time. So, from a purely practical point of view, it _____ to

1

get your studying done in the shortest possible _____. This selection

2

will cover the techniques you need to _____ this end.

3

1. **Set Your Goal.** Before you start any _____, decide what your

4

objective is and keep it clearly _____ mind. Industry has discovered

5

the value of setting production _____ for increasing productivity.

6

No organized fund-raising campaign or _____ program ever gets off

7

the ground until the goal _____ target has been defined. How can

8

your study activities _____ results if you don't know exactly what

9

results you _____ after?

10

When a student complains, "I do all my _____ and still get poor

11

grades," chances are good that _____ is studying without clearly

12

defined goals. When you sit _____ to study, your goal should be

13

subject oriented; it _____ relate to the study matter itself. In biology,

14

for _____, your objective may be to understand the functions of

15

_____ circulatory system; in history, to learn the causes of

16

_____ Civil War. Whatever the subject, you must set your

17

_____ on *learning* some aspect of it.

18

Further, your objective _____ be specific. Too broad a goal, such

19

as "learning _____ chapter" or "reading unit three" or "reading

20

pages 21 _____ 27 by tomorrow" is self-defeating. General aims like

21

_____ don't help you direct your efforts effectively.

22

You may _____, "How can I set a goal when I don't

23

_____ anything about this subject?" One thing you can do

24

_____ look over your classroom notes; find something stressed or

25

some question raised by the instructor. Or read the subheads of the textbook chapter or the discussion questions following the unit.

COMPREHENSION TEST 13-B

Directions: This is another passage from the selection, again with words omitted. Proceed as before, giving yourself two points for each blank filled correctly. Add this score to the one from Test A and enter your total score in the box at the end of the selection. Use the conversion table on page 254 to convert your *total* score to a comprehension percentage, and record that grade in the box also. A list of omitted words can be found on page 240.

Time is a limited resource. There are only twenty-four hours to do all _____ things we want to do in any one day. _____, it is
₁   ₂
very costly to study in an unplanned, _____ way. To save you
₃
valuable time, we want you _____ devise a study schedule. Following
₄
this selection you will _____ a form to use and instructions for
₅
setting up _____ personal study schedule. The value of planning
₆
and following _____ a program cannot be overemphasized.
₇

First, decide how much _____ you should spend studying each
₈
night. Depending on your _____ load, you may need to study an hour
₉
and _____ half each school night, two hours, three hours, or
₁₀
_____.
₁₁
Many high school courses will require no more than _____ half
₁₂
hour per night for you to stay current. _____-level courses, on the
₁₃
other hand, often demand two _____ of homework for every hour
₁₄
spent in class. Budget _____ time to match the difficulty of the
₁₅
course. If _____ doubt, ask your teacher for recommendations. More
₁₆
than likely _____ will have to revise your schedule as the school
₁₇
_____ progresses in order to devote more time to certain
₁₈
_____.
₁₉
It is generally recommended that no less than a _____ half hour
₂₀
of *productive* time be spent on any _____ subject. This means that
₂₁
you should devote the full _____ to each subject each day that class
₂₂
meets. When, _____ occasionally happens, you are able to complete
₂₃
the day's _____ with time remaining, you have an opportunity to
₂₄
strengthen _____ knowledge by reviewing. Frequent reviewing of the
₂₅
subject could result in a higher grade, boosting your overall average.

PLANNING HOW YOU WILL STUDY

Directions: The following exercise will help you develop more efficient study procedures. Take this opportunity to evaluate your present study habits. Consider ways in which you can organize your study time to best advantage.

1. In two separate columns, list the positive and negative aspects of your study area. In what ways can you improve or change your study area to increase your efficiency during study time?

2. In what ways can you strengthen your approach to your course work? Consider such questions as:
   a. How far in advance do you begin to prepare for an exam? Do you depend on cramming alone?
   b. How well organized are you? Do you study from well-ordered notes? Do you study in a hit-or-miss fashion or do you select certain aspects of the material to be learned?
   c. How soon after a written assignment has been given do you begin to work on it?
   d. What time blocks do you set aside for study? Are they periods when you are most alert and able to concentrate and work efficiently?

3. It is often true that, for various reasons, some courses require more hours of study than others. Determine how much study time you should devote each day to each of your courses in order to achieve success in school. To do this, you should evaluate each of your courses in terms of the amount of reading necessary, the number of written assignments required, your general knowledge and grasp of the subject, and the factual or theoretical nature of the material.

4. Make it a point to ask each of your instructors how much time he thinks a student of average ability should spend studying his subject in order to (a) just pass; (b) get a superior grade. How much time do *you* estimate is necessary to (a) just pass; (b) get a superior grade for each of your subjects?

5. Write a specific, clearly defined study goal or objective for each of your courses for the coming week.

6. Using the form provided on page **134**, create an efficient study schedule for yourself based on the suggestions presented in this selection.

SUBJECT	MONDAY	TUESDAY	WEDNESDAY	THURSDAY	FRIDAY

Show in the spaces above the time and day each class meets. Schedule in the spaces below at least one half hour of study for each academic subject on the same day that class meets. Use your final half hour each night for review and memorization.

List above the subjects you are carrying this term. List below your study periods using half-hour intervals.

> No one is born with a naturally poor memory. What we call forgetting is in reality faulty recall. Techniques can be applied to improve the ability to recall. The memory is a faculty which can be strengthened and developed.

Training Your Memory

Ask any student what his greatest problem is and his answer will invariably be, "Remembering."

This problem is not confined to students alone; it's quite common to hear people in all walks of life complain of poor memories. Almost everyone you meet will confess how poor he is at recalling names.

Psychiatrists, however, suggest that we never really lose anything once it enters our minds. Everything we have learned and experienced is indelibly etched in our memories. The problem is that it is not always possible for us to recall information when we need it. What occurs then is what we call "forgetting."

Upon closer examination, what we commonly call memory is made up of three faculties. One aspect of memory deals with retention; this is the storehouse, so to speak. Like the memory banks of a computer, this faculty receives and stores impressions passed along by our external senses.

The second faculty of memory is recall. When people speak of having a poor memory, they really mean they are unable to recall information readily. And recalling information and facts they have learned is what gives students the most trouble.

The third aspect of memory is recognition. We recognize people and things because our memories tell us we have seen or experienced them somewhere before.

AIDS TO RECALL

As mentioned above, there are techniques we all can learn and use to help improve our ability to recall what we have learned. It is simply not true that you have been cursed with a poor memory. You can improve your memory substantially by following these suggestions.

1. Plan to Remember. This bit of advice appears so obvious that we tend to overlook its value. Yet, it works. Tell yourself that you want to remember something and you will.

In the words of Thomas DeQuincey, "It is notorious that the memory strengthens as you lay burdens upon it, and becomes trustworthy as you trust it." If, like most people, you have trouble recalling the names of those you've just met, try this: The next time you are introduced to a group of people, plan to remember the names. Say to yourself, "I'll listen carefully, I'll repeat the names to be sure I've got them, and I will remember them." You'll probably recall those names for the rest of your life.

Transfer this same idea to your studying. Perhaps your approach to your assignments has not always been accompanied by a real resolve to remember. Except when you are reviewing for examinations, your purpose for studying may be to complete the assignment in the quickest way possible; your intention being not to remember but to get it done.

So, when we complain that we can't remember, the truth usually is that we never really planned to. From now on, make up your mind before you start to read or study; tell yourself that you've got to remember this. In this way you are putting your mind to work — you are *concentrating*.

2. **Review the Matter.** Psychologists tell us that most forgetting occurs shortly after the learning has been done. To overcome this, you must review. Go over the material again, either later the same day or early the next, or at both times if possible. Consider for a moment what good sense this makes: you may have spent an hour studying and learning something; five minutes devoted to reviewing is insurance that you won't forget and that the hour's study won't have been wasted.

A review need not be lengthy. A textbook chapter or lesson can be reviewed satisfactorily in five or ten minutes. A good review technique used by many students is to jot down on paper the five to seven main points of a chapter. (Rarely will you find more.) Then, recite from memory what you have learned about each point.

3. **Look for Principles.** It is a fact that no one can remember everything. The key to effective studying and remembering is in understanding what you are studying. Understanding comes from generalizing, as opposed to trying to remember isolated facts.

Look for major principles. Try not to think of the subject as lots of facts to be remembered. Instead, generalize the matter into several major ideas which you can readily repeat.

We mentioned that a well-organized textbook chapter develops no more than six or seven major points or principles. Further, these are normally quite easy to locate. Main ideas are usually identified by numbers in the margin, by bold headings, or in some other way. Let the headings form the core of your studying. As you read about the major points, try to see individual facts in relation to the main principles. Later, recalling the principles will help you remember the facts.

As the Dutch philosopher Spinoza put it: "The more intelligible a thing is, the more easily it is retained in the memory; and contrariwise, the less intelligible it is, the more easily we forget it." Seek out the principles and strive to understand them clearly; this is the efficient way to learn and remember.

4. **Schedule Memorization Last.** An additional fact about memorization is that forgetting sometimes results from new learning displacing what was previously learned. This means that if you study several subjects, the one you study last will probably be best recalled. This is so primarily because no new learning has been acquired to compete with it.

The application of such knowledge is obvious: if you know you will be called upon to remember something the next day, study that subject last. Review the major principles just before going to bed. This will ensure optimum conditions for retention.

5. **Think about the Matter.** Another way to improve retention is through evaluation of the material you are studying. After you have studied, work the matter over in your mind. Examine and analyze it. Use comparison or contrast: how does this information relate to other things you know? How is it similar to or different from related topics? If the learning concerns theory or opinion, do you tend to agree or disagree? Are there aspects of the subject which you can criticize? This kind of mental manipulation significantly improves recall.

6. **Apply the Learning.** When studying subjects which permit practical application, an excellent way of ensuring understanding and retention is through performing the application yourself or on yourself.

You may be studying physics and learning about simple machines. As you study, apply the principles using objects at hand. Learning through experience is extremely effective. You are learning by doing, not just by reading. In biology, when you study the structure of the human skeleton, move your body and feel your own bones as you read about them.

Seek out other opportunities for applying what you are studying and learning. In whatever way you can, make the instruction meaningful; make it come alive.

7. **Discuss the Material.** Retention is certain to be minimal whenever you do not clearly understand a subject.

As you study, you will more than likely encounter subjects which will give you trouble. This can present a dangerous situation if you let it. Because we find a subject hard to learn, we tend to wish it away. We convince ourselves that we can never learn it, and eventually we stop trying.

Use the buddy system to help you over this hurdle. Find a fellow student who is achieving well in the course, and discuss the work on a regular basis. Frequently, conversation of this kind brings meaning and organization to the jumble of words in the text.

Discuss the subject whenever you can, with anyone you can find. Certainly don't hesitate to discuss the material with your teacher. Ask questions in class. The effect of all this discussion is to open up another avenue of learning for you in the course, thus compensating for the difficulties you are experiencing.

8. Use Memory Formulas. Many students devise formulas to help them recall items on a list, steps to a procedure, or other things of a serial nature. Such memory aids usually consist of a word formed by the first letters of the items to be remembered. The name for these devices is *mnemonic*.

For example, to recall the names of the primary colors of the spectrum — red, orange, yellow, green, blue, indigo and violet — you might devise the mnemonic *ROY G. BIV*.

Artificial memory aids are no substitute for understanding, but they are useful when you are faced with memorizing a list of items which seem to bear no internal or natural kind of relationship.

Don't feel that you have been born with a poor memory. We all have the mental equipment we need for storing learning and experiences. The ability to recall can be developed. All of the suggestions presented here can help you improve your retention and recall of study material if you will apply them on a regular basis.

_____: Reading Time

_____: Reading Rate

_____: Score, Test A

_____: Score, Test B

_____: Total Score

_____%: Comprehension

COMPREHENSION TEST 14-A

Directions: The following passage, taken from the selection you have just read, has words omitted from it. Fill in each blank with the word that was omitted. Each blank filled correctly is worth two points. Ask your instructor if you may take credit for close synonyms. Enter your score in the box provided at the end of the selection. A list of the omitted words can be found on page 240.

Ask any student what his greatest problem is and his answer will invariably be, "Remembering."

This problem is not confined to students alone; it's _____ common 1 to hear people in all walks of life _____ of poor memories. Almost 2 everyone you meet will confess _____ poor he is at recalling names. 3

Psychiatrists, however, suggest _____ we never really lose anything 4 once it enters our _____. Everything we have learned and experienced 5 is indelibly etched _____ our memories. The problem is that it is not 6 _____ possible for us to recall information when we need 7 _____. What occurs then is what we call "forgetting." 8

Upon _____ examination, what we commonly call memory is made 9 up _____ three faculties. One aspect of memory deals with retention; 10 _____ is the storehouse, so to speak. Like the memory 11 _____ of a computer, this faculty receives and stores impressions 12 _____ along by our external senses. 13

The second faculty of _____ is recall. When people speak of having 14 a poor _____, they really mean they are unable to recall information 15 _____. And recalling information and facts they have learned is 16 _____ gives students the most trouble. 17

The third aspect of _____ is recognition. We recognize people and 18 things because our _____ tell us we have seen or experienced them 19 somewhere _____. 20

AIDS TO RECALL

As mentioned above, there are techniques _____ all can learn and 21 use to help improve our _____ to recall what we have learned. It 22 is simply _____ true that you have been cursed with a poor 23 _____. You can improve your memory substantially by following 24 these _____. 25

1. Plan to Remember. This bit of advice appears so obvious that we tend to overlook its value.

COMPREHENSION TEST 14-B

Directions: This is another passage from the selection, again with words omitted. Proceed as before, giving yourself two points for each blank filled correctly. Add this score to the one from Test A and enter your total score in the box at the end of the selection. Use the conversion table on page 254 to convert your *total* score to a comprehension percentage, and record that grade in the box also. A list of omitted words can be found on page 240.

7. **Discuss the Material.** Retention is certain to be minimal whenever you do not clearly understand a subject. As you study, you will more than likely encounter _____ which will give you trouble. This can present a

_____ situation if you let it. Because we find a _____ hard

to learn, we tend to wish it away. _____ convince ourselves that we

can never learn it, and _____ we stop trying.

Use the buddy system to help _____ over this hurdle. Find a

fellow student who is _____ well in the course, and discuss the work

on _____ regular basis. Frequently, conversation of this kind brings

meaning _____ organization to the jumble of words in the text.

_____ the subject whenever you can, with anyone you can

_____. Certainly don't hesitate to discuss the material with your

_____. Ask questions in class. The effect of all this _____

is to open up another avenue of learning for _____ in the course, thus

compensating for the difficulties you _____ experiencing.

8. **Use Memory Formulas.** Many students devise formulas to _____

them recall items on a list, steps to a _____, or other things of a

serial nature. Such memory _____ usually consist of a word formed

by the first _____ of the items to be remembered. The name for

_____ devices is *mnemonic*.

For example, to recall the names _____ the primary colors of the

spectrum — red, orange, yellow, _____, blue, indigo and violet — you

might devise the mnemonic _____ G. BIV.

Artificial memory aids are no substitute for understanding, _____

they are useful when you are faced with memorizing _____ list of

items which seem to bear no internal or natural kind of relationship.

Don't feel that you have been born with a poor memory.

AIDS TO REMEMBERING

Directions: As was mentioned in the selection you have just read, the ability to retain and recall what you have learned is a skill which can be developed and improved. The suggestions given in the selection for developing memory are summarized below. Study them and resolve to apply them on all occasions when remembering is essential.

1. **Plan to Remember.** One reason we forget is that we never really planned to remember. If you wish to commit a matter to memory, resolve to remember it. Concentrate!	5. **Think about the Matter.** Examine and analyze the matter to become familiar with it. Think about its different aspects. Relate the material to other things you know.
2. **Review.** To overcome forgetting, you must review the matter, bring it back to the forefront of your mind and refresh your memory. Reviewing is an essential step.	6. **Apply the Learning.** We forget what we don't use. Find a way to make the material personal and meaningful through applying and using it. Make it come alive.
3. **Look for Principles.** The key to retention is understanding. By trying to memorize many facts, we only complicate our task. Concentrate on remembering major ideas.	7. **Discuss.** Discussion gives meaning and organization to difficult matter, thus increasing your chances of remembering it later on. Discuss the material whenever possible.
4. **Memorize Last.** When you are faced with several learning tasks, schedule memorization work last. This prevents new learning from interfering with your recall ability.	8. **Use Memory Formulas.** When there is little relationship among items to be remembered, make up a word composed of the first letters of each item. This is a mnemonic.

PRACTICE REMEMBERING

Directions: The following exercise will help you to develop your ability to retain and recall what you have learned. Keep in mind the aids to remembering discussed in this chapter as you do each of the activities below.

1. Choose a chapter from a textbook you are currently using in a major subject. Skim through to locate and record the five to seven major points covered in the chapter. As you read the chapter carefully and thoroughly, try to see individual facts in relation to these main principles. When you have finished, recite what you remember about each main point on your list.

2. Using another chapter from a text you are now using in a major course, choose a section which covers one main principle. As you read this section, concentrate on evaluating and analyzing the material. Do you agree or disagree? How does it fit in with, or differ from, other information you have read about the topic? How will knowledge of this material benefit you? Test your memory the next day by seeing how much you can remember about this section of your text.

3. Discussion often brings meaning and organization to difficult material. Choose a topic which you find difficult in one of your major subjects, and discuss it with someone in your class. Be sure to choose a topic specific enough to be covered thoroughly in the discussion.

4. The eight aids to remembering discussed in this selection are summarized on the preceding page. Without looking, what are they? If you can't remember all of them, review the summary. Try listing the eight suggestions again. When you have it down pat, try recalling them again the next day.

5. In Item 3 of the selection, there is a quotation from Spinoza. Reread the quotation carefully. Think about the quotation for three full minutes by the clock. At the end of three minutes, see how close you can come to reproducing the main idea of the quotation. Try again from memory the next day.

6. At a social gathering, resolve to remember five people: their names, what each looks like, what each was wearing, and one fact about each. Test your recall at bedtime and again the next morning.

> Everyone suffers from a lack of concentration at times, but a chronic inability to sustain attention spells disaster for students. To improve concentration, students can avoid distracting influences and employ aids to acquire and develop the ability to concentrate.

Learning to Concentrate

As a student you probably suffer from a problem common to all students: there are times when you cannot concentrate. If it happens to you occasionally, don't be too concerned; everyone's concentration wanders sometimes. But if it happens to you most of the time, you're in trouble and you must do something about it.

Fortunately, you *can* do something. You can improve your ability to concentrate, and you can begin by understanding what concentration is all about. It is not a gift which some have and others do not. Think of the times when you have been concentrating. What were you doing? It's safe to say that you were totally involved in some matter which interested you. And this is precisely what concentration means: to fix your attention on something. To do this effectively, you must keep distracting thoughts away.

Keeping your attention fixed on a subject without yielding to distractions is not all that difficult; we all do it many times a day. Most drivers are able to concentrate effectively behind the wheel; TV viewers concentrate to the point of total involvement when watching favorite programs. When we need to, we seem to be able to concentrate.

Why, then, is concentration so difficult when it comes to study? The obvious answer is that the interest is just not there; lessons don't mean as much to us as these other things. It would seem then that finding ways to build interest in studies will contribute to greater concentration.

INTERFERENCES

1. **Hunger.** If you are hungry, don't try to settle down for a session of concentrated study. It can't be done. No matter how interested or preoccupied you become with the study matter, your body will be relentless in its demands for attention.

Food for the body must precede food for the mind. But settle for a light snack, enough to tide you over until the work is done. Don't use studying as an excuse to nibble yourself into a weight problem. Constant trips to the refrigerator can be as distracting as genuine hunger.

2. **Fatigue.** You cannot concentrate for long when you are tired. Again, the needs of the body predominate. Take a nap to satisfy your physical requirements and then get down to study.

It has been found that the body seems to operate on a "biological clock" which makes you more alert at certain times of the day and less alert at other times. Many people have a letdown between noon and 3:00 P.M. Some reach peak performance early in the day and again early in the evening. The wee hours of the morning are the lowest point in the day for most people so that burning the midnight oil is generally not a good idea. At test time, some students prefer to rise early in the morning rather than stay up late studying for exams. This way, the period of forgetting is reduced while the period of physical efficiency is approaching its peak.

The point is that you should find those times of the day when you are most alert to do your most important work.

3. **Distractions.** Distractions take many forms. What is distracting for you may just be soothing background noise for someone else. You must be the judge. Certainly, you are not giving yourself an even chance if you place yourself in circumstances likely to be distracting. Conversations, activity and loud music will compete for your attention and probably win out. You must avoid such situations if you plan to concentrate.

BUILDING CONCENTRATION

1. **Develop an Interest.** Because concentration comes easier when you are engrossed in something that interests you, try to generate an interest in the subject. An excellent way of doing this is through previewing. The preview, as you know, acquaints you with the subject and gives you some background information on it.

Many textbook chapters are followed by questions put there by the author to stimulate your interest. If there are no questions provided, make up some of your own and keep your interest alive by trying to discover answers in your reading.

2. **Set a Goal.** Another way to build the concentration you need is to formulate an immediate and clear objective or purpose. Student drivers find much to motivate them in studying for their operator's license. The goal of passing tomorrow's quiz often helps students concentrate quite effectively the night before.

Your objective should be realistic enough to make you want to study. Even a short-range goal might be enough to give you the motivation you need at the moment. For example, devising and answering three or four questions related to your reading could be an effective short-range goal.

3. **Prepare to Concentrate.** Plan seriously to get down to work. Have the books and supplies you need. Make certain before you begin that everything you require is on hand. If you have to get up to sharpen a pencil or find some paper, concentration will never take hold.

4. **Vary the Activity.** Concentration is a demanding mental task. No one can sustain peak attention over a prolonged period. Anticipate this by varying your activity. When studying, there may be an opportunity in the middle to jot down some notes. Do this for a break in the study routine.

Perhaps you will want to turn to the back of the chapter and see which questions you can answer. Or, try reciting for a few minutes; see if you can repeat some of the main points of the lesson. Give yourself some relief from the task of prolonged concentration. You will find that you will be able to study longer.

5. **Prevent Daydreaming.** Even the best students tend to daydream. Expect your mind to wander; in this regard you are no different from anyone else. The way to overcome the tendency to daydream is to correct it immediately. Don't give in to the inclination; fight it. Personal problems, conflicts, memories and plans for the future must be consciously put out of your mind before you can concentrate on the subject at hand.

A good way to start again is to review rapidly what has been covered to the point where you lost your concentration and then continue on.

6. **Relate Learning.** To sustain the concentration you have begun, you need to make meaningful associations. It is wise to relate what you are learning to what you already know about the subject.

Material you are currently learning is usually related in some way to matter you have learned in previous lessons and classroom lectures. Try to see the relationships; see how the new material fits. This way, your new learning becomes meaningful from the very start, keeping your attention and concentration focused.

7. **Set a Time.** Have you ever noticed how timing brings out peak performance? Almost every athletic event is either closely timed or the participants are competing against time. In track events, spectators are generally more interested in the winning time than they are in the winner's name.

Beating the clock is an irresistible target. Set a time for the completion of the task. Your inclination to beat the clock may bring the sustained concentration you need.

8. **Pace the Assignment.** Trying to do too much too fast destroys concentration. You know that you are not able to employ total concentration for very long periods, especially if you're not in the habit.

When an assignment is long or involved, it is best not to attempt to complete it at one sitting. Divide the learning into twenty-minute periods and spread out the periods of study. Returning to an unfinished project makes it easier for you to regain concentration. You naturally want to see the assignment completed, and this gets you off to a good start.

9. **Organize the Assignment.** One major reason students cannot concentrate is that they often have nothing to concentrate on. Their approach to an assignment is so unplanned that this in itself becomes a distraction.

Organize the assignment into a series of related and specific tasks. Use your preview skills to help you understand the work and what you expect to gain from it. Break the job down for yourself; keep in mind exactly what you wish to learn or accomplish from this study session.

10. **Practice.** The further you go in school, the more you will need to develop the ability to concentrate. More and more, you will be expected to see relationships, make generalizations and understand principles, not just accumulate facts. Learning of this kind requires independent study and research. You will be on your own and expected to keep up.

Because most students have not had much practice in this kind of self-generated study, you may lack the necessary discipline. The steps discussed above will help you get off to the right start. You will not be expected to apply all of these procedures every time you open a book. But look them over, become familiar with them and use the two or three suggestions which apply most directly to your current assignment.

_____: Reading Time

_____: Reading Rate

_____: Score, Test A

_____: Score, Test B

_____: Total Score

_____%: Comprehension

COMPREHENSION TEST 15-A

Directions: The following passage, taken from the selection you have just read, has words omitted from it. Fill in each blank with the word that was omitted. Each blank filled correctly is worth two points. Ask your instructor if you may take credit for close synonyms. Enter your score in the box provided at the end of the selection. A list of the omitted words can be found on page 240.

As a student you probably suffer from a problem common to all students: there are times when you cannot concentrate. If it happens to you occasionally, don't be too _____1_____; everyone's concentration wanders sometimes. But if it happens to _____2_____ most of the time, you're in trouble and you _____3_____ do something about it.

Fortunately, you *can* do something. _____4_____ can improve your ability to concentrate, and you can _____5_____ by understanding what concentration is all about. It is _____6_____ a gift which some have and others do not. _____7_____ of the times when you have been concentrating. What _____8_____ you doing? It's safe to say that you were _____9_____ involved in some matter which interested you. And this _____10_____ precisely what concentration means: to fix your attention on _____11_____. To do this effectively, you must keep distracting thoughts _____12_____.

Keeping your attention fixed on a subject without yielding _____13_____ distractions is not all that difficult; we all do _____14_____ many times a day. Most drivers are able to _____15_____ effectively behind the wheel; TV viewers concentrate to the _____16_____ of total involvement when watching favorite programs. When we _____17_____ to, we seem to be able to concentrate.

Why, _____18_____, is concentration so difficult when it comes to study? _____19_____ obvious answer is that the interest is just not _____20_____; lessons don't mean as much to us as these _____21_____ things. It would seem then that finding ways to _____22_____ interest in studies will contribute to greater concentration.

INTERFERENCES

1. _____23_____. If you are hungry, don't try to settle down _____24_____ a session of concentrated study. It can't be done. _____25_____ matter how interested or preoccupied you become with the study matter, your body will be relentless in its demands for attention.

Food for the body must precede food for the mind.

COMPREHENSION TEST 15-B

Directions: This is another passage from the selection, again with words omitted. Proceed as before, giving yourself two points for each blank filled correctly. Add this score to the one from Test A and enter your total score in the box at the end of the selection. Use the conversion table on page 254 to convert your *total* score to a comprehension percentage, and record that grade in the box also. A list of omitted words can be found on page 240.

8. **Pace the Assignment.** Trying to do too much too fast destroys concentration. You know that you are not able to employ _____ 1 concentration for very long periods, especially if you're not _____ 2 the habit.

When an assignment is long or involved, _____ 3 is best not to attempt to complete it at _____ 4 sitting. Divide the learning into twenty-minute periods and _____ 5 out the periods of study. Returning to an unfinished _____ 6 makes it easier for you to regain concentration. You _____ 7 want to see the assignment completed, and this gets _____ 8 off to a good start.

9. **Organize the Assignment.** One _____ 9 reason students cannot concentrate is that they often have _____ 10 to concentrate on. Their approach to an assignment is _____ 11 unplanned that this in itself becomes a distraction.

Organize _____ 12 assignment into a series of related and specific tasks. _____ 13 your preview skills to help you understand the work _____ 14 what you expect to gain from it. Break the _____ 15 down for yourself; keep in mind exactly what you _____ 16 to learn or accomplish from this study session.

10. **Practice.** _____ 17 further you go in school, the more you will _____ 18 to develop the ability to concentrate. More and more, _____ 19 will be expected to see relationships, make generalizations and _____ 20 principles, not just accumulate facts. Learning of this kind _____ 21 independent study and research. You will be on your _____ 22 and expected to keep up.

Because most students have _____ 23 had much practice in this kind of self-generated _____ 24, you may lack the necessary discipline. The steps discussed _____ 25 will help you get off to the right start. You will not be expected to apply all of these procedures every time you open a book.

PRACTICING CONCENTRATION

Directions: The following activities will help you develop your ability to concentrate more effectively.

1. Close your eyes and picture a large blackboard in your mind. Visualize numbers being written on the blackboard one at a time: 100, 200, 300, and so on. See how far you can get before stray thoughts push the number pictures from your mind. Then start over again, concentrating harder, and try to get further the second time, and still further the third time.

2. Concentration is an important part of careful observation and is essential for good remembering. Look at a picture of a group of people in a magazine or newspaper. Read the caption which gives the names of the people. Study the picture and caption for 30 seconds, concentrating on them as intensely as you can. Without looking at the picture, name and describe each person.

3. Many popular meditation systems promote deep relaxation by teaching you how to concentrate on relaxing. Since everyone's concentration wanders after a time, a preselected number, word or nonsense syllable is used to return your concentration to what you are doing. Try the following procedure at a time when you are reasonably alert. If you are tired, concentrating on relaxing will probably put you to sleep.
   a. Sit in a comfortable position with your eyes closed. Choose any word, name, number or nonsense syllables — Shangri-La would do, for example.
   b. Concentrate on relaxing every muscle in your body, starting with your scalp and moving slowly down to your toes.
   c. Once completely relaxed, think of something pleasant: a friend, a country scene. You will find you can't concentrate on the subject very long before distracting or unpleasant thoughts push it from your mind and your relaxed muscles begin to become tense again. This is where you use your word or number.
   d. Drive out the distracting thoughts by saying the word or number until you can return your concentration to relaxing and your pleasant thought. Each time you try you will find your span of concentration becomes longer.

4. Check the quality of your concentration with and without distractions. Select any two pictures in this book that have similar subjects. Study one of the pictures for one minute in a quiet atmosphere. Write as complete a description of the picture as you can under the same quiet circumstances. Do the same with the second picture, but have loud music playing all the while. Which is the better job? Which took longer?

> Listening is a lost art today for most people. Understanding listening faults is prerequisite to overcoming them. Suggestions for improving listening help you correct poor habits and cultivate good ones.

Listening Effectively

A wise man once said that listening is the hardest thing in the world to do.

Faulty listening leads to misunderstanding, and we all know from experience the problems that can cause. And there are those who feel, with good reason, that we might have universal peace at last if only people would really listen to one another.

In industry millions of dollars are lost annually as a result of poor listening. Consequently, it has become standard practice at most major companies to "write it down." Xerox, a leading corporation, has developed an employee listening improvement course which it now sells to other companies.

In school, students fail to listen properly to instructions and after every exam we hear about those who lost credit by not following directions. Teachers often repeat an important fact three or four times in class only to hear some students complain, "But I never heard you say that!"

LISTENING FAULTS

Causes of faulty listening are many and mixed. For purposes of discussion we can classify them as follows:

1. **Daydreaming.** This is probably the most troublesome listening fault because it affects everyone. Frequently a speaker will mention some person or thing which triggers an association in our minds and off we go. When we return to reality and start listening again, we discover that point three is being presented and we have no recollection of points one and two.

Opportunities for daydreaming are abundant because people speak much more slowly than we can think. Thus, while a speaker is talking at a rate of 125 words a minute, your mind is free to race along.

There are ways to overcome the natural tendency to daydream, and we will discuss them later in this selection.

2. Closed-mindedness. We often refuse to listen to ideas and viewpoints that run contrary to our preconceived notions about a subject. We say, in effect, "I know all I want to know, so there's no use listening."

Actually, this is an intellectual fault that leads to a listening problem. Closed-mindedness interferes with learning by causing you to shut out facts you need to know whether you agree with them or not.

Close attention and a fair appraisal of what's being said are all most teachers are after; they don't necessarily want or need your agreement.

3. False Attention. This is a protective device that everyone resorts to from time to time. When we're not really interested in what someone has to say, we just pretend to listen. We nod and make occasional meaningless comments to give the impression that we are paying attention, when actually our minds are somewhere else.

Some people become so skilled at this that they convince their teachers that they are the most attentive of students. But the teachers remain convinced only until exam time when it becomes obvious how much these false listeners have missed.

False attention will not do for school; don't let yourself form the habit. Even though a teacher may not be an interesting speaker, you will still be held responsible for all that is said. Golden nuggets of information often come in torrents of uninspired words. Unfortunately, to separate out the gold you must train yourself to be attentive to it all.

4. Intellectual Despair. Listening can be difficult at times. Often you have to sit through lectures on subjects hard to understand. Occasionally you may feel the urge to throw in the towel, to give up. You say to yourself: "No matter how hard I try, I don't get it. I may as well face facts; I just can't learn this stuff." With this kind of thinking it is easy to stop trying.

Obviously, you'll never understand if you give up. The thing to do is to listen more carefully than ever; ask questions when practical and, most important, discuss the material with a classmate. Attack the problem as soon as it appears. Catch up right away and you'll feel less inclined to adopt an attitude of futility.

5. Memorizing. Some listeners try to memorize every word spoken by the lecturer. You cannot remember everything a speaker says; it is impossible. When you try, you miss the sense of the lecture and come out remembering less. A student who displays this fault probably has never been taught the techniques for effective listening.

6. Personality Listening. It is only natural for listeners to appraise and evaluate a speaker. Our impressions should not interfere with our listening, however. The content must be judged on its own merit.

You will encounter instructors who bore you and others who have a distracting habit or characteristic. There's nothing much you can do about it. Unfortunately, grading systems don't make allowances for distracting or boring personalities. It is your responsibility to dredge whatever nuggets of information you can from every speaker no matter how difficult or unrewarding the job may seem. One way to deal with a difficult speaker is to concentrate twice as hard. Asking a question occasionally helps because then you are forcing a personal exchange with the speaker that helps keep both of you alert.

GOOD LISTENING

We've discussed faults to avoid when listening in class. Keep them in mind and avoid them. To help improve your listening, here are some positive steps you can take.

1. Prepare to Listen. Your attitude in attending class is important. If you feel that a particular class is a waste of time, you obviously will be in no mood to listen. Decide before class that the lecture period will be well spent; resolve to make it a learning experience.

The best way to prepare for lectures is to keep ahead in your textbook and other required reading. The more you know about a subject in advance the more interested you will be in hearing what your instructor has to say about it. For prepared students lectures become an exchange of ideas rather than a deluge of unfamiliar and seemingly unrelated facts. It is difficult and often impossible to get anything out of a lecture that you are not prepared for.

2. Watch the Speaker. Don't take your eyes off him. When you look away, you invite visual distractions which compete for your attention. In class, you've got to listen with your eyes as well as your ears.

Develop an awareness of the speaker's mannerisms. His gestures supplement his remarks. What a writer does with punctuation, bold print, headlines and italics, a speaker does with vocal inflection and body gestures. All speakers communicate physically as well as orally. You must watch as you listen.

3. Note Questions. Listen closely to questions asked in class. When an instructor asks a question, he is probably about to discuss something important and is calling for your attention. This is an important signal between a speaker and his listeners. Consider that he knows the answer; there is nothing he can learn from the question. He's asking it so *you* will learn; he wants you to understand and remember the answer. Speakers' questions are designed to help you listen and learn. Notice, too, questions asked by others in the class. Student questions signal the instructor; they tell him how his message is coming across. He will elaborate and illustrate, repeat and paraphrase to help his listeners understand the matter.

Questions from both teacher and student are valuable; pay attention to them.

4. **Listen Creatively.** You should not listen and think about other matters at the same time; you must give your entire attention to the speaker's words.

If you sit passively, like a sponge, expecting to soak up knowledge, you are really only half listening. To listen totally, you have to react; you must put your mind to work. Like a computer, start to process the data coming in. This forces you to think ahead. You become attuned to the speaker and can anticipate what is coming up. Get your mind running on a parallel track.

Ask questions. If questions are not permitted during a class session, write your questions in your notebook and get the answers later.

Bring questions to class. Your attention is sharpened when you are listening for answers. If your instructor calls for class participation, participate by all means. Don't be afraid or shy about speaking up. Your attention is focused most sharply when you are on the firing line; and if you are mistaken and are corrected in class, you can be sure you will never forget the correct response at exam time, when being right really counts.

Your success in school will depend largely on how well you listen in class. The suggestions offered here can substantially improve your ability in this vital area.

_____: Reading Time

_____: Reading Rate

_____: Score, Test A

_____: Score, Test B

_____: Total Score

_____%: Comprehension

COMPREHENSION TEST 16-A

Directions: The following passage, taken from the selection you have just read, has words omitted from it. Fill in each blank with the word that was omitted. Each blank filled correctly is worth two points. Ask your instructor if you may take credit for close synonyms. Enter your score in the box provided at the end of the selection. A list of the omitted words can be found on page 241.

A wise man once said that listening is the hardest thing in the world to do. Faulty listening leads to misunderstanding, and we all know _____ 1 experience the problems that can cause. And there are _____ 2 who feel, with good reason, that we might have _____ 3 peace at last if only people would really listen _____ 4 one another.

In industry millions of dollars are lost _____ 5 as a result of poor listening. Consequently, it has _____ 6 standard practice at most major companies to "write it _____ 7." Xerox, a leading corporation, has developed an employee listening _____ 8 course which it now sells to other companies.

In _____ 9, students fail to listen properly to instructions and after _____ 10 exam we hear about those who lost credit by _____ 11 following directions. Teachers often repeat an important fact three _____ 12 four times in class only to hear some students _____ 13, "But I never heard you say that!"

LISTENING FAULTS

_____ 14 of faulty listening are many and mixed. For purposes _____ 15 discussion we can classify them as follows:

1. Daydreaming. This _____ 16 probably the most troublesome listening fault because it affects _____ 17. Frequently a speaker will mention some person or thing _____ 18 triggers an association in our minds and off we _____ 19. When we return to reality and start listening again, _____ 20 discover that point three is being presented and we _____ 21 no recollection of points one and two.

Opportunities for _____ 22 are abundant because people speak much more slowly than _____ 23 can think. Thus, while a speaker is talking at _____ 24 rate of 125 words a minute, your mind is _____ 25 to race along.

There are ways to overcome the natural tendency to daydream, and we will discuss them later in this selection.

COMPREHENSION TEST 16-B

Directions: This is another passage from the selection, again with words omitted. Proceed as before, giving yourself two points for each blank filled correctly. Add this score to the one from Test A and enter your total score in the box at the end of the selection. Use the conversion table on page 254 to convert your *total* score to a comprehension percentage, and record that grade in the box also. A list of omitted words can be found on page 241.

3. Note Questions. Listen closely to questions asked in class. When an instructor asks a question, he is probably _____ to discuss something
                                                                    1
important and is calling for your _____. This is an important signal
                                            2
between a speaker and _____ listeners. Consider that he knows the
                            3
answer; there is _____ he can learn from the question. He's asking
                        4
it _____ *you* will learn; he wants you to understand and
        5
_____ the answer. Speakers' questions are designed to help you
        6
_____ and learn. Notice, too, questions asked by others in
        7
_____ class. Student questions signal the instructor; they tell him
        8
_____ his message is coming across. He will elaborate and
        9
_____, repeat and paraphrase to help his listeners understand the
        10
_____.
        11

Questions from both teacher and student are valuable; pay _____
                                                                        12
to them.

4. Listen Creatively. You should not listen and _____ about other
                                                            13
matters at the same time; you must _____ your entire attention to
                                            14
the speaker's words.

If you _____ passively, like a sponge, expecting to soak up
            15
knowledge, _____ are really only half listening. To listen totally,
                16
you _____ to react; you must put your mind to work.
        17
_____ a computer, start to process the data coming in.
        18
_____ forces you to think ahead. You become attuned to
        19
_____ speaker and can anticipate what is coming up. Get
        20
_____ mind running on a parallel track.
        21
Ask questions. If _____ are not permitted during a class session,
                        22
write your _____ in your notebook and get the answers later.
                23
Bring _____ to class. Your attention is sharpened when you are
            24
_____ for answers. If your instructor calls for class participation,
        25
participate by all means.

PRACTICE LISTENING

Directions: DO NOT READ THE FOLLOWING PASSAGES; have someone read them to you. Listen carefully to determine the *main idea* presented in each passage. Have your reader offer you the four choices at the end of each passage. From these select the main idea. (Answer Key Page 249)

1. By learning to decide for yourself, you will improve greatly, and will not have to be running continually to your mother when she is reading or sewing, and disturbing her with questions. You know how annoying it is to be disturbed when you are doing anything.

The main point of this selection is
- ☐ a. that mother enjoys reading and sewing.
- ☐ b. that questions are disturbing.
- ☐ c. to learn to make your own decisions.
- ☐ d. that running continually will improve you greatly.

2. Mr. and Mrs. Snagsby are not only one bone and one flesh, but, to the neighbors' thinking, one voice too. That voice, appearing to proceed from Mrs. Snagsby alone, is heard in Cook's Court very often. Mr. Snagsby, otherwise than as he finds expression through these dulcet tones, is rarely heard.

The central focus of this paragraph is that
- ☐ a. Mr. Snagsby doesn't like to talk.
- ☐ b. Mrs. Snagsby does the talking for both.
- ☐ c. Mrs. Snagsby has a sweet voice.
- ☐ d. Mrs. Snagsby talks a lot.

3. The word science is constantly undergoing a change of meaning. In bygone days it was practiced and associated with various skills often having nothing to do with any branch of science as we know it today. Alchemy, magic and the black arts were defined as sciences.

This passage is intended to show that
- ☐ a. science involves the black arts.
- ☐ b. science has always been associated with the same skills.
- ☐ c. the meaning of science is constant.
- ☐ d. the meaning of science undergoes change with time.

4. People attach too much importance to words. They are under the illusion that talking effects great results. Yet words are, as a rule, the shallowest part of all the argument. They but dimly represent the great surging feelings and desires which lie behind. When the distraction of the tongue is removed, the heart listens.

The central thought is that
- ☐ a. deep feelings and desires are beyond description.
- ☐ b. people should talk less and listen more.
- ☐ c. people communicate best with their emotions and feelings.
- ☐ d. people do not know how to communicate with words.

5. Rose was a large girl of twenty-five or thereabouts and was called an old maid. She radiated good-nature from every line of her buxom self. Her black eyes were full of drollery, and she was on the best of terms with Howard at once. She had been a teacher, but that did not prevent her from assuming a peculiar directness of speech. Of course, they talked about old friends.

The main point of the paragraph is that Rose
- □ a. has pretty eyes.
- □ b. is a good talker.
- □ c. seems to have a friendly personality.
- □ d. was quite satisfied being an old maid.

7. I was at a loss in my thoughts to conclude at first what this gentleman designed; but I found afterward he had had some drink in his head, and that he was not very unwilling to have some more. He carried me to the Spring Garden, at Knightsbridge, where we walked in the gardens, and he treated me very handsomely; but I found he drank freely. He pressed me also to drink, but I declined it.

The focus of this paragraph is on the fact that
- □ a. the man drinks quite liberally.
- □ b. the woman was concerned about her welfare.
- □ c. the woman wasn't having a good time.
- □ d. the man was acting foolishly.

6. Where we had stranded we had nothing but pools of water and wet patches of coral about us, and farther in lay the calm, blue lagoon. We were aware that the tide was going out. We continually saw more corals sticking up out of the water round us, while the surf, which thundered without interruption along the reef, sank down, as it were, a floor lower. What would happen there on the narrow reef when the tide began to flow again was uncertain. We must get away.

The people stranded on the reef realized that
- □ a. they were caught at high tide.
- □ b. they would be safe when the tide came in.
- □ c. their situation was dangerous.
- □ d. the surf was more and more threatening.

8. The next meal, when the family party assembled, there was not a trace of displeasure in Madame de Bernstein's countenance. Her behavior to all the company, Harry included, was perfectly kind and cordial. She praised the cook this time, declared the fricassee was excellent, and that there were no eels anywhere like those in the Castlewood moats; would not allow that the wine was corked, or hear of such extravagance as opening a fresh bottle for a useless old woman like her.

The main idea of this passage concerns
- □ a. Madame de Bernstein's change to more pleasant behavior.
- □ b. the people at a dinner party.
- □ c. the woman's commonly pleasant disposition.
- □ d. the meal when the family party assembled.

Panic time comes when an inexperienced student is expected to take notes. With confidence, the skill is readily mastered. Suggestions help the notetaker develop the resources needed to record classroom lectures successfully.

How to Take Notes

When students are confronted with the need to take notes for the first time, they often discover that note-taking is a skill which requires forethought and practice. Never having had to take notes before, they have no idea how or where to begin. Since it is not unusual for a student to be expected to take notes in class and be responsible for the content of the class lecture, it is important that you develop your skill at note-taking.

Following are four methods of taking notes. Two are recommended as successful techniques; two are *not* recommended.

1. **Verbatim Transcript (Not Recommended).** Many students, faced with taking notes for the first time, try to copy the lecture word for word. Those who do soon discover that it is impossible and become frustrated. But the real danger in trying is that no time is left for understanding; the student is too busy writing.

To take notes on what is being said, you must be listening and understanding — not hearing and copying. A word-for-word copy of the lecturer's message is neither useful nor necessary.

2. **Selected Quotations (Not Recommended).** Students who give up trying to record the speaker's every word often adopt the method of copying certain quotations they hope are important. This is a desperation exercise which reveals the student's basic insecurity. Not trusting his own judgment, he is only comfortable recording the speaker's exact words. The obvious shortcoming of this method is that one is never sure of selecting the major statements of the lecture.

There are times when the speaker's words are important, as in the case of definitions, and you will want to record them completely and exactly. Normally, the lecturer will alert his listeners on such occasions by announcing that what is coming up is important to know and remember. Moreover, when the speaker wants you to get his exact words, he interrupts his normal delivery and dictates or records the facts he wants you to get on the chalkboard, leaving no doubt about what he considers important.

3. **Headings and Statements (Recommended).** This is a very popular method of note-taking. It consists of recording the main points (headings) and writing complete and meaningful phrases (statements) about them.

The advantages of this system are several. First, you are able to organize as you write. By recording the main points and writing about them, you are distinguishing between what is major and what is supplementary to it. There are techniques to help you take notes effectively in this fashion, and we will discuss them later in this selection.

A second advantage is that this system encourages listening. You wait to hear what the speaker says about the topic before recording your statement. This overcomes a common student fault: writing, instead of listening. If you do not understand the lecture in the classroom, you'll never piece it together meaningfully from your notes. The first task of the notetaker, then, is to listen.

A third advantage is that you create your own statement. You do not quote the speaker; you paraphrase him. You condense the message into a brief, meaningful statement. In this way, you are assured that you understand the lecture.

Still another advantage is that you are writing full statements, not isolated groups of words which become cryptic and meaningless later. To be useful, your notes must be understandable; this system guarantees that they will be.

4. **Pre-class Outline (Recommended).** This fourth method of note-taking is by far the best and the one

you should use when the opportunity permits. Under this system, you prepare an outline to use in class as the foundation for your notes. The organizing, then, is all done and you just have to fill in the statements. The advantages of using the method are obvious: you have your headings and main topics all nicely laid out and you know before the lecture starts what topics will be discussed.

A shortcoming of the system is that it can be used only with highly organized teachers. If you discover that one of your instructors generally follows the plan of the text, then each night before class you can prepare a topical outline to use as the basis for your notes. This system presupposes that the speaker will follow the pattern established by the text. Few do. Most teachers use the text as a springboard, elaborating on some matters and glossing over others. They vary their presentation to suit the needs of a particular group of students or to discuss interesting, related points.

Nevertheless, having an outline in advance gives you a remarkable head start on the day's lecture and provides the bonus of preparing you to understand better what is being discussed. So be on the alert for opportunities to use this method of note-taking. It guarantees excellent notes.

TAKING USEFUL NOTES

Since the method of recording headings and statements offers the most advantages, it is the system we suggest you use in most cases.

To become proficient in taking notes, you must become secure in your own ability. You must develop the confidence needed to evaluate and organize as you listen. This is not as difficult as it first sounds. By applying and practicing the following suggestions, you will find yourself rapidly growing in skill as a notetaker.

1. **Prepare for Lectures.** This means

two things. First, come to class ready to study and learn; this is not the time to relax and be entertained.

Next, do the necessary preparations before class. Read ahead in the text the night before. Since it is natural to become confused if you know nothing about the subject of the lecture, read enough about the topic to understand the substance. This will help you evaluate the lecture and decide what to record.

Very early in a course, you should discover the lecturer's plan and how his lectures relate to the text. Once you know this, you can prepare for them. If you discover that the speaker often discusses matters that are well covered in the text, you need not copy down his words; merely make a note beside the topic to see the text. Or if your teacher follows the plan of the text, you can best prepare by composing a pre-class outline each day.

2. **Listen before Writing.** The first job of the notetaker is to listen. Notes are of no use to the student who does not understand to begin with.

Speakers use many examples to help their listeners see the point. Listen long enough to be sure you've got it and then write it down. Chances are you will not recall the speaker's original words. Good! Then you are forced to record what you have understood. Any time you can paraphrase, you show that you understand.

If you find you don't have time to write before the speaker goes on to something new, put down just a single word or two to recall the topic and leave a blank space. After class, ask the lecturer or another student what was said in order to refresh your memory. Then fill in the blank space in your notes. Use this same method if you don't understand enough to put down anything useful. In this case, no notes are better than poor notes; you know what you've missed and you can correct the omission.

3. Write Complete Statements. This suggestion follows naturally from the one above. As you listen, try to construct a complete statement which best expresses the thought. Don't just jot down unrelated words; say what you know about them.

When you return to your notes later in the semester, single words and meaningless phrases won't be enough to refresh your memory on the subject. You need statements containing complete, accurate information.

4. Write Selectively. Notes are best when they are brief, concise. Evaluate and select what needs to be recorded. The speaker's illustrations, anecdotes and examples need not be preserved; they are presented to help you understand some point. Make sure that just the most important points are covered in your notes.

5. Organize. The way you arrange your notes should indicate the organization of the lecture. For example, you should begin with a title for the lecture; this goes at the top of a new page. When the speaker changes topics and discusses something new (this may be the next class or several classes later), start a new page with a new title at the top.

Next, record your notes in outline style. Main points are listed at the margin, followed by a statement or two about them. Secondary ideas on the same point should be indented as subheadings and followed by a statement of explanation. Further indentions indicate more subordinate ideas. When reviewing your notes, a glance down the left-hand margin will reveal all the main points of the lecture at a glance.

Note-taking is not the difficult task that students fear and imagine. Follow these suggestions to build your confidence. Practice each day and, before long, you will develop a very comfortable and rewarding system of recording classroom lectures.

_____: Reading Time

_____: Reading Rate

_____: Score, Test A

_____: Score, Test B

_____: Total Score

_____%: Comprehension

COMPREHENSION TEST 17-A

Directions: The following passage, taken from the selection you have just read, has words omitted from it. Fill in each blank with the word that was omitted. Each blank filled correctly is worth two points. Ask your instructor if you may take credit for close synonyms. Enter your score in the box provided at the end of the selection. A list of the omitted words can be found on page 241.

Following are four methods of taking notes. Two are recommended as successful techniques; two are *not* _____.
1

1. Verbatim Transcript (Not Recommended). Many students, faced with taking _____ for the first time, try to copy the lecture _____ for
2   3
word. Those who do soon discover that it _____ impossible and
4
become frustrated. But the real danger in _____ is that no time is
5
left for understanding; the _____ is too busy writing.
6

To take notes on what _____ being said, you must be listening
7
and understanding — not _____ and copying. A word-for-word
8
copy of the _____ message is neither useful nor necessary.
9

2. Selected Quotations (Not _____). Students who give up trying
10
to record the speaker's _____ word often adopt the method of
11
copying certain quotations _____ hope are important. This is a
12
desperation exercise which _____ the student's basic insecurity. Not
13
trusting his own judgment, _____ is only comfortable recording the
14
speaker's exact words. The _____ shortcoming of this method is that
15
one is never _____ of selecting the major statements of the lecture.
16
There _____ times when the speaker's words are important, as in
17
_____ case of definitions, and you will want to record
18
_____ completely and exactly. Normally, the lecturer will alert
19
his _____ on such occasions by announcing that what is coming
20
_____ is important to know and remember. Moreover, when the
21
_____ wants you to get his exact words, he interrupts
22
_____ normal delivery and dictates or records the facts he
23
_____ you to get on the chalkboard, leaving no doubt
24
_____ what he considers important.
25

3. Headings and Statements (Recommended). This is a very popular method of note-taking.

COMPREHENSION TEST 17-B

Directions: This is another passage from the selection, again with words omitted. Proceed as before, giving yourself two points for each blank filled correctly. Add this score to the one from Test A and enter your total score in the box at the end of the selection. Use the conversion table on page 254 to convert your *total* score to a comprehension percentage, and record that grade in the box also. A list of omitted words can be found on page 241.

3. Write Complete Statements. This suggestion follows naturally from the one above. As you listen, try to construct a complete statement _____ best expresses the thought. Don't just jot down unrelated _____; say what you know about them.
₁ ... ₂

When you return _____ your notes later in the semester, single words and _____ phrases won't be enough to refresh your memory on _____ subject. You need statements containing complete, accurate information.

4. Write _____. Notes are best when they are brief, concise. Evaluate _____ select what needs to be recorded. The speaker's illustrations, _____ and examples need not be preserved; they are presented _____ help you understand some point. Make sure that just _____ most important points are covered in your notes.

5. Organize. _____ way you arrange your notes should indicate the organization _____ the lecture. For example, you should begin with a _____ for the lecture; this goes at the top of _____ new page. When the speaker changes topics and discusses _____ new (this may be the next class or several _____ later), start a new page with a new title _____ the top.

Next, record your notes in outline style. _____ points are listed at the margin, followed by a _____ or two about them. Secondary ideas on the same _____ should be indented as subheadings and followed by a _____ of explanation. Further indentions indicate more subordinate ideas. When _____ your notes, a glance down the left-hand margin _____ reveal all the main points of the lecture at _____ glance.

Note-taking is not the difficult task that _____ fear and imagine. Follow these suggestions to build your confidence.

PRACTICE TAKING NOTES

Practice Exercise 1

Directions: In the following discussion about questioning the author when studying textbook material, the lecturer mentions four questions you should ask to focus your reading. Explanations of why you should question and what you can learn from each of the four questions are also given. See if you can record these four questions as someone reads the selection to you. It is not necessary to take detailed notes at this point; rather, concentrate on listening and understanding the lecturer's main ideas. When you finish, compare your notes with the model on page 250.

QUESTION THE AUTHOR

You've probably heard it said that you'll never learn if you don't ask questions.

Why is inquisitiveness associated with learning? We speak of the student seeking knowledge, or of the inquiring mind, and both of these concepts imply asking or questioning.

This is because learning is not a passive process; it is something we do. Learning is an activity—it requires us to go after it, seek it out. This is why we say that questioning is part of learning.

A technique good students use is to question the author. We question following previewing by asking, "What can I expect to learn from this chapter or article? Based on my prereading, what are some of the things to be covered or presented? What will the author tell me about this subject?" Questions like these "frame" the subject for us, give us an outline to fill in when reading.

Another question we hope to find the answer to is "What is the author's method of presentation?" There are many different methods the author can use in presenting material. He or she may ask questions and answer them, adopting this technique to make the subject easier to learn. The author may give details, describe and illustrate, or use comparison and contrast. Whatever the method, discover it and put it to use when studying.

In many books the questions are already there waiting to be used. Check your textbooks. Are there questions following the chapters? If so, use them during previewing to instill the inquisitiveness so necessary to learning. These are special questions—they tell us what the author considers important in each chapter, what he or she really expects us to learn.

Develop the technique of questioning. Try whenever you study to create questions you expect to find answered.

PRACTICE TAKING NOTES

Practice Exercise 2

Directions: This exercise will give you an opportunity to practice taking a more complete set of notes. In the following discussion of *The Nature of Comprehension*, the lecturer organizes his ideas into four main categories. The first one is a discussion of the student view of reading — make this your first heading.

As someone reads the selection to you, concentrate on recording the title, four main headings and four complete but brief summary statements. To formulate each summary statement in your own words, you must listen carefully to understand the lecturer's main idea in each category. Organize your notes in the form suggested in this chapter. When you finish, compare your notes with the model suggested on page 250.

THE NATURE OF COMPREHENSION

Reading is one of those subjects, like politics and religion, that everyone knows something about. For purposes of examination, let us classify common views of reading into the following groups.

What is the student view of reading? Most students, unfortunately, approach the reading assignment in a very mechanical and passive fashion. They feel that reading involves sitting before the open book and moving the eyes over the lines of print. If comprehension results, fine. If not, the student contends that it's not his fault; he did his part; he fulfilled his end of the bargain. Teachers hear this concept expressed when a student reports: "I read it but I don't get it," or "I went over it twice and I still don't get it."

Contrary to student thinking, the reader is not a sponge soaking up comprehension from the printed page. The reader must search out comprehension; there is no formula guaranteeing that comprehension will follow automatically. In other words, reading is an active, not a passive, process; there is no easy road to comprehension.

The story is told of the freshman student who inquired at the college bookstore for a manual to help him study better. When the clerk replied that he had just the thing, that "this book can cut your study time in *half*," the student said, "Great! I'll take *two*."

What is the parent view of reading? Many parents become anxious when a child starts school and begins learning to read. If after a few weeks the child comes home and can read, that is pronounce, the simple words in his basal reader, the parents relax. The school is doing its job, they feel. If the child cannot pronounce the words, does not know how to sound them out, then the schools "aren't teaching kids to read like they used to."

Parents cannot be faulted for taking this view. Their only means of appraising their child's progress is through oral reading, by listening to the child read aloud.

PRACTICE TAKING NOTES

This places great emphasis on phonics and oral reading skills. Too great a concentration on any one aspect of learning to read can lead to an imbalance in the beginning reading program. Most basal reading programs stress a balanced approach, incorporating comprehension and silent reading skills as well.

What is the Madison Avenue view of reading? Inevitably, the techniques of mass marketing and national promotion found their way into the field of reading improvement. Thus, the adult consumer is sold on the desirability of knowing how to read at thousands of words per minute. We are told that we are not living up to our potential in reading, while television portrays course graduates comfortably consuming entire books in seconds. In true Madison Avenue fashion, the enrollee is guaranteed his money back if his reading speed is not tripled with "satisfactory" comprehension.

Actually, it is unrealistic for the student to imagine that fact-laden textbooks can be skimmed at thousands of words per minute. To your instructor, "satisfactory" comprehension means an understanding of the facts and details, as well as the principles and generalizations of his course.

What is a more realistic view of reading? Perhaps one that incorporates elements of these other views. First, the student does have to sit down before the open book with the determination to read actively and to spend the necessary time. Second, a balanced dose of phonics does contribute to growth in reading ability. And third, high-speed skimming is a valuable tool of the efficient reader.

Because reading implies comprehension, the reader must make this his goal. He must demand comprehension of himself in everything he reads.

Practice Exercise 3

Directions: The topic of the following lecture is *Vision and Reading*. As someone reads it to you, take notes using a system of headings and statements. In addition, include subheadings and substatements where needed. Try to record as complete a set of notes as you can. When you finish, compare your notes with the model on page 250.

VISION AND READING

To help you understand the relationship between vision and reading, let us examine the visual requirements for successful school achievement.

First, *visual acuity*. This refers to the ability to see small objects clearly. A person with normal visual acuity is said to have 20/20 vision. This simply means that he is able to read a letter which is 11/32 inches high from a distance of twenty feet.

As an index to visual acuity, the description 20/20 has limitations. Eye specialists caution that it designates *normal* vision. Someone scoring outside this range may or may not have *faulty* vision; only a comprehensive visual screening can determine for certain.

Visual acuity is affected by three optical defects. They are myopia (nearsightedness), hyperopia (farsightedness), and astigmatism. The most common of these is myopia or nearsightedness, characterized by blurred vision. This type of problem is easily corrected with eye glasses.

Hyperopia refers to farsightedness. In less severe cases with children, the eye is able to adjust its focus, solving the problem. Severe cases require corrective glasses.

Astigmatism, characterized by blurring or discomfort, usually accompanies myopia or hyperopia and is corrected by glasses.

A second basic visual skill is *fixation ability*. Fixation ability has three aspects: (a) the ability to aim the eyes at a motionless object; (b) the ability to follow a moving object; and (c) the ability to shift the eyes from one object to another. The importance of the fixation skills to reading and school work is apparent.

A third basic visual skill is *accommodation*. This describes the ability to adjust the focus of the eye between objects at different distances. For students, the skill of accommodation is frequently used when shifting vision from the book to the blackboard. This ability reaches its performance peak at adolescence and declines with age.

A fourth visual skill is *binocular fusion*. Binocular fusion is the ability to combine data from the two eyes to form a single image. The brain, you see, receives two images (a picture from each eye) because each eye is separately equipped with its own muscles and optic nerve which report directly to the brain. There is no connection of any kind linking the left and right eye. It is the function of the brain to fuse the two pictures into a single image. Double vision occurs when binocular fusion is faulty. In such a situation, the vision of one eye will be suppressed or ignored in an attempt to eliminate the confusion.

A fifth skill involves having an *adequate field of vision*. Normally, your eyes are able to see to the sides and above and below the object being viewed. This peripheral vision is essential for normal functioning. In driving an automobile, playing sports and for general safety, you must be aware of movement and action on both sides, even while looking ahead. While clear vision is not possible, the eyes must be sensitive to the movement of objects in the field of vision.

Finally, a sixth visual skill is *form perception*. This is the ability to recognize shapes. In terms of reading ability, this may well be the most important visual skill.

Writing need not be the chore many students make it. Organization is the key to effective writing. A step-by-step approach will help you structure and compose your work. Editing will improve the quality and effectiveness of your writing as well as disclose any errors in it.

How to Write Effectively

It seems that many students hate to write, and yet reading, writing and speaking are the student's tools of learning. We all have good ideas suitable for writing about. The trouble arises in expressing our ideas in an organized way, and it is usually this lack of organization which makes students dislike writing. If you will become organized in your approach to writing, you will find the experience rewarding and probably enjoyable.

PLANNING TO WRITE

In writing, preparation is the all-important consideration. There are procedures to follow which can help you when you start to write.

1. Define Your Subject. Think first and carefully about your subject. Then write down a brief description of your subject. This should not be just a short title. Rather, it should be a statement describing or defining the subject you plan to discuss and also what you plan to say about it. You should be able to state clearly in a sentence or two the main ideas you wish to present.

Many students fail right here, before they even begin, by not knowing what their main ideas are. Obviously, you cannot write effectively if you don't know what you're going to say. Take enough time at the beginning to write your subject statement. It will pay dividends in time saved later and will produce a more effective piece of writing.

2. Limit the Subject. You should know before you begin writing how long your paper will be or how long you want it to be. This means that your presentation will have to be limited to just those topics which can be suitably covered in the space and time allowed. Many students try to cover too much ground in too little space. The result is that they never really present anything of value; their writing consists of a series of unrelated facts with no real point or substance.

You must stop, think and define the limitations of your subject. Decide exactly on the two or three points you want to cover, and know before you write what you intend to say. A few notes, a brief outline, or just referring to your subject statement will help you to control your thoughts.

3. **Clarify Your Purpose.** Every student has a purpose in mind when writing, but too often it is a vague, poorly defined idea. Words are tools employed to convey the exact meanings intended by the author. This presupposes that as a writer you know beforehand which exact meanings you want to convey. You must know clearly what your purpose in writing is. Take a position regarding your subject and defend or support it.

Purposeless writing is ineffective writing. Unless your reader knows where you are leading him, your writing will not make sense. Aimless writing creates aimless and dull reading.

4. **Support Your Ideas.** Every paper, essay or theme must do more than merely present ideas; your ideas must be supported. You cannot expect your reader to accept your position unless it is properly presented and well substantiated.

This does not mean that everything you write has to take a stand on some controversial issue. It means that, whatever your subject and purpose, your writing must include the facts, details, definitions, descriptions, illustrations, or arguments that make your ideas reasonable and acceptable to the reader.

Examine paragraphs from your textbooks. Observe how skilled writers flood the reader with all kinds of support for their generalizations.

5. **Fact and Opinion.** In every essay or theme, a writer presents both facts and opinions about a subject. Student writers frequently fail to identify which of their ideas are facts and which are opinions. As you might expect, this leaves the reader hanging and confused, uncertain of the validity of your conclusions.

Present the facts clearly for the reader to see and understand. Then state opinions based on those facts for the reader to appraise and evaluate. This way readers can agree or disagree with you in an intelligent fashion.

6. **Structure the Presentation.** Your organization must be clear to your readers; they must be able to see how your theme or essay is structured. Unstructured writing is disorganized; readers do not know where you are leading them and they are unable to see the logic of your discussion. Readers need to be aware of the divisions of your presentation, when you have completed discussion of one idea and have moved on to the next. Readers need to be aware of the transitions from one idea to the next as you develop a major theme. Only then can your readers put the pieces together intelligently.

7. **Justify Conclusions.** A sign of an inexperienced writer is a statement of a conclusion that is not justified or supported by the evidence. Your conclusion may be obvious to you because of your research into the subject. The reader, however, cannot be expected to "buy" your conclusion unless you have presented enough facts to support it.

EDITING YOUR WORK

After you finish writing a theme or essay, it needs to be read and edited. This is the time to polish your writing, smooth out the rough spots and correct any errors.

It is a mistake to suppose that a satisfactory piece of work can result from just one writing. Everyone needs to work from a rough draft, polishing and editing to arrive at a truly finished product. Skilled writers revise

the effect you intended. Does it sound the way you want it to?

Certain errors of agreement and usage will be obvious when you hear them. Generally, though, you are listening for impact, to determine if your paper puts across your ideas in the way you intended.

2. Review Sentence Structure. Be alert for incomplete thoughts (sentence fragments) and run-on sentences or comma splices. Each sentence should express a complete thought. Excessively long, involved, unclear sentences confuse the reader. Search for a more concise and accurate way to express your ideas. Look for ways to combine thoughts; connect sentences which are related.

Check every sentence. It is usually here where themes first start to break down.

3. Check Punctuation. Punctuation is intended to help the reader understand your writing. It is a way of showing on paper the pauses and inflections we make when we speak.

Be sure to use the proper mark of punctuation. Consult your dictionary or composition and usage text for assistance.

4. Check Pronouns. Pronouns, as you know, replace nouns. The antecedent of every pronoun must be clear to your reader. There should be no doubt what every "it," "he," "they," or "him" refers to.

Check, too, to be sure that each pronoun agrees with its antecedent in person and number. A frequent error is to use a plural pronoun (these, they) to replace a singular noun.

5. Improve Nouns and Verbs. We all tend to use the same nouns and verbs over and over. This makes our writing dull and unimaginative. Try to replace with a more specific and expressive word each important noun and verb in your paper. Help the reader see and feel your thoughts. However, avoid artificial or over-inflated language. You want to produce impact, not poetry.

several times because they have learned that each editing produces an improved version. At least one rewrite is essential to make your paper acceptable. When proofing and editing your first copy, follow these steps.

1. Read for Effect. After you have finished writing your paper, read it aloud to see if your words create

6. Add Adjectives. Sometimes sentences you write can be improved by adding a colorful adjective. Try it; it often works. Practice doing this with simple sentences, and see how interesting they can become. This one technique can double the effectiveness of your writing. But be careful; sometimes a simple, unadorned statement is best, depending on the effect you are trying to create.

7. Use Appropriate Language. There are, as you know, levels of language usage. Formal occasions demand the use of formal language, while conversations with friends permit the use of fragmented, informal speech. The language you use must be suitable for your subject, purpose and reader.

ANALYZE OTHER WRITING

The final bit of advice we can pass along to developing writers is to study the writings of others. By others, we refer, of course, to published authors and professional writers.

Most composition courses include the use of readers. These are books containing different kinds and styles of writing for students to analyze and imitate. The selections in the reader are designed to serve as models for you.

Take a paragraph or two from an effective piece of writing and study it. Judge each sentence against the suggestions presented above for editing your work. Especially notice the nouns and verbs. Are they specific and image-provoking? They are certain to be in good writing.

Check the adjectives, too. See how experienced writers create word pictures through descriptive terms. Notice how the professionals organize their work and develop every idea.

Writing need not be a chore for you. Try following the suggestions given here, and see if you don't become a more expressive and more competent writer.

_____: Reading Time

_____: Reading Rate

_____: Score, Test A

_____: Score, Test B

_____: Total Score

_____%: Comprehension

COMPREHENSION TEST 18-A

Directions: The following passage, taken from the selection you have just read, has words omitted from it. Fill in each blank with the word that was omitted. Each blank filled correctly is worth two points. Ask your instructor if you may take credit for close synonyms. Enter your score in the box provided at the end of the selection. A list of the omitted words can be found on page 241.

PLANNING TO WRITE

In writing, preparation is the all-important consideration. There are procedures to follow which can help you _____ you start to write.
                                           1

1. Define Your Subject. Think first _____ carefully about your
                                          2
subject. Then write down a brief _____ of your subject. This should
                                  3
not be just a _____ title. Rather, it should be a statement describing
               4
or _____ the subject you plan to discuss and also what
     5
_____ plan to say about it. You should be able _____
6   7
state clearly in a sentence or two the main _____ you wish to present.
                                             8

Many students fail right here, _____ they even begin, by not
                                9
knowing what their main _____ are. Obviously, you cannot write
                         10
effectively if you don't _____ what you're going to say. Take enough
                          11
time at _____ beginning to write your subject statement. It will pay
         12
_____ in time saved later and will produce a more _____
13   14
piece of writing.

2. Limit the Subject. You should know _____ you begin writing
                                           15
how long your paper will be _____ how long you want it to be.
                             16
This means _____ your presentation will have to be limited to just
            17
_____ topics which can be suitably covered in the space
18
_____ time allowed. Many students try to cover too much
19
_____ in too little space. The result is that they _____
20   21
really present anything of value; their writing consists of _____
                                                             22
series of unrelated facts with no real point or _____.
                                                 23
You must stop, think and define the limitations of _____ subject.
                                                     24
Decide exactly on the two or three points _____ want to cover, and
                                            25
know before you write what you intend to say. A few notes, a brief outline, or just referring to your subject statement will help you to control your thoughts.

COMPREHENSION TEST 18-B

Directions: This is another passage from the selection, again with words omitted. Proceed as before, giving yourself two points for each blank filled correctly. Add this score to the one from Test A and enter your total score in the box at the end of the selection. Use the conversion table on page 254 to convert your *total* score to a comprehension percentage, and record that grade in the box also. A list of omitted words can be found on page 242.

5. **Improve Nouns and Verbs.** We all tend to use the same nouns and verbs over and over. This makes our writing dull and unimaginative. Try to _____ 1 with a more specific and expressive word each important _____ 2 and verb in your paper. Help the reader see _____ 3 feel your thoughts. However, avoid artificial or over-inflated _____ 4. You want to produce impact, not poetry.

6. **Add Adjectives.** _____ 5 sentences you write can be improved by adding a _____ 6 adjective. Try it; it often works. Practice doing this _____ 7 simple sentences, and see how interesting they can become. _____ 8 one technique can double the effectiveness of your writing. _____ 9 be careful; sometimes a simple, unadorned statement is best, _____ 10 on the effect you are trying to create.

7. **Use** _____ 11 **Language.** There are, as you know, levels of language _____ 12. Formal occasions demand the use of formal language, while _____ 13 with friends permit the use of fragmented, informal speech. _____ 14 language you use must be suitable for your subject, _____ 15 and reader.

ANALYZE OTHER WRITING

The final bit of _____ 16 we can pass along to developing writers is to _____ 17 the writings of others. By others, we refer, of _____ 18, to published authors and professional writers.

Most composition courses _____ 19 the use of readers. These are books containing different _____ 20 and styles of writing for students to analyze and _____ 21. The selections in the reader are designed to serve _____ 22 models for you.

Take a paragraph or two from _____ 23 effective piece of writing and study it. Judge each _____ 24 against the suggestions presented above for editing your work. _____ 25 notice the nouns and verbs. Are they specific and image-provoking?

DESCRIBING AND DEFINING A SUBJECT

Directions: Assume that you have been given the following writing assignments. All of the subjects are too general — too broad — to handle effectively as assigned. Write one or two sentences which describe, define and limit each subject as you would write about it. The first one has been done for you.

1. Compare the American and French Revolutions.

   Both the American and French revolutions were revolts against monarchy and attempts to establish governments more responsive to the needs of people. However, the conditions in France and America at the time were vastly different.

2. What is pollution?

3. Why is a two-party system good (or bad) in a democracy?

4. Is socialism the threat or promise of the future?

5. Do prisons prevent or cause crime?

6. Describe the federal government of the United States.

7. How does music affect you?

8. Suggest a solution to the income tax mess.

9. Explain what career you would choose, and why, if you had to make a choice tomorrow.

10. What is the most urgently needed reform in your school?

EDITING

Directions: It was suggested that you reread and edit all of your writing assignments for effect, sentence structure, punctuation, pronouns, spelling and other potential problems. Practice doing this on your own work, and read and criticize the work of others whenever possible.

Deliberate errors have been introduced into the following passage. See how many corrections and improvements you can make. When you finish, compare your answers with those suggested on page 251.

JOHN ROSS AND THE CHEROKEES

1   In October of 1828, a blue-eyed, fair-skinned man stood before   1

2   the General Council of the Cherokees. Raising his right hand he took   2

3   the oath of office in being the Principle Chief of the Cherokee   3

4   Nation.   4

5   John Ross, the man who took that oath, had many white relatives   5

6   but his Scottish imigrant father had bought John up as an Indian   6

7   among Redskins. John Ross thought of himself as a Cherokee grew   7

8   up to marry a Cherokee girl and devoted his life to heading up the   8

9   people he loved.   9

10   By the time Ross took his oath as Principal Chief, the tribe had   10

11   gone far toward civilization. They were acomplished farmers, cattle-   11

12   men and weavers. They had built roads, schools and churches,   12

13   through the invention of a Cherokee alphabet, they were largely   13

14   literate.   14

15   But the Cherokees' golden age was to be a brief one, for as early as   15

16   1802, the federal government had promised the state of Georgia that   16

17   Indians would be taken away from their lands. In 1822 the House of   17

18   Representatives voted to take away Cherokee land titles. The Cher-   18

19   okee Counsel responded by voting to make no more treaties with the   19

20   United States, neither persuasion, threats, nor the bribery attempts   20

21   of two comissioners sent to the tribe from Washington could change   21

22   Cherokee opposition attempts.   22

23   Since Georgia held forth that the Indians were only tenants on   23

24   their lands, the legislature ruthlessly stripped the Cherokees of all   24

25   their civil rights. When gold was discovered on trible lands, the fate   25

26   of the Cherokees was sealed and answering demands of the Georgia   26

27   legislature, the U.S. Congress layed out $50,000 for the taking away   27

28   of the tribe.   28

> Faulty handwriting is actually a cause of low grades for many students. Factors of fatigue and muscle cramp affect responses to exam questions. A review of correct letter formations can help students develop a legible hand.

Improving Handwriting

A most common student deficiency, according to instructors, is poor handwriting. How you write is important because most of your grade is based on your instructor's evaluation of your written work and exams.

That faulty handwriting can account in part for poor grades makes sense when you consider that poor writers suffer from muscle cramp and fatigue in situations requiring prolonged writing. Take essay tests, for example. If possible, examine one of your old test papers to see if your handwriting deteriorated as you progresssed through the test. If it did, your paper became harder to read and your knowledge of the subject more difficult to assess as the instructor read on. Under such circumstances it is not unreasonable for the instructor to become convinced that the quality of your response was declining with the quality of your writing.

In truth, teachers try not to let a student's handwriting interfere with their judgment and, for the most part, they succeed. However, teachers are human and, after hours of reading papers, they find outright carelessness, deliberate sloppiness, or a penciled scrawl as offensive as you would if the situation were reversed. Chances are your paper will be judged purely on the quality of the contents, but if the contents are obscured by a sloppy appearance, you can lose points needlessly.

Moreover, faulty writing actually *causes* poor answers. As fatigue sets in, your tendency is to shorten answers. As writing becomes difficult, you may compensate by writing less, leaving out elements of your response. When you write less, you signal the instructor that you know less. Obviously, your grade will suffer.

Poor writers are often slow writers. Students with faulty handwriting are forced to write slowly to keep their work legible. Thus, they take fewer notes in class and end up having less to study at exam time. During exams, their slow hand prevents them from telling all they know about a subject. Good writers are those who can write well *and* rapidly; thus, when the chips are down and pressure mounts, they can still produce to their potential. In school, where almost everything is timed, or is limited by time, slow writing won't do. Check an old exam again to see if your answers became shorter as you progressed. If so, correct the problem now; improve your handwriting and your performance at the same time.

BEGINNING WRITING

Most students first learned to write using manuscript letters (printing style). Cursive writing was not taught until later.

Beginning with manuscript is believed to be easier for a child. His eye-hand-arm coordination is such that the letters are easier to form. In terms of motor development, the first grade child is not ready to learn cursive writing.

In addition, manuscript letters also resemble the ones the child is learning to read. Learning to write, therefore, reinforces learning to read. The case is made for not teaching the child two sets of symbols at the same time; that is, cursive letters for writing and manuscript letters for reading. Manuscript writing is believed to be less confusing to learn at this period of development.

A third reason is that manuscript writing is more legible, to the child himself and to his teacher. Thus, children can read each other's writing and parents can read their children's writing with little difficulty.

In the third grade, the transition is made to cursive writing. At this time the child is taught to recognize and use the new letter shapes. He is also taught proper slant. A slight slant to the letters improves the appearance and legibility. The child must also be taught to connect the letters in each word. Having made the transition, the child now knows how to write.

Somewhere along the line, however, something goes awry in the process and thousands of students develop faulty writing habits and illegible letter formation. A recent study of the writing of both students and adults revealed the following errors:

1. **Illegible Numbers.** In cases where numbers are involved, the ones most often found to be unreadable are *5, 0* and *2*. These cause the most confusion and misreading. Look over some of your recent writing and check how well you write these numbers.

2. **Illegible Letters.** The study also revealed that 45 percent of handwriting errors involve the four letters *a, e, r, t.* Thus, most of us can make a vast improvement in our handwriting by correcting just four letters.

3. **Writing *e* Like *i*.** Fifteen percent of errors involve the single fault of writing the letter *e* like *i*. If this is one of your problems, the solution is obvious: take extra care in forming the letter *e*; keep the loop open.

4. **Letter Formation.** Three errors of letter formation recur commonly: (1) failure to close letters like *a, d, etc.*, (2) closing loops, as in *b, f, etc.*, and (3) putting loops in nonloop letters like *t* and *w*.

IMPROVING HANDWRITING

Handwriting is a skill. Like any skill it can be developed through instruction and refined through practice. Use the following suggestions to help you improve your skills.

1. **Proper Grip.** Look at the way you normally hold your pen or pencil. If you use a tight grip with your fingers compressed against the writing instrument, you invite muscle cramp and fatigue.

Hold the pen or pencil between the thumb and index finger, resting it against the third finger. Use an easy but firm grip, just tight enough to keep the pen from slipping.

Practice writing with this grip and observe the difference. Because the finger muscles are not tensed, writing is effortless and rapid. Strain is greatly reduced and the onset of cramp and fatigue is delayed. You should feel as though you could write for hours without tiring. Continue to practice until the grip becomes comfortable and feels natural.

Make sure your pen or pencil is a decent writing instrument that feels comfortable in your hand. Pens that are too fat, too skinny, or too short and aging pens that skip and scratch make your hand and arm tire rapidly.

2. **Finger Position.** A great many poor writers hold the pen or pencil too close to the point. Check your usual finger placement. The fingers should leave about 3/4 of an inch of pen showing.

When you hold the pen too close to the point, you block your view; you cannot see what you're writing without bending your head around close to the page. This is an unnatural position for the head and shoulders and results in premature fatigue. For some students, the position becomes so extreme that the side of the face is almost against the desk.

There's an accompanying tendency to "draw" the letters under these conditions. Obviously, handwriting speed is significantly reduced for those with this habit.

Left-handed writers will need to grip the pen still further up to see the page clearly.

3. **Straight Downstrokes.** Letters are made up of curves and strokes. Whenever you make a downstroke,

keep it a straight line. Do not curve it to finish the letter or to connect it to the next letter until you have reached the bottom of the letter at the line.

This results in a uniformity of appearance in your letters. Examine your present writing. When downstrokes are curved, every letter is different; there are no regular features.

Once you incorporate this feature into your handwriting, you'll notice a tremendous improvement in legibility.

4. **Uniform Slant.** Along with the straight downstrokes, your handwriting should also display a uniform slant. A slight slant to the right (for right-handed writers) creates a pleasing effect and improves legibility.

Poor writers slant their letters many ways. These opposing lines "pull" the eyes of the reader in different directions, causing distractions and illegibility.

Combine practice on straight downstrokes and proper slant to develop the techniques together. The combined effect will be most impressive.

5. **Letter Forms.** There are four basic letter forms used in writing twenty-four of the twenty-six letters. The forms for *r* and *s* are different.

a) One basic form is used in writing the letters *a, c, d, g, o, q.*

b) A second basic form appears in *m, n, v, x, y, z.*

c) A third form is used to write the letters *b, f, h, k, l, e.*

d) The last basic form is needed for the letters *i, j, p, u, w, t.*

The exercise following this selection illustrates the forms and their letters. Learn the forms and practice them. It is important that you develop the habit of writing them easily and naturally. Use a comfortable, easy grip on the pen and let the letters flow. Avoid any kind of muscle tension in practice and the problem won't occur when you write.

Handwriting can be a liability or an asset to your school career. It is an indispensable tool of your trade.

_____: Reading Time

_____: Reading Rate

_____: Score, Test A

_____: Score, Test B

_____: Total Score

_____%: Comprehension

Directions: The following passage, taken from the selection you have just read, has words omitted from it. Fill in each blank with the word that was omitted. Each blank filled correctly is worth two points. Ask your instructor if you may take credit for close synonyms. Enter your score in the box provided at the end of the selection. A list of the omitted words can be found on page 242.

A most common student deficiency, according to instructors, is poor handwriting. How you write is important because most of your _____ is
                                                                          1
based on your instructor's evaluation of your written _____ and
                                                                2
exams.

That faulty handwriting can account in part _____ poor grades
                                                        3
makes sense when you consider that poor _____ suffer from muscle
                                                    4
cramp and fatigue in situations requiring _____ writing. Take essay
                                                    5
tests, for example. If possible, examine _____ of your old test papers
                                                  6
to see if your _____ deteriorated as you progressed through the test.
                    7
If it _____, your paper became harder to read and your knowledge
          8
_____ the subject more difficult to assess as the instructor
        9
_____ on. Under such circumstances it is not unreasonable for
      10
_____ instructor to become convinced that the quality of your
      11
_____ was declining with the quality of your writing.
      12
In _____, teachers try not to let a student's handwriting interfere
        13
_____ their judgment and, for the most part, they succeed.
      14
_____, teachers are human and, after hours of reading papers,
      15
_____ find outright carelessness, deliberate sloppiness, or a penciled
      16
scrawl _____ offensive as you would if the situation were reversed.
            17
_____ are your paper will be judged purely on the _____
      18   19
of the contents, but if the contents are obscured _____ a sloppy
                                                              20
appearance, you can lose points needlessly.

Moreover, _____ writing actually *causes* poor answers. As fatigue
                21
sets in, _____ tendency is to shorten answers. As writing becomes
              22
difficult, _____ may compensate by writing less, leaving out elements
                23
of _____ response. When you write less, you signal the instructor
      24
_____ you know less. Obviously, your grade will suffer.
      25

COMPREHENSION TEST 19-B

Directions: This is another passage from the selection, again with words omitted. Proceed as before, giving yourself two points for each blank filled correctly. Add this score to the one from Test A and enter your total score in the box at the end of the selection. Use the conversion table on page 254 to convert your *total* score to a comprehension percentage, and record that grade in the box also. A list of omitted words can be found on page 242.

1. **Proper Grip.** Look at the way you normally hold your pen or pencil. If you use a tight grip with your fingers _____ against the writing
                                                                        1
instrument, you invite muscle cramp and _____.
                                          2

Hold the pen or pencil between the thumb and _____ finger,
                                                3
resting it against the third finger. Use an _____ but firm grip, just
                                             4
tight enough to keep the _____ from slipping.
                          5

Practice writing with this grip and observe _____ difference.
                                              6
Because the finger muscles are not tensed, writing _____ effortless
                                                     7
and rapid. Strain is greatly reduced and the _____ of cramp and
                                                8
fatigue is delayed. You should feel _____ though you could write
                                     9
for hours without tiring. Continue _____ practice until the grip
                                     10
becomes comfortable and feels natural.

_____ sure your pen or pencil is a decent writing _____
  11   12
that feels comfortable in your hand. Pens that are _____ fat, too
                                                     13
skinny, or too short and aging pens _____ skip and scratch make your
                                      14
hand and arm tire _____.
                    15

2. **Finger Position.** A great many poor writers hold the _____ or
                                                            16
pencil too close to the point. Check your _____ finger placement.
                                           17
The fingers should leave about 3/4 of _____ inch of pen showing.
                                        18

When you hold the pen _____ close to the point, you block your
                        19
view; you _____ see what you're writing without bending your head
            20
around _____ to the page. This is an unnatural position for
         21
_____ head and shoulders and results in premature fatigue. For
  22
_____ students, the position becomes so extreme that the side
  23
_____ the face is almost against the desk.
  24
There's an _____ tendency to "draw" the letters under these
             25
conditions. Obviously, handwriting speed is significantly reduced for those with this habit.

IMPROVING LETTER FORMATION

Directions: Take this opportunity to evaluate your own handwriting. Work to improve the legibility and appearance of your writing by keeping in mind the suggestions listed below.

1. Straight Downstrokes and Uniform Slant. Each downstroke of the pen should be a straight line. Do not curve the letter until the stroke has been completed. Keeping the straight strokes slanted at a similar angle gives a regular appearance to your writing and improves its legibility.

2. Letter Forms. These four forms are basic to twenty-four of the twenty-six letters in the alphabet. Practice writing the forms first; then practice writing the letters which they make.

Form A

Form B

Form C

Form D

Learn to write these forms rapidly, clearly and effortlessly. If you can avoid muscle tension while you develop a rapid hand, premature fatigue and muscle cramp can be avoided in prolonged writing situations.

PRACTICING HANDWRITING

Directions: Copy each of the numbered sentences three times using the following method.

 a. The first time write slowly, being sure that all the letters match the forms on the preceding page.

 b. The second time, write a little faster, copying your first effort.

 c. The third time, cover your first two attempts with a blank card and write the sentence easily and naturally, letting the letters flow. If you are not satisfied with the result, repeat the process.

1. The tall young woman had a perfect figure.

_____

_____

_____

2. All employees were kept very busy during the holidays.

_____

_____

_____

3. The author's main point is that life is incredible.

_____

_____

_____

4. He was quite frank in accusing his father of laziness.

_____

_____

_____

5. Life is a foolish play of passions.

_____

_____

_____

6. It was on a morning of May that Peter Featherstone came home.

_____

_____

_____

7. Those who had visited the islands before were anxious to begin the journey.

_____

_____

_____

8. The solitary horseman traversed the border of the Dead Sea.

_____

_____

_____

9. On the following day, the mayor called a press conference.

_____

_____

_____

> When exam time comes, students must put their knowledge on the line. With good notes and continuous review, successful exam preparation is assured. Exam jitters or panic will not plague the student who is well prepared.

Reviewing for Examinations

For students, the expression "Into every life a little rain must fall" pertains to the inevitability of final examinations. Although many schools are adopting pass-fail grades for courses, and others are revising the portion of final grade based on examinations, most students will be taking exams for most courses. Face it — exams are a fact of academic life.

Unfortunately (and unnecessarily), many students panic at examination time. They worry so much that they cannot study and review effectively. This results in poor performance on the test and causes even more apprehension on future tests. You must break the cycle. Success on your next set of finals can reverse the process.

The main reason students panic is lack of adequate preparation. To most students, final review means cramming — a do-or-die, headlong plunge into the unfamiliar waters of the subject matter. Cramming can be beneficial; any brief, intensive review is sure to do more good than harm. As your only method of exam preparation, however, cramming lets you down. There's just too much to be covered.

Successful preparation has two prerequisites: suitable notes and continuous review. You cannot begin to study well with unsatisfactory notes. In addition to knowing what is in the text, you must be able to recall and review what was emphasized in class. You need a good set of notes to do this. Other selections in this text have covered the areas of listening in class, taking useful notes, and using your textbook efficiently. If you follow the suggestions presented in those chapters, your notes will be in good shape for successful reviewing.

You must review regularly and faithfully all through the term, not just before exams. This approach will not only ease the load at exam time, but will also lead to a better understanding of the subject matter with each review.

This sounds like a lot of extra work, but it actually makes your life much easier. By keeping up with your work, you are more relaxed and more confident. You will actually save time in the long run.

If you have not been reviewing during the term, start now. It will probably be necessary for you to outline the course to date; this is the best way to be sure you have covered everything. Schedule a week for the task, and review and outline a segment each night. Anticipate as much reviewing as possible now.

With these two conditions in order, you are ready to get down to the business of studying for final exams.

STUDYING FOR FINALS

1. **Establish a Review Schedule.** As you have learned from working with your regular study schedule, you must be organized to study successfully. Set up a new schedule a week or two before final exams, spreading the material to be reviewed and studied over the allotted time. Save the final day (the night before the actual test) for cramming; we'll see later how to cram intelligently. Divide the course work among the other days so that every aspect of the subject can be covered.

Assign a reasonable length of time to your daily study period. If a subject is one of your "good" ones, an hour a day of concentrated study might be sufficient. If, on the other hand, this subject has been giving you trouble, you will need to devote more time to it. Schedule accordingly.

Draw up your review schedule on paper, showing the time allotment each day for the subject. Obviously, for the system to work, you must spend the full time in actual study.

2. **Develop a New Approach.** This can be a technique of real value to you. Rehashing the same old stuff is not very exciting and certainly nothing to look forward to. Try approaching the subject differently; get a fresh outlook on the material.

For example, put yourself in the role of instructor. Imagine that next semester you will be teaching this subject and you want to review it now so you'll know it well enough to teach.

For biology, take the point of view of a doctor. What does science mean to him? How can he use it in his practice?

Use your imagination. Be both quizmaster and contestant. Ask yourself questions aloud, and answer them aloud for a "prize" of a million dollars and a free trip to Tahiti.

However you do it, adopt a fresh point of view and make the material you are studying come alive.

3. **Outline the Course.** This may appear to be an enormous task to undertake at the end of the semester, but it need not be. Keep your outline brief; do not exceed three pages. The thinking that goes into outlining makes for excellent reviewing.

When you have completed your outline, you will have a picture of your knowledge of the subject. Your study assignment is now organized for you. Each night attack a new part of the outline and fill in the gaps.

Actually, this technique combines two steps in one. When outlining the matter, you are forced to deal with principles and generalizations. All of your study should be to this end: an understanding and retention of main points and principles.

You know from your own experience that you cannot recall everything about a subject. You must become selective and choose only the most important elements of the subject. As you do this, you'll be pleased to observe how the recall of major points triggers the recall of accompanying details. You'll find yourself remembering much more than you had originally thought you could.

4. **Know What to Expect.** There is

a great deal you can learn about an examination beforehand. If you are "exam-wise," you can plan the best way to study and the kinds of answers to prepare.

First, discover the kind of exam to be given. Essay exams require you to organize and compose your own answers. Objective tests require you to select the best response to multiple-choice questions, or to label statements true or false, or to fill in or match items. The best way to study for both types of examinations will be covered in later selections.

Most instructors don't mind discussing upcoming exams in a general way. Others are very specific in advising you what to prepare for. By all means, be in class and be alert when a coming exam is being discussed.

It may also be possible to talk to those who have already taken the course to discover what sort of test the instructor gives. Does he look for facts and details? If so, study accordingly. Does he look for an understanding of principles? Does he expect his students to reason, to apply knowledge to a specific case? The answers to these questions require a suitable kind of study on your part.

Does the instructor have a favorite question? Is there one item that appears again and again on his tests? If so, plan your response in advance.

Don't worry yourself or your instructor to death trying to get advance "tips," but use wisely whatever solid information is legitimately available to you to help plan your studying.

5. **Study Quizzes.** Study the other tests and quizzes you have taken during the term. Some of the same questions, or variations of them, might be asked again.

All teachers stress what they consider important on quizzes during the term. Reviewing past tests will assure that you will be covering many of the most important topics in the course.

6. **Review Class Questions.** Like the rest of us, teachers are creatures of habit. They tend to repeat themselves. During the term, make notes on the questions your instructor asked in class. You can feel confident that questions like these will appear again.

Be sure to copy down accurately everything mentioned by the instructor in his pre-exam review. Many lecturers devote their final class to summarizing the course. Questions asked at this time are particularly significant because the instructor is speaking with the exam in mind.

7. **Cram.** Devote the final night to cramming. Spend your last moments in an intensive review of all the major facts, principles and generalizations. Do not be concerned with details at this time; they'll come back to you later.

Cover the items on your outline fully. Be sure that you can define, explain, or describe what is important or essential to each major point.

8. **Be Ready.** Do not stay up too late the night before. Staying up may create worry and anxiety — just the situation you want to avoid in the morning.

On the day of the exam, get up early and have breakfast. Even if it is not your custom to eat, have something. Nervousness can bring on distracting hunger pangs.

Have confidence in your ability. Follow the procedures suggested here, and you'll give a good performance. The best cure for exam jitters is preparation.

_____: Reading Time

_____: Reading Rate

_____: Score, Test A

_____: Score, Test B

_____: Total Score

_____%: Comprehension

190   THE COLLEGE STUDENT

COMPREHENSION TEST 20-A

Directions: The following passage, taken from the selection you have just read, has words omitted from it. Fill in each blank with the word that was omitted. Each blank filled correctly is worth two points. Ask your instructor if you may take credit for close synonyms. Enter your score in the box provided at the end of the selection. A list of the omitted words can be found on page 242.

Unfortunately (and unnecessarily), many students panic at examination time. They worry so much that they cannot study and _____ effectively.
1

This results in poor performance on the test _____ causes even more
2

apprehension on future tests. You must _____ the cycle. Success
3

on your next set of finals _____ reverse the process.
4

The main reason students panic is _____ of adequate preparation.
5

To most students, final review means _____ — a do-or-die, headlong
6

plunge into the unfamiliar _____ of the subject matter. Cramming
7

can be beneficial; any _____, intensive review is sure to do more good
8

than _____. As your only method of exam preparation, however,
9

cramming _____ you down. There's just too much to be covered.
10

_____ preparation has two prerequisites: suitable notes and
11

continuous review. _____ cannot begin to study well with unsatis-
12

factory notes. In _____ to knowing what is in the text, you must
13

_____ able to recall and review what was emphasized in
14

_____. You need a good set of notes to do _____. Other
15   16

selections in this text have covered the areas _____ listening in class,
17

taking useful notes, and using your _____ efficiently. If you follow
18

the suggestions presented in those _____, your notes will be in good
19

shape for successful _____.
20

You must review regularly and faithfully all through the _____, not
21

just before exams. This approach will not only _____ the load at
22

exam time, but will also lead _____ a better understanding of the
23

subject matter with each _____.
24

This sounds like a lot of extra work, but _____ actually makes
25

your life much easier. By keeping up with your work, you are more relaxed and more confident.

COMPREHENSION TEST 20-B

Directions: This is another passage from the selection, again with words omitted. Proceed as before, giving yourself two points for each blank filled correctly. Add this score to the one from Test A and enter your total score in the box at the end of the selection. Use the conversion table on page 254 to convert your *total* score to a comprehension percentage, and record that grade in the box also. A list of omitted words can be found on page 242.

5. Study Quizzes. Study the other tests and quizzes you have taken during the term. Some of the same questions, or variations of them, _____(1)_____ be asked again.

All teachers stress what they consider _____(2)_____ on quizzes during the term. Reviewing past tests will _____(3)_____ that you will be covering many of the most _____(4)_____ topics in the course.

6. Review Class Questions. Like the _____(5)_____ of us, teachers are creatures of habit. They tend _____(6)_____ repeat themselves. During the term, make notes on the _____(7)_____ your instructor asked in class. You can feel confident _____(8)_____ questions like these will appear again.

Be sure to _____(9)_____ down accurately everything mentioned by the instructor in his _____(10)_____ review. Many lecturers devote their final class to summarizing _____(11)_____ course. Questions asked at this time are particularly significant _____(12)_____ the instructor is speaking with the exam in mind.

7. _____(13)_____. Devote the final night to cramming. Spend your last _____(14)_____ in an intensive review of all the major facts, _____(15)_____ and generalizations. Do not be concerned with details at _____(16)_____ time; they'll come back to you later.

Cover the _____(17)_____ on your outline fully. Be sure that you can _____(18)_____, explain, or describe what is important or essential to _____(19)_____ major point.

8. Be Ready. Do not stay up too _____(20)_____ the night before. Staying up may create worry and _____(21)_____ — just the situation you want to avoid in the _____(22)_____.

On the day of the exam, get up early _____(23)_____ have breakfast. Even if it is not your custom _____(24)_____ eat, have something. Nervousness can bring on distracting hunger _____(25)_____.

Have confidence in your ability.

THINKING ABOUT REVIEWING

Directions: The following exercise will help you develop an effective approach to reviewing for exams.

1. One of the ways to become "exam-wise" is to familiarize yourself with the thought processes that go into making up an exam. Assume that you are an instructor and create a quiz based on this lesson. Compose at least two essay questions and five multiple-choice questions. If other students participate in this activity, exchange questions and criticize one another's work.

2. Assume that you are going to have an important exam in one of your major subjects in one week. You have determined that there will be four essay questions and twenty multiple-choice questions.
   a. Make a list of all the things you should do to get ready for the exam.
   b. Create a time schedule that will enable you to complete your studying by exam time.

3. Identify a course you are taking this term which you consider difficult. Make a list of ways to make the material come alive when you do your studying. List any game or gimmick you can think of. Compare your list with those of other students participating and discuss your ideas.

4. Look at some old exams and quizzes you have taken. What could you have done before those tests that might have improved your grades? You may want to do this in an open class discussion.

> You can't pass a test if you don't know the subject. But it is possible to improve your test performance through a knowledge of test-taking techniques, thus ensuring that your knowledge of the subject is used to best advantage.

Taking Objective Exams

In the previous selection we discussed procedures to use when reviewing for examinations. This selection will examine one type of examination and methods to use to help you obtain high scores.

If you do not know the subject matter and are unprepared for a test, there is not much which will bail you out. You can't pass a test if you don't know the answers. However, all things being equal, you can earn a higher score by following certain procedures which reduce careless errors and ensure that you use your knowledge of the subject to best advantage.

FEATURES OF OBJECTIVE TESTS

This kind of test consists of multiple choice, fill-in, true-false, matching and similar questions requiring only a mark of the pencil or a single-word response. Frequently, answers are recorded on a separate sheet.

Students generally prefer objective tests over the essay type which requires written answers. Apparently they feel that, because the objective test is easier to answer, they do better on it. Actually, this is not the case at all; you have much more control over your grade on essay exams. Once you learn techniques for handling them well, you may begin to prefer written examinations.

One advantage of objective tests for teachers is their ease of correction. Using a template or scoring key, a teacher can correct an entire test in 15 or 20 seconds. The corresponding disadvantage is that the tests are difficult and time consuming to construct. Most teachers do not have sufficient time to create valid tests and, therefore, rely on the essay type for evaluating the progress of students taking their courses.

Once a good objective test has been constructed, it can be re-used. This is another feature which makes it attractive to teachers. However, it is necessary to number and keep track of all copies so that the test does not become available to succeeding classes.

Objective tests are corrected objectively. This means that there is no possibility of your answer being misread or misinterpreted. No bias or unfavorable attitude on the part of the scorer can affect or influence your grade. Many students regard this as an advantage; everyone has the same opportunity to pass or fail.

REVIEWING FOR THE TEST

In preparing for essay tests, some answers can be organized and composed in advance. This cannot be done with objective tests. With the essay type, only a limited number of questions can be asked; the student knows that only the important topics will be covered. On objective tests, almost anything and everything can be included. For this reason, everything must be studied and learned.

From quizzes and questions asked in class, determine what kinds of questions your instructor favors. Is he interested in details? If so, you must pay particular attention to names, dates, places, and other information of this nature. Make it a point to study these things well.

Does the lecturer frequently ask for definitions in class? Be sure you devote sufficient study time to them when reviewing. Many definitions are (or should be) already marked off in your textbook, making them easy for you to locate and learn.

Analyze the kind of information

your instructor covers on his quizzes. Chances are the same preferences will be repeated on his examinations as well. Once you know this, you can study accordingly.

TAKING THE TEST

1. **Read Directions.** On any test there is always someone who loses credit because he does not follow directions. As a result, neither he nor his instructor knows his true achievement in the subject. Don't let this happen to you. Before anything else, read *all* of the directions for *all* of the test. Make sure, before starting, that you know what is expected of you.

2. **Arrange Questions.** Certain parts of the test are generally worth more credit than others. The point values should be given for each section of the test. Number each section according to value and work in this order. As you go through the test each time, begin again at the section worth the most points. This ensures that the most valuable part of the test will be completed even if time runs out.

3. **Apportion Time.** Before starting to answer the questions, apportion the time into three segments of equal duration. This will enable you to go through the examination three times.

4. **Answer Easy Questions.** During the first time segment, read *all* the questions and answer those you know immediately. This procedure assures that you will not run out of time, leaving easy questions unanswered.

Also, you have seen the entire test. Everyone is anxious at the start of a test; however, anxiety should not be permitted to interfere with test performance. To most students the anticipation is worse than the reality; seeing the whole test and answering the easy questions will relieve the pressure and give you confidence.

As you read through, mark only those answers which occur to you immediately. If you must pause to consider a response, go on to the next question. Go through the whole test this way before starting over again with section one.

5. **Answer Questions of Moderate Difficulty.** The second time through, mark those questions whose answers you can supply after brief consideration. Skip only the questions whose answers you definitely don't know. If time does run out, you will have at least answered all those questions you are likely to get correct. Put a mark of some kind in the margin for those you skip and continue through the test.

6. **Answer Difficult Questions Last.** During the last time segment, answer the remaining questions. Consider each one carefully, and use whatever techniques you can to arrive at the correct answer. Try rewording the questions. State them in your own words to see if they make more sense. Study the questions and underline significant words and words which puzzle you. Extra attention to them might trigger an association, giving you an indication of the right answer.

Look for clue words which point to certain answers. Words like *only, all, always, never,* indicate finality. These responses are not usually the correct ones. Choose an option containing the words *generally, usually, sometimes, may,* and so on. These words imply the possibility of a correct answer.

Cross out options which you know are definitely wrong. By elimination you may arrive at the correct one, or at least be left with choosing from two remaining options, thus improving the odds of your selecting the right one. Be sure to answer all remaining questions before time is called.

OTHER SUGGESTIONS

If you have followed the procedures explained above, you have improved your chances of earning the highest score possible. Here are other suggestions to keep in mind.

1. Answer All Questions. There are differences of opinion regarding this advice. Some tests are corrected for guessing. This is done by subtracting the number of wrong answers from the number of right ones. In this way, students who guess and are wrong are penalized. Under these conditions, the student is advised not to guess, to answer only those questions he is sure of. Educational research has revealed, however, that your chances of scoring higher are increased if you follow a hunch rather than leave a question unanswered.

On standardized tests, those that employ a machine-scored answer sheet, it is helpful for you to know whether or not wrong answers will reduce your score. If not, if your score is simply the number of correct answers, it is possible on closely timed tests to make random responses to any remaining questions when time is called. Some of these answers might happen to be correct and will increase your score.

2. Do Not Change Answers. As a rule, stick with your first choice. Of course, if you discover an error, correct it. It's possible that something later in the test will indicate that one of your answers is wrong. But if you are not convinced that your first answer is positively wrong, don't change it. Statistics have established that your score will not be increased by changing answers without having a very good reason to do so.

3. Use All Available Time. Do not be tempted to finish early. Give yourself every advantage by using all the time allotted to you. Check your paper over carefully. A good technique is to check off each question as you review to eliminate the possibility of skipping any answers. Read the directions again to be sure that you have followed them exactly and completely. Check your test paper thoroughly before handing it in.

_____: Reading Time

_____: Reading Rate

_____: Score, Test A

_____: Score, Test B

_____: Total Score

_____%: Comprehension

COMPREHENSION TEST 21-A

Directions: The following passage, taken from the selection you have just read, has words omitted from it. Fill in each blank with the word that was omitted. Each blank filled correctly is worth two points. Ask your instructor if you may take credit for close synonyms. Enter your score in the box provided at the end of the selection. A list of the omitted words can be found on page 243.

In the previous selection we discussed procedures to use when reviewing for examinations. This selection will examine one type of examination and _____ to use to help you obtain high scores.
1

If _____ do not know the subject matter and are unprepared
2
_____ a test, there is not much which will bail _____
3   4
out. You can't pass a test if you don't _____ the answers. However,
5
all things being equal, you can _____ a higher score by following
6
certain procedures which reduce _____ errors and ensure that you use
7
your knowledge of _____ subject to best advantage.
8

FEATURES OF OBJECTIVE TESTS

This _____ of test consists of multiple choice, fill-in, true-false,
9
matching _____ similar questions requiring only a mark of the pencil
10
_____ a single-word response. Frequently, answers are recorded on
11
_____ separate sheet.
12
Students generally prefer objective tests over the _____ type
13
which requires written answers. Apparently they feel that, _____
14
the objective test is easier to answer, they do _____ on it. Actually,
15
this is not the case at _____; you have much more control over your
16
grade on _____ exams. Once you learn techniques for handling them
17
well, _____ may begin to prefer written examinations.
18
One advantage of _____ tests for teachers is their ease of correc-
19
tion. Using _____ template or scoring key, a teacher can correct an
20
_____ test in 15 or 20 seconds. The corresponding disadvantage
21
_____ that the tests are difficult and time consuming to
22
_____. Most teachers do not have sufficient time to create
23
_____ tests and, therefore, rely on the essay type for
24
_____ the progress of students taking their courses.
25
Once a good objective test has been constructed, it can be re-used.

COMPREHENSION TEST 21-B

Directions: This is another passage from the selection, again with words omitted. Proceed as before, giving yourself two points for each blank filled correctly. Add this score to the one from Test A and enter your total score in the box at the end of the selection. Use the conversion table on page 254 to convert your *total* score to a comprehension percentage, and record that grade in the box also. A list of omitted words can be found on page 243.

If you have followed the procedures explained above, you have improved your chances of earning the highest score possible. Here are other suggestions to keep in mind.

1. Answer _____ Questions. There are differences of opinion
　　　　　　　　1
regarding this advice. _____ tests are corrected for guessing. This is
　　　　　　　　　　　　2
done by _____ the number of wrong answers from the number of
　　　　　　　3
_____ ones. In this way, students who guess and are _____
　　　4　　　　　　　　　　　　　　　　　　　　　　　　　　　　　5
are penalized. Under these conditions, the student is advised _____ to
　　　　　　　　　　　　　　　　　　　　　　　　　　　　　　　6
guess, to answer only those questions he is _____ of. Educational
　　　　　　　　　　　　　　　　　　　　　7
research has revealed, however, that your chances _____ scoring
　　　　　　　　　　　　　　　　　　　　　　　　　　8
higher are increased if you follow a hunch _____ than leave a question
　　　　　　　　　　　　　　　　　　　　9
unanswered.

On standardized tests, those _____ employ a machine-scored
　　　　　　　　　　　　　　　　10
answer sheet, it is helpful _____ you to know whether or not wrong
　　　　　　　　　　　　　11
answers will _____ your score. If not, if your score is simply
　　　　　　　12
_____ number of correct answers, it is possible on closely
　13
_____ tests to make random responses to any remaining questions
　14
_____ time is called. Some of these answers might happen
　15
_____ be correct and will increase your score.
　16

2. Do Not _____ Answers. As a rule, stick with your first choice.
　　　　　　　17
_____ course, if you discover an error, correct it. It's
　18
_____ that something later in the test will indicate that
　19
_____ of your answers is wrong. But if you are _____
　20　　　　　　　　　　　　　　　　　　　　　　　　　　　　　　21
convinced that your first answer is positively wrong, don't _____ it.
　　　　　　　　　　　　　　　　　　　　　　　　　　　　　　22
Statistics have established that your score will not _____ increased
　　　　　　　　　　　　　　　　　　　　　　　　　23
by changing answers without having a very good _____ to do so.
　　　　　　　　　　　　　　　　　　　　　　24

3. **Use All Available Time.** Do not _____ tempted to finish early.
　　　　　　　　　　　　　　　　　　　25
Give yourself every advantage by using all the time allotted to you.

PRACTICE CREATING AN OBJECTIVE EXAMINATION

Directions: It has been noted that when you get a feeling for how objective exams are created, you have a better feeling for how to answer them.

Using a textbook from any course you are taking this semester, create an objective examination based on one chapter. If you keep a good set of notes, make the exam from them if you prefer.

The test should consist of:

    a. five multiple choice questions

    b. a matching question with eight pairs of items to be matched

    c. six sentences, each with one blank to be filled in

    d. eight true-false statements

Try to pair up with another student who is using the same textbook and take each other's exams. Compare the results.

Following is a list of things to watch for as you make up questions.

    a. Is there more than one possible answer for any question?

    b. Is every statement absolutely clear?

    c. Avoid "catch" questions. The object is to test knowledge, not trick someone.

    d. Can any of the true-false questions be answered *maybe*?

    e. Avoid testing for obscure details. Test for important main ideas, key definitions, essential facts and details.

Perhaps you have realized at this point that this is a good way to focus your attention on important information when studying for a real examination.

> Essay examinations permit you to influence the kind of grade you receive to a considerable extent. Because much can be organized and prepared in advance, you have an opportunity to demonstrate your knowledge of the subject most effectively.

Taking Essay Exams

Because they involve composition and punctuation, spelling and writing, students dislike taking essay-type exams. You should not feel this way because you can exercise much greater control over your grade on this type of exam than on any other. Once you learn the correct techniques to use, you may come to prefer the essay test.

There are several advantages. First, limited examination time forces an instructor to limit the number of questions. Thus, he has to concentrate on the most important aspects of the subject, and you are less likely to be caught unprepared. Also, because you usually have some degree of choice on essay exams, you can select those questions you know most about.

Another advantage is that you can prepare some of your answers in advance. As we will see a little later, it is possible to guess correctly at least half of the questions to be asked. This permits you to study selectively and purposefully.

A third advantage is that you can influence the grade you receive on the essay exam. Through pleasing handwriting, sound organization, and concise presentation of information, you can create a favorable attitude in the mind of the scorer.

STUDYING FOR ESSAY EXAMS

1. **List Fifteen Questions.** As we mentioned above, your study task is simplified when you review for this type of test. Only so many aspects of the subject can be covered, and you can probably guess most of them.

Go through your notes first, selecting those topics stressed in class. Refer to questions asked at midterm. Listen carefully to the teacher's review. He will mention the topics likely to be covered on the final.

Go through your text looking for points which the author emphasized. Take special note of review questions at the end of chapters; something stressed there indicates its importance.

From all of these sources, create fifteen questions. It is important that you frame your questions in broad terms; make them comprehensive.

2. **Prepare Outlines.** Review your notes and text with the questions in mind. Study and make notes until you have on hand complete information to answer all the questions adequately.

It is not advisable to write out and try to memorize answers word-for-word. Learning by rote will let you down on the actual exam. Instead, prepare a good outline answer for each question. Make your outline complete; cover all that is essential to the topic. Practice writing your outlines until you are able to reproduce all the important points.

You will study everything about the questions, of course, but you need not try to memorize all the details. On the exam, the major points will trigger recall of the supplementary facts.

3. **Learn Definitions.** Find out if the instructor includes definitions on his exams. If so, the question may be worded: "Define three of the following four terms . . . ."

A question like this can be of real value to you. Learn the important definitions given in your text and notes. If you have marked your text well, the definitions should be easy to locate. Spend time memorizing and learning them. The sure points earned on this kind of question can help your overall score on the test.

If you have prepared definitions and they are not asked on the test, you'll surely be able to incorporate some of them in your answers to other questions, thus improving the quality of those responses.

4. **Prepare Opening Sentences.** Your instructor will be correcting many papers in addition to yours. A strong, well-organized beginning to your answer immediately demonstrates the careful study you have done in the subject.

For each of your fifteen questions, create a comprehensive summary statement to use as an opener. Avoid weak, ineffective sentences like: "It is when . . ." or "This means that . . . ." Also, avoid repeating the question in your opening sentence; start right off with a fact-loaded statement.

5. **Understanding Key Terms.** Be sure you know exactly what is meant when your instructor asks you to *define, illustrate, enumerate, explain, describe, state, compare* or *contrast.*

Be certain that you answer questions explicitly. If you are asked to define, be sure to give a definition, not a description or explanation. If you are asked to compare, tell how things are alike *and* how they are different; if you are to contrast, tell only how they are different. If you are to illustrate, use concrete examples.

Examine the terms your instructor uses and prepare answers that correspond to them specifically.

6. **Practice Condensing.** Your paper will be read, not weighed. Wordy, overlong answers weaken your performance. Your instructor is interested in facts; don't conceal your knowledge behind extra words.

You can improve your performance on essay tests through practice. A good technique is to write a few answers to your sample questions. Think before you write. Concentrate on writing concise, to-the-point answers.

Next, examine your answers to see how they can be improved. Write them out again eliminating unnecessary words, combining ideas, and substituting expressive terms for weak, vague ones. Be sure that in the condensing process, however, you don't sacrifice important information.

TAKING THE TEST

Here are the procedures to follow once the examination has begun.

1. **Divide the Time.** Apportion your time among the questions. Base your time allotments on the credit value of the questions. Spend more time on the ones that are worth more. If all of the questions are of equal value, devote equal time to each one.

Dividing your time appropriately among the questions has the advantage of preventing you from spending too much time on any one. It is not unusual for a student to lose track of the time and find the testing period fast disappearing as he scrambles to answer the last question. Also, students often tend to spend more time than they should on the first question. The result, of course, is that little time is left for the rest of the test and the quality of the responses declines accordingly. Don't lose points in this way; assign an appropriate amount of time to each question before you begin and stick to it.

2. **Outline All Answers First.** Before writing, outline your answers to *all* of the questions. You will have prepared many of these in advance and ought to be able to write them down rapidly.

Confine the outlines to headings and subheads only. Try to list all the main headings that apply, even if you can't recall any subheads at the moment. As you work on other parts of the test, associations may help you to recall the information you need.

If you have a choice of questions, you might want to outline responses to all questions and then select those whose outlines appear the strongest.

3. **Balance the Outlines.** Next, look over your outlines. Some will be complete; others will be weak. Wherever possible, transfer headings from the strong answers to the weak ones. This will give you confidence on the test because you will know something about each question. The test frequently deals with a single subject, so a little deliberation will indicate how you can transfer headings and make them applicable to another question.

This procedure also ensures that you will not be unnecessarily disclosing a weakness in any one area of the test. Incomplete responses alert the instructor to a gap in your knowledge of the subject.

4. **Write the Answers.** After your outlines are complete, start to write. Remember to write clear, concise sentences. A good practice is to create a single, well-constructed sentence for each heading and subhead on your outline. If necessary, expand your answer from there.

Begin your answer, if possible, with one of your prepared openers. This will start you off well. Remember to include definitions wherever you can, showing that you have studied the subject thoroughly.

Write legibly. This is most important. Your teacher has to read many exam papers. Anything you can do to make your answers more readable will create a favorable impression.

Keep your pen moving. If an important fact escapes you for the moment, leave a space and come back to it later.

Check off the questions as you answer them. Mark questions you wish to return to later.

5. **Review.** Make a final check before handing in your paper. First of all, see if you have answered all the questions required.

Check next to see if you have answered each question explicitly. Be sure you have answered the same question that was asked. Did you give a definition if the question said *define*? Did you offer an explanation where you were asked *why* or to *explain*?

Finally, correct spelling, punctuation and any mechanical errors before handing in your paper.

Use as much of the allotted time as you need. Don't give up early with a "what's the use" attitude. Keep working until you have squeezed out the last drop of pertinent information.

_____: Reading Time

_____: Reading Rate

_____: Score, Test A

_____: Score, Test B

_____: Total Score

_____%: Comprehension

COMPREHENSION TEST 22-A

Directions: The following passage, taken from the selection you have just read, has words omitted from it. Fill in each blank with the word that was omitted. Each blank filled correctly is worth two points. Ask your instructor if you may take credit for close synonyms. Enter your score in the box provided at the end of the selection. A list of the omitted words can be found on page 243.

Because they involve composition and punctuation, spelling and writing, students dislike taking essay-type exams. You should not feel this way because you can _____ much greater control over your grade on this type
                        1
_____ exam than on any other. Once you learn the _____
        2   3
techniques to use, you may come to prefer the _____ test.
                                                            4
There are several advantages. First, limited examination time _____
                                                                            5
an instructor to limit the number of questions. Thus, _____ has to
                                                                6
concentrate on the most important aspects of _____ subject, and
                                                            7
you are less likely to be caught _____. Also, because you usually
                                        8
have some degree of choice _____ essay exams, you can select those
                              9
questions you know _____ about.
                        10
Another advantage is that you can prepare some _____ your
                                                                11
answers in advance. As we will see a _____ later, it is possible to
                                            12
guess correctly at least _____ of the questions to be asked. This
                              13
permits you _____ study selectively and purposefully.
                14
A third advantage is that _____ can influence the grade you receive
                              15
on the essay _____. Through pleasing handwriting, sound organiza-
                16
tion, and concise presentation of _____, you can create a favorable
                                        17
attitude in the mind _____ the scorer.
                        18

STUDYING FOR ESSAY EXAMS

1. List Fifteen Questions. _____ we mentioned above, your study
                              19
task is simplified when _____ review for this type of test. Only so
                              20
many _____ of the subject can be covered, and you can
        21
_____ guess most of them.
22
Go through your notes first, _____ those topics stressed in class.
                                    23
Refer to questions asked _____ midterm. Listen carefully to the
                              24
teacher's review. He will _____ the topics likely to be covered on
                              25
the final.

Go through your text looking for points which the author emphasized.

COMPREHENSION TEST 22-B

Directions: This is another passage from the selection, again with words omitted. Proceed as before, giving yourself two points for each blank filled correctly. Add this score to the one from Test A and enter your total score in the box at the end of the selection. Use the conversion table on page 254 to convert your *total* score to a comprehension percentage, and record that grade in the box also. A list of omitted words can be found on page 243.

3. Balance the Outlines. Next, look over your outlines. Some will be complete; others will be weak. Wherever _____ 1, transfer headings from the strong answers to the weak _____ 2. This will give you confidence on the test because _____ 3 will know something about each question. The test frequently _____ 4 with a single subject, so a little deliberation will _____ 5 how you can transfer headings and make them applicable _____ 6 another question.

This procedure also ensures that you will _____ 7 be unnecessarily disclosing a weakness in any one area _____ 8 the test. Incomplete responses alert the instructor to a _____ 9 in your knowledge of the subject.

4. Write the Answers. _____ 10 your outlines are complete, start to write. Remember to _____ 11 clear, concise sentences. A good practice is to create _____ 12 single, well-constructed sentence for each heading and subhead _____ 13 your outline. If necessary, expand your answer from there.

_____ 14 your answer, if possible, with one of your prepared _____ 15. This will start you off well. Remember to include _____ 16 wherever you can, showing that you have studied the _____ 17 thoroughly.

Write legibly. This is most important. Your teacher _____ 18 to read many exam papers. Anything you can do _____ 19 make your answers more readable will create a favorable _____ 20.

Keep your pen moving. If an important fact escapes _____ 21 for the moment, leave a space and come back _____ 22 it later.

Check off the questions as you answer _____ 23. Mark questions you wish to return to later.

5. Review. _____ 24 a final check before handing in your paper. First _____ 25 all, see if you have answered all the questions required.

Check next to see if you have answered each question explicitly.

PRACTICE ANSWERING ESSAY QUESTIONS

The discomfort most students feel when faced with essay questions is the same discomfort they feel when faced with any writing assignment: *What shall I say? How shall I say it?*

The *what* — knowledge of the subject — can only come from reading and studying. The *how* — how to write effectively — can come from practice. (Review the selection "How to Write Effectively.") Practice writing and rewriting as much as possible; this, after all, is your main stock in trade as a student. Read the work of professional writers carefully and critically. Accept criticism of your own work and advice for improvement at every opportunity.

Directions: Following are essay questions about the Civil War that you can probably answer without studying. (If you prefer, create your own questions from any course you are taking this semester.) Select any five of the eight questions and prepare a 100-word answer for each.

    a. You have *one* hour to answer five questions.
    b. Outline each response before writing.
    c. Use the entire hour, but no more. If you have time to spare, use it to improve your answers.
    d. Ask someone to criticize or "grade" your exam.

1. Identify and discuss two causes of the American Civil War. Which of the causes do you believe was more important in leading to war? State the reasons for your opinion.

2. In what ways was the American Revolution a "civil war"?

3. Confederate soldiers were called "rebels." Explain why you think this was or was not an appropriate label.

4. Why might Lincoln's Emancipation Proclamation, which freed the slaves, be considered a military strategy?

5. Define the terms "civil war" and "revolution." How are they the same? How are they different?

6. Why did the Union win the Civil War?

7. By and large, freedom for Black Americans in 1865 meant exchanging one set of problems for another set of problems. What, then, is so important about freedom?

8. Compare the American Civil War with any other civil war or revolution you know about. (French or Russian Revolutions; conflicts in Vietnam, Ireland, Lebanon, and so on.)

> Asking why, what and how isn't for children only. Intelligent people of all ages are insatiably curious. An active curiosity can help you "get into" subjects you might have thought dull and uninteresting, and active participation in your courses will help keep your interest level, and your grades, high.

Making Curiosity and Interest Work for You

Curiosity and interest in the world around you are natural responses that you can use to good advantage.

As a small child you probably drove your parents to distraction by curiously asking "Why?" and by demanding explanations for everything from why the sky is blue to what makes an automobile go or how babies are born. *Why, what* and *how* should still be counted among the words you use most — especially in school.

Curiosity represents a desire to learn. But as you well know, curiosity can be a fleeting thing. We tend to pass quickly from one thing to another if we feel that the object of our curiosity is not worth the time and trouble it might take to find an answer or explanation.

So while curiosity can start you on the road to learning, it takes something more — sustained interest — for learning to actually occur. Pursuit of a hobby is a good example of curiosity that turns to sustained interest and produces learning.

You might become curious about raising house plants, for example, by seeing an attractive display in a friend's home. Purchasing a few plants of your own, you begin asking questions about watering and feeding them; you might get a book about plants from the library. Anyone who has become hooked on a hobby knows the rest of the story. As your interest grows you spend more and more time and money on your hobby. You read more and exchange information with other hobbyists. In the process, a tremendous amount of learning occurs.

There are many things that arouse our curiosity and many things that we become interested in to a greater or lesser degree. Thus, we may be interested in a television show long enough to watch it through; we may be interested in some parts of the newspaper but not others; we may be interested enough in an election to vote, but not enough to work actively for a candidate. We are always interested in learning how to do things that are "fun" – playing sports, driving a car, whistling, popping bubble gum and other things too numerous to mention.

But as you mature, you should become accustomed to directing your curiosity and interest both to things that you want to learn and to things you know you should learn or must learn in order to achieve certain goals: success in school and progress toward a satisfying career, for example.

Fortunately, since curiosity and interest are innate responses that you have experienced since earliest childhood, they are not attitudes that you have to go to great pains to acquire. However, you might have to learn to channel your curiosity and interest and practice applying these very potent forces to make them work where you want them to work.

MAKING CURIOSITY WORK

Our most accomplished people are insatiably curious. You will find scientists, inventors, artists, musicians, top-level executives and leaders in every walk of life always curious and always asking questions. They are curious about everything they encounter. A common denominator among those whom we call genius is an unfailing curiosity born of an active imagination. These people are always trying to relate one thing to another and often get excited over anything that is new or different to them.

You have an imagination, too; it's a basic human characteristic. And as we have pointed out, there is no one who doesn't have the ability to be curious. So, while no one will ask you to be a genius, there's no reason why you can't use your curiosity – sparked by your imagination – to generate a bit of excitement in your classes and study sessions.

You must first make up your mind, however, that everything you encounter in school has some use or value and is worthy of your attention. If you can't see the use in what you are doing, that's the very time to get curious about it and find out *why* what you are doing is important.

Ask yourself how a particular subject relates to your life now or in the future. How is the subject important to others in the world? A course needn't always serve a practical need; it might serve to make you a better person in some way or sharpen your reasoning faculties. Explore all the possibilities.

This is easy in the case of a potential scientist who takes a science course. But what if you are taking the course simply to fulfill a requirement for

graduation and your main interest is music?

A little thought should make you realize that as a consumer in a scientifically oriented world, it behooves all of us to have a basic knowledge of science. For a musician, the relationships between music and science should be apparent: the mechanics of a tuning fork, how musical tones can be made and amplified electronically, how a column of air makes music in a wind instrument, and so on.

"But what can be more dull than learning irregular verbs in a foreign language?" you may ask.

First apply the rule of asking yourself why taking a foreign language has value in the first place. Then use your imagination to try to relate the foreign language to your own vocabulary.

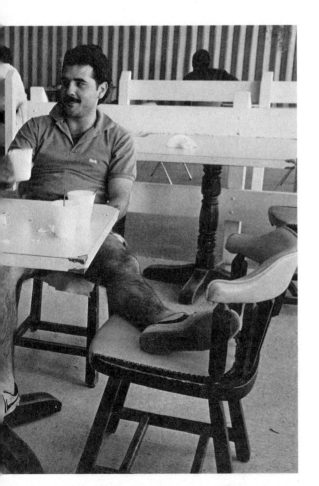

Just as an example, you might be curious to know if the French verb *aller* is related to the English word it sounds like — *alley*. A quick trip to the dictionary will satisfy your curiosity, and you'll probably never forget that *aller* means to go (down an alley perhaps). In Spanish, *vamos* sounds suspiciously like the American slang *vamoose*. If you're curious about it, you will find that the two words are, indeed, first cousins. It is little tricks like these that make learning not only palatable but enjoyable, and you have the added advantage of expanding your knowledge beyond what is required of you.

When you begin a new subject, it is a good idea to find out why that subject appeals to specialists in the field. The best place to find this information is in the preface or introduction to your textbook. It is here that the author makes a special effort to communicate his own interest or personal feeling for the subject.

Given a chance, many instructors will tell you what keeps their curiosity and interest alive in a subject. Enthusiasm is catching, and if you listen with an open mind you may become infected with an itching curiosity in the subject, too.

Give vent to your natural curiosity. Remember the *why, what* and *how* syndrome of your childhood. Practice and develop curiosity by asking questions. Apply them to your reading or ask them silently as you listen to lectures. There is just nothing so dull that it can't be made appealing with the use of creative curiosity.

MAKING INTEREST WORK

It can be said that interest is sustained curiosity. Once you have succeeded in arousing your interest, via curiosity, to the level needed to get you off to a good start in a subject, you must be able to sustain that interest in order to maintain the effort it will take to get you through the semester.

Since sustained interest implies a personal concern or involvement in a matter, the best way to maintain your interest in a subject is to plunge actively into the middle of it. In a classroom situation this means participation. When reading, it means pursuing the subject with a critical, questioning and analytical attitude. Intelligent marking of your text, as described in an earlier selection, is an excellent way to maintain active interest in a subject.

The more difficult you think it will be to maintain interest in a subject, the more you should ask questions, argue about it and discuss it. The excitement and tension you create this way works to arouse genuine interest not only for yourself but for everyone in the class.

If a class is one where you can't participate actively, listen critically; jot down questions and comments, reactions and opinions. If a teacher is dull and uninteresting, don't compound the problem by being dull and uninteresting yourself. Good students learn in spite of poor teaching because they are able to create their own interest and excitement.

Look for ideas behind facts. It is both pointless and dull to accumulate facts without understanding them. If what you read or hear has meaning for you, meaning that you have helped create through analytical thinking, you are bound to find it interesting.

Find out and be sure you understand what it is you are trying to do at all times. You soon lose interest in what seems like work without a purpose.

With a little effort, it's not hard to become "hooked" on a subject in school just as you can with an interesting hobby. And even though you may have to force yourself to become interested, you will find you get markedly better grades in subjects where interest is high.

_____: Reading Time

_____: Reading Rate

_____: Score, Test A

_____: Score, Test B

_____: Total Score

_____%: Comprehension

COMPREHENSION TEST 23-A

Directions: The following passage, taken from the selection you have just read, has words omitted from it. Fill in each blank with the word that was omitted. Each blank filled correctly is worth two points. Ask your instructor if you may take credit for close synonyms. Enter your score in the box provided at the end of the selection. A list of the omitted words can be found on page 243.

Curiosity and interest in the world around you are natural responses that you can use to good advantage.

As a small child you probably drove your parents _____ distraction
                                                            1
by curiously asking "Why?" and by demanding explanations _____
                                                                        2
everything from why the sky is blue to what _____ an automobile
                                                        3
go or how babies are born. *Why,* _____ and *how* should still be
                                          4
counted among the words _____ use most — especially in school.
                                  5
Curiosity represents a desire _____ learn. But as you well know,
                                        6
curiosity can be _____ fleeting thing. We tend to pass quickly from
                      7
one _____ to another if we feel that the object of _____
        8   9
curiosity is not worth the time and trouble it _____ take to find an
                                                        10
answer or explanation.

So while _____ can start you on the road to learning, it
                11
_____ something more — sustained interest — for learning to actually
        12
occur. _____ of a hobby is a good example of curiosity
            13
_____ turns to sustained interest and produces learning.
        14
You might _____ curious about raising house plants, for example,
                15
by seeing _____ attractive display in a friend's home. Purchasing
                16
a few _____ of your own, you begin asking questions about watering
            17
_____ feeding them; you might get a book about plants
        18
_____ the library. Anyone who has become hooked on a
        19
_____ knows the rest of the story. As your interest _____
        20   21
you spend more and more time and money on _____ hobby. You
                                                        22
read more and exchange information with other _____. In the
                                                            23
process, a tremendous amount of learning occurs.

_____ are many things that arouse our curiosity and many
        24
_____ that we become interested in to a greater or lesser degree. Thus,
        25
we may be interested in a television show long enough to watch it through; we
may be interested in some parts of the newspaper but not others; we may be
interested enough in an election to vote, but not enough to work actively for a
candidate.

COMPREHENSION TEST 23-B

Directions: This is another passage from the selection, again with words omitted. Proceed as before, giving yourself two points for each blank filled correctly. Add this score to the one from Test A and enter your total score in the box at the end of the selection. Use the conversion table on page 254 to convert your *total* score to a comprehension percentage, and record that grade in the box also. A list of omitted words can be found on page 244.

It can be said that interest is sustained curiosity. Once you have succeeded in arousing your interest, via _____, to the level needed to get you off
        1
to _____ good start in a subject, you must be able _____
        2   3
sustain that interest in order to maintain the effort _____ will take
                                                                      4
to get you through the semester.

Since _____ interest implies a personal concern or involvement
          5
in a _____, the best way to maintain your interest in a
          6
_____ is to plunge actively into the middle of it. _____
          7   8
a classroom situation this means participation. When reading, it _____
                                                                              9
pursuing the subject with a critical, questioning and analytical _____.
                                                                              10
Intelligent marking of your text, as described in an _____ selection,
                                                                    11
is an excellent way to maintain active interest _____ a subject.
                                                              12

The more difficult you think it will _____ to maintain interest
                                                      13
in a subject, the more you _____ ask questions, argue about it and
                                      14
discuss it. The _____ and tension you create this way works to
                          15
arouse _____ interest not only for yourself but for everyone in
            16
_____ class.
      17
If a class is one where you can't _____ actively, listen critically;
                                                    18
jot down questions and comments, reactions _____ opinions. If a
                                                          19
teacher is dull and uninteresting, don't _____ the problem by being
                                                      20
dull and uninteresting yourself. Good _____ learn in spite of poor
                                                    21
teaching because they are _____ to create their own interest and
                                    22
excitement.

Look for _____ behind facts. It is both pointless and dull to
              23
_____ facts without understanding them. If what you read or
      24
_____ has meaning for you, meaning that you have helped create
      25
through analytical thinking, you are bound to find it interesting.

Find out and be sure you understand what it is you are trying to do at all times.

TOPICS FOR DISCUSSION

Directions: The ten topics listed below concern making curiosity and interest work for you in school. Consider each carefully and apply the ideas suggested in this selection to your studies. Discuss your ideas with other students.

1. It can be argued that some subjects are so painfully boring that there is just no way to arouse your interest in them. Which subjects do you find most boring and why? How might you approach these subjects in order to make them at least tolerable for you?

2. Students tend to do well in courses that interest them. Students are generally interested in courses in which they do well.
   a. Which comes first, in your opinion: interest or success?
   b. What is the relationship between interest and doing well?

3. How might the following subjects be considered interesting?
   a. Solid geometry
   b. The Battle of Waterloo
   c. Rembrandt's paintings
   d. Geography of Europe
   e. Harriet Beecher Stowe's biography
   f. George Eliot's novel *Silas Marner*
   g. Greek mythology
   h. Latin grammar
   i. Botany
   j. Investment economics

4. If you have a hobby or other special interest, try to describe what makes it interesting for you.

5. Are there other things besides interest that might attract you to a subject and cause you to do well?

6. It is a truism that in any class of thirty students, no more than five will participate actively in discussions when asked to. Why do you think this is so?

7. How can you prepare yourself to participate in class more actively than you do now?

8. Some teachers are scholars and vast reservoirs of information, but they are not very exciting to listen to in class. How can you benefit most from this kind of teacher?

9. Some teachers conduct very interesting or amusing classes but convey very little information. Then, at exam time, you find yourself in trouble. How can you best cope with this kind of situation to assure yourself a good grade?

10. Some teachers contend that they are not obliged to make a subject interesting. They call this spoon feeding people who are supposed to be adults.
    a. What is your opinion of this attitude?
    b. Whose responsibility is it to make a subject interesting?

The demands on a student's time are heavy. You must find time to attend classes, enjoy some sort of leisure activity, perhaps hold a paying job, and actually sit down and study. Learning how to manage your time takes a little common sense and a lot of discipline. It can be the most valuable lesson you'll ever learn.

How to Manage Your Time

Tonight's the night you tackle that big term project. So after supper, you get down to the business of serious studying. First, you call all your friends now so they won't interrupt you with *their* calls later on. Next, you finish that magazine article so it can't tempt you anymore. Now you're ready to sit down and crack the books. But who can study without a cup of coffee? And besides, it's beginning to look like you'll be up all night. As you fix a snack to go with it, you remember that your favorite TV program is on tonight. You know you'll feel sorry for yourself all evening if you miss it, so it makes good sense to watch it, right?

When it's over, you take a second cup of coffee to your desk and consider, "Besides that big project that's been weighing heavy on my mind, there are a couple of smaller assignments I might as well get out of the way first." Later, feeling rather pleased with your brief spurt of industry, you reward yourself with a peek at the late show.

Finally, the time is right for that big assignment. But now it's one o'clock in the morning! A person can't start a project like that at one A.M. You'd get it done twice as fast if you waited until your mind was fresh. And, you recall, you need some books from the library. No sense starting without them. Besides, there's that game (debate, meeting) tomorrow; you can't let your friends down by not being in shape for it. So you might just as well turn in for the night. Tomorrow night's the night you'll tackle that important term project.

Sound familiar? Every student occasionally has trouble settling down to work. However, if this sounds more like the rule than the exception for you, then maybe you need to think more about how to manage your time.

Of your basic educational tools — books, teachers and time — time is your most limited commodity. A wasted evening is never recovered. Some teachers do not accept an assignment after it's due. And chances are that teachers who do accept a late assignment will penalize your grade because of it. But don't give up on yourself. If the scene above sounds like someone's been eavesdropping on your study sessions, here are some ways to make the most of your time.

1. **Establish a Routine.** The most important thing you can do is make studying part of your daily routine. Forget everything you ever heard about routine being a rut and about dead-of-the-night inspiration as a source of brilliant thinking. The most creative people in the world have to discipline themselves with a routine.

Decide what part of your day is the most practical time to set aside for studying. Consider when you are most alert, when you can study in relative quiet, and when you won't have other things demanding your attention. Once you have decided on a routine for study, stick to it. Regular sessions add up to steady progress. Setting aside a certain time every day for studying is a much more painless way to get it done than fretting and putting it off, waiting for a right time that never comes.

2. **Start All Your Assignments.** You usually have a variety of assignments demanding your attention every day — short ones, such as a chapter to read in your textbook, a laboratory experiment to write up, some math problems to complete, and one or two long-range assignments, such as a term paper or research project. It's tempting to complete the short assignments right away and put off the big ones until you have more time, energy or ambition. But it's critically important to make a start at everything.

A semester project or a term paper involving independent research and original thinking may boggle your mind at first, but this kind of project has a way of taking on more manageable proportions once you get started. Put your other work aside for a few minutes and think about what you'll be investigating. Decide what kind of reference materials you'll need and work up a rough timetable to use as a schedule. Suddenly you'll be able to put the whole project into a more realistic perspective and see it as a series of smaller assignments rather than one big one.

If the assignment you're avoiding is a daily exercise in a difficult subject, start this one, too, even if you believe you can't do it. Open the book, read the instructions and review the

material. Then, in class, you'll be better able to ask those questions that will result in helpful answers for you.

3. **Limit Your Course Load.** Don't take on more course work than you can handle well. It's tempting to take on extra subjects to get through school sooner, to sign up for advanced courses, or to sign up for extra electives simply because they sound interesting. But don't try it unless you know you are disciplined enough to devote the extra studying time they will require.

It's better to have a strong, solid grasp of the required subjects than a weak, superficial understanding of an accelerated program. What you don't learn thoroughly now will plague you later on.

4. **Outside Activities.** We all need some relaxation in our lives, but plan the fun around your study routine. Don't rush to join everything at once. Choose a variety of relaxing activities that don't take too much of your time, until you know for sure how much time you have. Biking or walking, a game of tennis or basketball, short visits with friends, or recreational reading are the sorts of things that can fit into a tight schedule. If you must become heavily involved in team athletics or club or organization work, choose the one activity that gives you the most pleasure. Avoid spreading your time and energy too thin.

Be careful about what you take on in the way of outside jobs. Many successful people relate with pride how they worked their way through school. But for each of those successes there are countless others who couldn't juggle both school and a job. Give yourself a fair chance at being a good student. If you do have to work your way through school, consult with your adviser first. He can tell you how many hours you ought to work in relation to the course load you are carrying. He might be able to help you find a job that isn't too demanding on your energy or one that allows some time for studying while working; some child care and some guard or gatekeeping jobs allow time for reading, for example. Some schools have work-study programs through which students can work with local businesses in jobs related to their academic programs and receive both pay and academic credit.

Remember — if you are carrying a full academic program, that is a full-time job by itself and don't let anyone tell you it isn't. Anything you do beyond that means you are working at two jobs or a double shift.

5. Analyze Your Time. Since there are only twenty-four hours in a day, a very simple way to find out if you are trying to fit too much into your schedule is to add up the hours you use each day. Include everything you do.

You must set aside 8 hours for sleep, 2 hours for eating and at least 2 hours for dressing and other personal needs. That's half a day right there. When you add time spent in class, travel time, time for small errands and some rest and relaxation, there is precious little time left for studying.

In high school, you are expected to spend at least half an hour studying for each course each day. That's two or three hours a day, not counting library research and writing term themes.

In college, you are advised to spend *three hours working outside of class for each hour spent in class* in order to get fairly good grades when everything is going well. So a rather light program — 12 hours a week of classes — demands *36 hours* of outside study. That is a 48-hour work week all by itself.

People who have not been to college tend to regard these figures with disbelief. Most entering freshmen have absolutely no idea of the vast quantity of work that will be demanded of them. And the failure rate in freshman classes is upwards of fifty percent, not because most students are incapable of doing college work, but because they don't put in the time that is required.

Managing your time is a great responsibility and no one else can do it for you. Don't try to be a hero by taking on more than you can handle. And don't underestimate the amount of time it takes to do well in school. In the end, your success will be measured by what you did well, not by how many things you did in a mediocre or unsatisfactory way.

_____: Reading Time

_____: Reading Rate

_____: Score, Test A

_____: Score, Test B

_____: Total Score

_____%: Comprehension

COMPREHENSION TEST 24-A

Directions: The following passage, taken from the selection you have just read, has words omitted from it. Fill in each blank with the word that was omitted. Each blank filled correctly is worth two points. Ask your instructor if you may take credit for close synonyms. Enter your score in the box provided at the end of the selection. A list of the omitted words can be found on page 244.

Tonight's the night you tackle that big term project. So after supper, you get down to the business _____ (1) serious studying. First, you call all your friends now _____ (2) they won't interrupt you with *their* calls later on. _____ (3), you finish that magazine article so it can't tempt _____ (4) anymore. Now you're ready to sit down and crack _____ (5) books. But who can study without a cup of _____ (6)? And besides, it's beginning to look like you'll be _____ (7) all night. As you fix a snack to go _____ (8) it, you remember that your favorite TV program is _____ (9) tonight. You know you'll feel sorry for yourself all _____ (10) if you miss it, so it makes good sense _____ (11) watch it, right?

When it's over, you take a _____ (12) cup of coffee to your desk and consider, "Besides _____ (13) big project that's been weighing heavy on my mind, _____ (14) are a couple of smaller assignments I might as _____ (15) get out of the way first." Later, feeling rather _____ (16) with your brief spurt of industry, you reward yourself _____ (17) a peek at the late show.

Finally, the time _____ (18) right for that big assignment. But now it's one _____ (19) in the morning! A person can't start a project _____ (20) that at one A.M. You'd get it done twice _____ (21) fast if you waited until your mind was fresh. _____ (22), you recall, you need some books from the library. _____ (23) sense starting without them. Besides, there's that game (debate, _____ (24)) tomorrow; you can't let your friends down by not _____ (25) in shape for it. So you might just as well turn in for the night.

COMPREHENSION TEST 24-B

Directions: This is another passage from the selection, again with words omitted. Proceed as before, giving yourself two points for each blank filled correctly. Add this score to the one from Test A and enter your total score in the box at the end of the selection. Use the conversion table on page 254 to convert your *total* score to a comprehension percentage, and record that grade in the box also. A list of omitted words can be found on page 244.

5. **Analyze Your Time.** Since there are only twenty-four hours in a day, a very simple way to find out if you are trying to fit too much into your schedule is to add up the hours you use each day. Include everything you do.

You must set aside 8 _____ for sleep, 2 hours for eating and at least _____ hours for dressing and other personal needs. That's half _____ day right there. When you add time spent in _____, travel time, time for small errands and some rest _____ relaxation, there is precious little time left for studying.

_____ high school, you are expected to spend at least _____ an hour studying for each course each day. That's _____ or three hours a day, not counting library research _____ writing term themes.

In college, you are advised to _____ *three hours working outside of class for each hour* _____ *in class* in order to get fairly good grades _____ everything is going well. So a rather light program — _____ hours a week of classes — demands *36 hours* of _____ study. That is a 48-hour work week all by _____.

People who have not been to college tend to _____ these figures with disbelief. Most entering freshmen have absolutely _____ idea of the vast quantity of work that will _____ demanded of them. And the failure rate in freshman _____ is upwards of fifty percent, not because most students _____ incapable of doing college work, but because they don't _____ in the time that is required.

Managing your time _____ a great responsibility and no one else can do _____ for you. Don't try to be a hero by _____ on more than you can handle. And don't underestimate _____ amount of time it takes to do well in school. In the end, your success will be measured by what you did well, not by how many things you did in a mediocre or unsatisfactory way.

QUESTIONS FOR DISCUSSION

Directions: Below are ten discussion questions for you to consider involving the best use of time. Share your thoughts in a discussion with other students. Consider the suggestions presented in this selection and apply them to better management of your time.

1. In your opinion, why is it often so difficult to take the first step in beginning a major assignment?

2. What positive measures can you suggest to avoid wasting a whole evening that is needed for serious work?

3. What factors sometimes interfere with the best planned routines? How can you handle unavoidable interruptions of routine?

4. Recount an experience that you have had with putting off a term paper until the last minute.

5. The time is just after supper on Friday. Early Monday you will face a quiz and a major examination. A term report is due on Tuesday. You have been keeping abreast of your work and estimate that one day's work will see the report finished and one day of review for the exams should be enough. *But* you have a date for Saturday night and a family obligation for Sunday. What will you do?

6. What are your feelings about working hard to manage an accelerated course load and getting average grades versus carrying a light course load and getting superior grades?

7. What do you do to earn extra income? How do you fit this work into your class and study schedule?

8. Consult with several teachers and counselors. What is the recommended amount of study time per class hour in your school?

9. Who works harder and has more demands placed on their time: students or people in the working world? Give examples to support your opinion.

10. You are a member of the tennis team, you have a part-time job to enable you to pay your bills, and you are carrying a full academic load. You are failing two courses and just passing two others. If you perform well in tennis this year, you have a chance at an athletic scholarship — *if* your academic average is satisfactory. What will you do?

> Choosing courses can be a bewildering experience. You are expected to seek out required courses, choose from a tantalizing array of electives, and fit everything into a convenient schedule — all without even being sure where your interests lie and what you want to do when you graduate. But making decisions is an important part of your education, and this selection offers ways to minimize your mistakes.

Choosing Courses

One of the most unsettling problems that you have to face as a student is choosing courses and planning a program.

Young adults are rarely ready to make career choices at age sixteen or eighteen, or even at twenty-one; nevertheless you are continually asked to make many important decisions about what you want to do with your life and about the direction your education will take.

Even in high school, where programs are largely structured for you, you are faced with choices you are often ill-prepared to make. Do you want business, vocational or college prep courses? Will you take a foreign language, and if so, which one? What about science and math? Which social studies elective will you choose?

The problems seem endless and the consequences frightening and irreversible. Students fret about them and families have disagreements over them.

College students have additional problems: they are often asked to indicate a career choice or major interest even if they don't know what career they want, what they are most suited for, or what the various majors entail. They are asked to choose from dozens of courses they know nothing about and have to work them into a suitable schedule.

Advice pours in from family, friends and advisers. There are catalogs full of instructions to contend with, endless forms to fill out, people to confer with, questions to answer and a procedure to muddle through that rivals joining the Army. And then, finally, you have to make up your mind and choose.

Making important decisions is never easy, but you needn't be traumatized by the experience. Learning to make choices is part of your growth process and you should accept it as such. You will make mistakes; they are inevitable. Even experienced business executives, whose stock in trade is decision making, make mistakes — and some of their mistakes are beauties. Mistakes in choosing courses are rarely fatal, however, and learning from your mistakes is usually more beneficial in the long run than never learning how to choose at all. Here are some suggestions that might help.

1. **Seeking Advice and Counsel.** Acquaint yourself with the choices available to you as far in advance of registration as possible. Obtain a copy of course listings as soon as it is issued. Study it carefully and make a preliminary selection of courses you think you may want to take.

Consult with your counselor or adviser early — as far ahead of registration as possible. This has several advantages: you can see your adviser when there is more time to talk and explore options before the last minute crush; there will be time for a second consultation if it is needed later; and you will have the necessary information and time to consider your course options carefully and make the wisest choices for your needs and interests.

Ask questions. Someone once said, "The rewards in life often go to the person who knows when and how to ask the right questions." Find out as much as you can about course contents, prerequisites and recommended skills. Be sure you understand how each course contributes to getting your degree or how it fulfills other goals you may have.

Advisers can't know everything about every course. If you have doubts or fears about course content, make an appointment to speak to the instructor. Find out what kind of background you should have, how much reading there will be, and how many papers will have to be written. Students sometimes miss out on good courses because of fears raised by false rumors and misinformation.

Seek the advice of family and friends. Listen with an open mind,

without relinquishing your freedom of choice. Don't fall prey to misinformed rumors. If you speak to someone who has had trouble with a course, also speak to someone who has done well. If someone raises a question you can't answer, seek an answer from a qualified source.

2. **Making a Program.** Make a list of all the courses that are available for you to take. Eliminate those courses which fit in with neither your plan of study nor your preferences. Next, keeping in mind your course requirements and preferences, group the remaining courses into three categories: those which are your first choices, those which are your second choices, and those which are your third choices.

It's generally a good idea to fill your program with required courses as much as you can in your first few semesters. Some schools insist that you do this. The reason is that since you have to take the required courses sooner or later, you might as well take them early and give yourself time to find out where your interests and abilities lie.

Make out two or three schedules that seem acceptable. Check the days and times of the courses you want to take. Your courses should be spread out over the whole week. Avoid scheduling too many classes in any one day to eliminate the possibility of tests and report due-dates coming on the same day.

These schedules, together with your list of priorities, will prepare you to choose alternatives at registration time if preferred courses are closed or canceled. Try to avoid making last minute, on-the-spot decisions.

Register as early as possible. If your school has an advance registration alternative, take advantage of it. The earlier you register the more chance you have of getting the courses you want.

3. Avoiding Overload. It is tempting to take more courses than you can handle in order to shave half a year or so from your time in school. High school honors students who have carried heavy loads in their junior and senior years tend to assume that if they could do it in high school they can do it in college.

Most entering freshmen are rather naive about the amount of work it takes to succeed in college. They gasp in disbelief at the amount of outside work that is assigned. They think that the teacher couldn't possibly be serious or that there must be an "easy" way to do all the reading and write all the papers. Go slow until you know for sure how much you can handle.

If you have to work at an outside job, limit your program accordingly. Working students must expect to take a little longer to finish their degree work. There's no point in working your way *through* college if what you are really doing is working your way *out* of college. College teachers may sympathize with an ambitious student who carries a heavy course load and holds down a job as well, but they can't make special allowances at examination time.

So when making up a program, you must consider all the demands that will be made on your time and limit your course load accordingly. Your adviser can tell you the number of courses that are recommended for students working full or part-time and those who are heavily involved in athletics. If necessary, make a schedule of your outside activities, class periods and study times.

4. Experimenting. If you have a strong urge to try a course that doesn't exactly fit any long-range plan, it still might be worthwhile trying it. College is a time for experimentation, growth and change. Many students searching for a major interest have "found themselves" simply by playing a hunch. Others have found a secondary interest that greatly expanded their career opportunities. Just avoid large numbers of purposeless courses.

If you are uncertain about your long-range goals, try to choose electives that will be useful no matter what you decide to do later. Time is never wasted on such things as literature and composition, basic mathematics and science, psychology and foreign languages.

5. Changing and Dropping Courses. Most schools have procedures for helping you to correct mistakes or change your mind. Find out what these procedures are and don't be afraid to use them if you have to. But be sure you know what the time limits are for dropping or changing courses and what the penalties are, if any.

Use these options judiciously and quickly. Don't wait until you fail a course or have to withdraw with a prejudicial grade. Don't abuse the change privileges or use them capriciously. Some students intentionally overload their programs until they see if they are going to get Dr. Scrooge or Mr. Niceguy for an instructor and then use their drop privilege. This sort of decision making is immature and frequently penalizes a serious student who may be kept from a place in a class that you have no intention of filling.

6. Making Your Own Decisions. When planning a program, make up your mind at the outset that your final decisions will be your own. Decision making is a vital skill that you need all of your life, and there is no better place than school to learn how to make decisions.

Listen to the advice of parents and friends with an open mind. Don't discount any suggestions that are made in your interest. But don't yield to suggestions to take a course because it is fashionable or "the thing to do" if you feel in your bones it is not right for you.

Evaluate all the advice and opinions you receive and then *make your own decision*. In the long run it is more important that your choices be your own than that they all be correct.

Then, accept wrong decisions gracefully; learn to live with them and make the most of them. That is part of the game, too. Being more experienced in decision making, you will do better next time.

_____: Reading Time

_____: Reading Rate

_____: Score, Test A

_____: Score, Test B

_____: Total Score

_____%: Comprehension

COMPREHENSION TEST 25-A

Directions: The following passage, taken from the selection you have just read, has words omitted from it. Fill in each blank with the word that was omitted. Each blank filled correctly is worth two points. Ask your instructor if you may take credit for close synonyms. Enter your score in the box provided at the end of the selection. A list of the omitted words can be found on page 244.

One of the most unsettling problems that you have to face as a student is choosing courses and planning a program.

Young adults are rarely ready to make career choices _____ age 1 sixteen or eighteen, or even at twenty-one; nevertheless _____ are 2 continually asked to make many important decisions about _____ 3 you want to do with your life and about _____ direction your 4 education will take.

Even in high school, _____ programs are largely structured for 5 you, you are faced _____ choices you are often ill-prepared to make. 6 Do you _____ business, vocational or college prep courses? Will 7 you take _____ foreign language, and if so, which one? What about 8 _____ and math? Which social studies elective will you choose? 9 _____ problems seem endless and the consequences frightening 10 and irreversible. _____ fret about them and families have disagree- 11 ments over them.

_____ students have additional problems: they are often asked 12 to _____ a career choice or major interest even if they 13 _____ know what career they want, what they are most 14 _____ for, or what the various majors entail. They are 15 _____ to choose from dozens of courses they know nothing 16 _____ and have to work them into a suitable schedule. 17 _____ pours in from family, friends and advisers. There are 18 _____ full of instructions to contend with, endless forms to 19 _____ out, people to confer with, questions to answer and 20 _____ procedure to muddle through that rivals joining the Army. 21 _____ then, finally, you have to make up your mind 22 _____ choose. 23

Making important decisions is never easy, but you _____ be 24 traumatized by the experience. Learning to make choices _____ 25 part of your growth process and you should accept it as such. You will make mistakes; they are inevitable.

COMPREHENSION TEST 25-B

Directions: This is another passage from the selection, again with words omitted. Proceed as before, giving yourself two points for each blank filled correctly. Add this score to the one from Test A and enter your total score in the box at the end of the selection. Use the conversion table on page 254 to convert your *total* score to a comprehension percentage, and record that grade in the box also. A list of omitted words can be found on page 244.

4. Experimenting. If you have a strong urge to try a course that doesn't exactly fit any long-range plan, it still might be worthwhile trying it. College is a time for experimentation, growth and change. _____ students searching for $\underset{1}{}$ a major interest have "found themselves" _____ by playing a hunch. $\underset{2}{}$ Others have found a secondary _____ that greatly expanded their $\underset{3}{}$ career opportunities. Just avoid large _____ of purposeless courses. $\underset{4}{}$

If you are uncertain about your _____-range goals, try to choose $\underset{5}{}$ electives that will be _____ no matter what you decide to do later. $\underset{6}{}$ Time _____ never wasted on such things as literature and $\underset{7}{}$ composition, _____ mathematics and science, psychology and foreign $\underset{8}{}$ languages.

5. Changing and _____ Courses. Most schools have procedures $\underset{9}{}$ for helping you to _____ mistakes or change your mind. Find $\underset{10}{}$ out what these _____ are and don't be afraid to use them if $\underset{11}{}$ _____ have to. But be sure you know what the _____ $\underset{12}{}$ $\underset{13}{}$ limits are for dropping or changing courses and what _____ penalties $\underset{14}{}$ are, if any.

Use these options judiciously and _____. Don't wait until you fail $\underset{15}{}$ a course or have _____ withdraw with a prejudicial grade. Don't $\underset{16}{}$ abuse the change _____ or use them capriciously. Some students $\underset{17}{}$ intentionally overload their _____ until they see if they are going $\underset{18}{}$ to get _____ Scrooge or Mr. Niceguy for an instructor and then $\underset{19}{}$ _____ their drop privilege. This sort of decision making is $\underset{20}{}$ _____ and frequently penalizes a serious student who may be $\underset{21}{}$ _____ from a place in a class that you have _____ $\underset{22}{}$ $\underset{23}{}$ intention of filling.

6. Making Your Own Decisions. When planning _____ program, $\underset{24}{}$ make up your mind at the outset that _____ final decisions will be $\underset{25}{}$ your own. Decision making is a vital skill that you need all of your life, and there is no better place than school to learn how to make decisions.

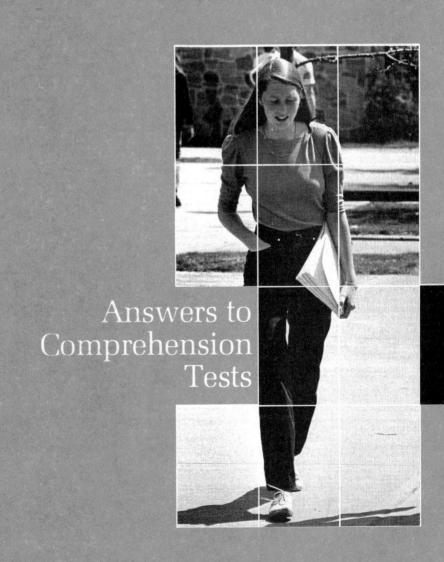

Answers to
Comprehension
Tests

Comprehension Test 1-A

1. a	6. hinder	11. well	16. strengths	21. strengthening
2. and	7. is	12. a	17. job	22. to
3. attitude	8. capable	13. bookkeeper	18. you	23. that
4. isn't	9. is	14. a	19. as	24. your
5. going	10. a	15. book	20. dealing	25. habits

Comprehension Test 1-B

1. error	6. about	11. own	16. give	21. short
2. how	7. in	12. you	17. you	22. succeed
3. it	8. with	13. high	18. from	23. are
4. them	9. study	14. continually	19. the	24. in
5. inventory	10. the	15. you	20. situation	25. it's

Comprehension Test 2-A

1. apprehend	6. eye	11. you	16. than	21. this
2. and	7. printed	12. for	17. so	22. of
3. most	8. for	13. order	18. a	23. reading
4. you	9. stop	14. percent	19. sweep	24. the
5. and	10. stops	15. one	20. a	25. line

Comprehension Test 2-B

1. cane	6. this	11. reading	16. had	21. can't
2. vowels	7. your	12. your	17. are	22. a
3. certain	8. quickly	13. good	18. students	23. common
4. shape	9. to	14. recognized	19. sight	24. them
5. English	10. in	15. it	20. some	25. you

Comprehension Test 3-A

1. content	6. take	11. to	16. hole	21. what
2. knows	7. your	12. road	17. you	22. game
3. consulting	8. doubt	13. any	18. or	23. some
4. that	9. to	14. it	19. coach	24. from
5. where	10. an	15. may	20. and	25. better

Comprehension Test 3-B

1. exactly	6. reader	11. the	16. find	21. discuss
2. opening	7. do	12. any	17. through	22. help
3. what	8. anecdote	13. reader	18. to	23. can
4. others	9. mood	14. to	19. watch	24. now
5. what	10. paragraph	15. it	20. presentation	25. read

Comprehension Test 4-A

1. is	6. through	11. subject	16. read	21. that
2. terms	7. vocabulary	12. field	17. already	22. sources
3. mastered	8. student	13. acquired	18. explains	23. and
4. who	9. flaunting	14. fact	19. learning	24. the
5. facts	10. to	15. than	20. foundation	25. key

Comprehension Test 4-B

1. they	6. ends	11. words	16. particular	21. and
2. the	7. meaning	12. root	17. will	22. for
3. in	8. speech	13. biology	18. word	23. and
4. un-	9. hateful	14. you	19. the	24. you
5. word	10. Latin	15. many	20. lesson	25. their

Comprehension Test 5-A

1. context	6. ambiguous	11. so	16. to	21. of
2. meaning	7. when	12. thought	17. understanding	22. where
3. surrounded	8. a	13. in	18. or	23. encompasses
4. word	9. reader	14. and	19. heard	24. other
5. is	10. sink	15. conventional	20. mean	25. words

Comprehension Test 5-B

1. unfamiliar	6. making	11. the	16. further	21. explain
2. the	7. understood	12. same	17. the	22. and
3. the	8. modified	13. that	18. in	23. be
4. words	9. information	14. recognized	19. by	24. unknown
5. context	10. shine	15. it	20. detectives	25. understanding

Comprehension Test 6-A

1. 3	6. c	11. we	16. word	21. a
2. frequently	7. to	12. or	17. of	22. find
3. are	8. in	13. as	18. phrases	23. occur
4. knows	9. practice	14. prominent	19. similar	24. up
5. may	10. prefer	15. it	20. list	25. sections

Comprehension Test 6-B

1. presentation	6. thought	11. signals	16. a	21. a
2. reading	7. still	12. ideas	17. finality	22. noticeable
3. two	8. critical	13. up	18. while	23. presentation
4. signals	9. suggests	14. are	19. where	24. talking
5. and	10. is	15. signal	20. author	25. said

Comprehension Test 7-A

1. construct	6. the	11. definition	16. for	21. introductory
2. authors	7. fat	12. or	17. for	22. the
3. from	8. is	13. entire	18. reading	23. to
4. carefully	9. purpose	14. will	19. what	24. is
5. accomplish	10. paragraphs	15. use	20. follow	25. guideposts

Comprehension Test 7-B

1. although	6. we	11. in	16. finally	21. will
2. conclusion	7. lesson	12. with	17. a	22. one
3. entire	8. to	13. to	18. the	23. transitional
4. however	9. every	14. facts	19. saying	24. similarly
5. too	10. though	15. most	20. aware	25. introduce

Comprehension Test 8-A

1. books	6. books	11. what	16. the	21. that
2. been	7. editors	12. if	17. their	22. next
3. all	8. setting	13. must	18. many	23. be
4. from	9. purchasing	14. production	19. newcomer	24. and
5. today	10. completed	15. will	20. of	25. in

Comprehension Test 8-B

1. that	6. that	11. the	16. has	21. you're
2. throughout	7. for	12. policy	17. words	22. is
3. works	8. contain	13. likely	18. to	23. it
4. appendix	9. the	14. work	19. textbooks	24. two
5. a	10. and	15. back	20. reaching	25. want

Comprehension Test 9-A

1. focuses	6. much	11. in	16. is	21. some
2. while	7. these	12. an	17. more	22. regard
3. to	8. to	13. read	18. material	23. grain
4. other	9. a	14. the	19. well	24. that
5. activity	10. short	15. have	20. you'll	25. all

Comprehension Test 9-B

1. series	6. presenting	11. write	16. the	21. point
2. phrases	7. something	12. is	17. exams	22. want
3. steps	8. series	13. may	18. is	23. intro.
4. them	9. to	14. a	19. beside	24. to
5. aid	10. the	15. it	20. be	25. use

Comprehension Test 10-A

1. entry	6. moments	11. rest	16. entries	21. locations
2. that	7. entry	12. the	17. and	22. find
3. into	8. from	13. left	18. to	23. measures
4. take	9. can	14. are	19. commonly	24. grammar
5. sense	10. looking	15. the	20. characters	25. like

Comprehension Test 10-B

1. follow	6. near	11. meaning	16. uses	21. word
2. tells	7. these	12. entry	17. appear	22. alphabetical
3. also	8. of	13. antonyms	18. given	23. the
4. origins	9. gradually	14. synonyms	19. used	24. have
5. word	10. show	15. be	20. locating	25. you

Comprehension Test 11-A

1. and	6. what	11. the	16. card	21. you'll
2. so	7. consult	12. the	17. have	22. number
3. author	8. all	13. place	18. you'll	23. the
4. either	9. you	14. there	19. it	24. book
5. the	10. card	15. when	20. card	25. today

Comprehension Test 11-B

1. areas	6. articles	11. investigating	16. consumer	21. forget
2. magazine	7. York	12. students	17. may	22. collections
3. Guide	8. people	13. publications	18. States	23. nice
4. popular	9. interest	14. the	19. issued	24. reference
5. New	10. so	15. problems	20. most	25. library

Comprehension Test 12-A

1. they	6. school	11. technique	16. during	21. successful
2. habits	7. spent	12. problem	17. reader	22. briefs
3. the	8. of	13. to	18. that	23. applying
4. to	9. satisfied	14. novel	19. this	24. inflexible
5. situation	10. develop	15. that	20. continue	25. easy

Comprehension Test 12-B

1. reading	6. by	11. follow	16. words	21. and
2. in	7. any	12. spent	17. of	22. eyes
3. courses	8. ever	13. when	18. the	23. line
4. this	9. preview	14. page	19. natural	24. are
5. these	10. you	15. read	20. eyes	25. seconds

Comprehension Test 13-A

1. pays	6. goals	11. assignments	16. the	21. through
2. time	7. advertising	12. he	17. the	22. these
3. accomplish	8. or	13. down	18. sights	23. argue
4. assignment	9. produce	14. must	19. should	24. know
5. in	10. are	15. example	20. this	25. is

Comprehension Test 13-B

1. the	6. a	11. more	16. in	21. academic
2. therefore	7. such	12. a	17. you	22. time
3. unprogrammed	8. time	13. college	18. term	23. as
4. to	9. course	14. hours	19. subjects	24. assignment
5. find	10. a	15. your	20. full	25. your

Comprehension Test 14-A

1. quite	6. in	11. this	16. readily	21. we
2. complain	7. always	12. banks	17. what	22. ability
3. how	8. it	13. passed	18. memory	23. not
4. that	9. closer	14. memory	19. memories	24. memory
5. minds	10. of	15. memory	20. before	25. suggestions

Comprehension Test 14-B

1. subjects	6. you	11. find	16. help	21. of
2. dangerous	7. achieving	12. teacher	17. procedure	22. green
3. subject	8. a	13. discussion	18. aids	23. ROY
4. we	9. and	14. you	19. letters	24. but
5. eventually	10. discuss	15. are	20. these	25. a

Comprehension Test 15-A

1. concerned	6. not	11. something	16. point	21. other
2. you	7. think	12. away	17. need	22. build
3. must	8. were	13. to	18. then	23. hunger
4. you	9. totally	14. it	19. the	24. for
5. begin	10. is	15. concentrate	20. there	25. no

Comprehension Test 15-B

1. total	6. project	11. so	16. wish	21. requires
2. in	7. naturally	12. the	17. the	22. own
3. it	8. you	13. use	18. need	23. not
4. one	9. major	14. and	19. you	24. study
5. spread	10. nothing	15. job	20. understand	25. above

Comprehension Test 16-A

1. from	6. become	11. not	16. is	21. have
2. those	7. down	12. or	17. everyone	22. daydreaming
3. universal	8. improvement	13. complain	18. which	23. we
4. to	9. school	14. causes	19. go	24. a
5. annually	10. every	15. of	20. we	25. free

Comprehension Test 16-B

1. about	6. remember	11. matter	16. you	21. your
2. attention	7. listen	12. attention	17. have	22. questions
3. his	8. the	13. think	18. like	23. questions
4. nothing	9. how	14. give	19. this	24. questions
5. so	10. illustrate	15. sit	20. the	25. listening

Comprehension Test 17-A

1. recommended	6. student	11. every	16. sure	21. up
2. notes	7. is	12. they	17. are	22. speaker
3. word	8. hearing	13. reveals	18. the	23. his
4. is	9. lecturer's	14. he	19. them	24. wants
5. trying	10. recommended	15. obvious	20. listeners	25. about

Comprehension Test 17-B

1. which	6. selectively	11. the	16. classes	21. statement
2. words	7. and	12. of	17. at	22. reviewing
3. to	8. anecdotes	13. title	18. main	23. will
4. meaningless	9. to	14. a	19. statement	24. a
5. the	10. the	15. something	20. point	25. students

Comprehension Test 18-A

1. when	6. you	11. know	16. or	21. never
2. and	7. to	12. the	17. that	22. a
3. description	8. ideas	13. dividends	18. those	23. substance
4. short	9. before	14. effective	19. and	24. your
5. defining	10. ideas	15. before	20. ground	25. you

Comprehension Test 18-B

1. replace	6. colorful	11. appropriate	16. advice	21. imitate
2. noun	7. with	12. usage	17. study	22. as
3. and	8. this	13. conversations	18. course	23. an
4. language	9. but	14. the	19. include	24. sentence
5. sometimes	10. depending	15. purpose	20. kinds	25. especially

Comprehension Test 19-A

1. grade	6. one	11. the	16. they	21. faulty
2. work	7. handwriting	12. response	17. as	22. your
3. for	8. did	13. truth	18. chances	23. you
4. writers	9. of	14. with	19. quality	24. your
5. prolonged	10. read	15. however	20. by	25. that

Comprehension Test 19-B

1. compressed	6. the	11. make	16. pen	21. close
2. fatigue	7. is	12. instrument	17. usual	22. the
3. index	8. onset	13. too	18. an	23. some
4. easy	9. as	14. that	19. too	24. of
5. pen	10. to	15. rapidly	20. cannot	25. accompanying

Comprehension Test 20-A

1. review	6. cramming	11. successful	16. this	21. term
2. and	7. waters	12. you	17. of	22. ease
3. break	8. brief	13. addition	18. textbook	23. to
4. can	9. harm	14. be	19. chapters	24. review
5. lack	10. lets	15. class	20. reviewing	25. it

Comprehension Test 20-B

1. might	6. to	11. the	16. this	21. anxiety
2. important	7. questions	12. because	17. items	22. morning
3. assure	8. that	13. cram	18. define	23. and
4. important	9. copy	14. moments	19. each	24. to
5. rest	10. pre-exam	15. principles	20. late	25. pangs

Comprehension Test 21-A

1. methods	6. earn	11. or	16. all	21. entire
2. you	7. careless	12. a	17. essay	22. is
3. for	8. the	13. essay	18. you	23. construct
4. you	9. kind	14. because	19. objective	24. valid
5. know	10. and	15. better	20. a	25. evaluating

Comprehension Test 21-B

1. all	6. not	11. for	16. to	21. not
2. some	7. sure	12. reduce	17. change	22. change
3. subtracting	8. of	13. the	18. of	23. be
4. right	9. rather	14. timed	19. possible	24. reason
5. wrong	10. that	15. when	20. one	25. be

Comprehension Test 22-A

1. exercise	6. he	11. of	16. exam	21. aspects
2. of	7. the	12. little	17. information	22. probably
3. correct	8. unprepared	13. half	18. of	23. selecting
4. essay	9. on	14. to	19. as	24. at
5. forces	10. most	15. you	20. you	25. mention

Comprehension Test 22-B

1. possible	6. to	11. write	16. definitions	21. you
2. ones	7. not	12. a	17. subject	22. to
3. you	8. of	13. on	18. has	23. them
4. deals	9. gap	14. begin	19. to	24. make
5. indicate	10. after	15. openers	20. impression	25. of

Comprehension Test 23-A

1. to	6. to	11. curiosity	16. an	21. grows
2. for	7. a	12. takes	17. plants	22. your
3. makes	8. thing	13. pursuit	18. and	23. hobbyists
4. what	9. our	14. that	19. from	24. there
5. you	10. might	15. become	20. hobby	25. things

Comprehension Test 23-B

1. curiosity
2. a
3. to
4. it
5. sustained
6. matter
7. subject
8. in
9. means
10. attitude
11. earlier
12. in
13. be
14. should
15. excitement
16. genuine
17. the
18. participate
19. and
20. compound
21. students
22. able
23. ideas
24. accumulate
25. hear

Comprehension Test 24-A

1. of
2. so
3. next
4. you
5. the
6. coffee
7. up
8. with
9. on
10. evening
11. to
12. second
13. that
14. there
15. well
16. pleased
17. with
18. is
19. o'clock
20. like
21. as
22. and
23. no
24. meeting
25. being

Comprehension Test 24-B

1. hours
2. 2
3. a
4. class
5. and
6. in
7. half
8. two
9. and
10. spend
11. spent
12. when
13. 12
14. outside
15. itself
16. regard
17. no
18. be
19. classes
20. are
21. put
22. is
23. it
24. taking
25. the

Comprehension Test 25-A

1. at
2. you
3. what
4. the
5. where
6. with
7. want
8. a
9. science
10. the
11. students
12. college
13. indicate
14. don't
15. suited
16. asked
17. about
18. advice
19. catalogs
20. fill
21. a
22. and
23. and
24. needn't
25. is

Comprehension Test 25-B

1. many
2. simply
3. interest
4. numbers
5. long
6. useful
7. is
8. basic
9. dropping
10. correct
11. procedures
12. you
13. time
14. the
15. quickly
16. to
17. privileges
18. programs
19. Dr.
20. use
21. immature
22. kept
23. no
24. a
25. your

Answers to
Practice Exercises

PRACTICE WITH WORD ELEMENTS

Practice Exercise 1

Word Elements and Their Meanings		Literal Meaning
1. bio = life	graph = write	write about life
2. post- = after	script = write	after the writing
3. super- = over	vis(e) = see	to oversee
4. re- = back	vert = turn	to turn back
5. cred = belief	-ible = capable of being	capable of being believed
6. mort(u) = death	-ary = place where	a place where death is
7. trans- = across	mit = send	to send across
8. pater(n) = father	-al = like	like a father
9. sol(i) = alone	-tude = condition	the condition of being alone
10. bi- = two	ped = foot	having two feet

Practice Exercise 2

Word Defined	Word Defined	Word Defined
1. omniscient	6. postmortem	11. retrogress
2. polychromatic	7. circumscribe	12. interstellar
3. prescience	8. triarchy	13. antecede
4. aqueous	9. concur	14. acrophobia
5. biogenesis	10. corporeal	15. abduce

PRACTICE IN USING CONTEXTUAL AIDS

Practice Exercise 1

1. small
2. round
3. water
4. rain
5. days
6. less
7. heat
8. plumber (repairman)
9. day
10. death
11. suburbs (country)
12. operation (surgery)
13. license
14. polls (voting booths)
15. pollution
16. breakfast (meal)
17. lines
18. headache (pain)
19. secret (surprise)
20. suspects (witnesses)

Practice Exercise 2

1. an overwhelming quantity
2. insulting
3. innocent; naive
4. courage
5. incapable of correction or rehabilitation
6. decreased; lessened
7. lowest point
8. conspicuous
9. stormy
10. cowardly
11. moral principles; ethical standards
12. one who takes advantage of a situation for self gain
13. insignificant; miserly
14. babbled; chattered
15. an interest in; a liking for
16. to regain
17. a setback
18. showed (her fine clothes) to be false or misleading; contradicted
19. talkative; loquacious; long-winded
20. was noncommittal; appeared to favor both sides

PRACTICE FINDING SIGNS AND SIGNALS

1. many other reasons
2. Finally; a single alternative; many other possible alternatives; For instance; All these; and
3. three pillars; (1), (2), (3)
4. two attitudes; however; One, The other; And
5. certain characteristics; First of all; Then; Again
6. therefore; but
7. then; moreover; Thus; At the same time
8. two facets; First; Second
9. For example; So also; Similarly; As a result
10. on the other hand
11. One last word; because; or; In either case

IDENTIFYING PARAGRAPH ROLES

1. Introduction: An emotional tone catches the reader's attention. *The question of capital punishment* states what the general subject matter will be.

2. Transition: This paragraph moves the reader from a statement of the problem in the first paragraph to a discussion of the answers in the succeeding paragraphs by pointing out that *the struggle for answers . . . is one to which every American should lend his voice.*

3. Information: *it is my belief* indicates that the author's opinions will follow.

4. Information: *At the same time* indicates that the author is about to show the other side of the coin; he is going to balance or round out the picture presented in the previous paragraph by continuing to give information.

5. Information and Transition: The author is continuing to give information by presenting facts (*Experience has clearly demonstrated*) and by presenting a beginning step in his argument (*however* indicates that the author has begun to favor one side of the coin). At the same time, the paragraph serves as a transition from the balanced view of the subject in the preceding paragraphs to the author's stand on the issue in succeeding paragraphs.

6. Illustration: The author uses two examples to prove his point.

7. Illustration: *just like* is a sure sign that an illustration is being given. The author is reinforcing his point through illustration by comparison.

8. Conclusion: *We must never* is emphatic and final. The author is stating his conclusion, the conclusion he hopes his readers will draw and remember.

9. Introduction: The questions asked indicate what will be discussed.

10. Definition: *It was* and *it was called* indicate a definition. Also, words are called out and quickly explained.

11. Information and Definition: The paragraph obviously starts with a historical account. The words *happened* and *advent of* indicate a historic narration. The words *known as* and *was used to* indicate a definition is nearby.

DICTIONARY SKILLS

Alphabetizing	Using Guide Words	Variant Spellings	Appropriate Meaning
1. afford	1. peace	1. dine	1. b
2. again	2. penurious	2. busy	2. c
3. bait	3. perhaps	3. ferry	3. a
4. believe	4. protection	4. fix	4. d
5. cancel	5. recent	5. curriculum	5. b
6. cycle	6. recollect	6. galosh	
7. effect	7. redoubt	7. garrote	
8. emulate	8. reversal	8. gaudy	
9. fissure	9. rural	9. gauge	
10. frighten	10. security	10. glamour	

PREFIXES, SUFFIXES AND ROOTS

Prefixes	Suffixes	
1. hemisphere	1. -able	adjective
2. hyperkinetic	2. -ment	noun
3. antebellum	3. -ize	verb
4. malefactor	4. -ly	adverb
5. circumlocution	5. -ward	adverb
6. antibiotic	6. -some	adjective
7. penultimate	7. -en	verb
8. nontoxic	8. -fy	verb
9. ambilateral	9. -ist	noun
10. emit	10. -ful	adjective

Roots

Words Derived from the Root	Words Derived from the Root
1. anthropoid, anthropology, misanthrope	11. grammar, graphology, homograph
2. astrology, astroid, astronavigation	12. heliocentric, heliotherapy, heliotropism
3. benefit, benevolent, beneficent	13. phonetics, stereophonic, homophone
4. chronological, chronical, chronic	14. position, deposit, compose
5. circumference, circumfuse, circumvent	15. rupture, interrupt, disrupt
6. cognizant, recognize, incognito	16. scribble, manuscript, inscribe
7. cosmography, cosmopolite, cosmopolis	17. septennial, septuagenarian, septet
8. dictator, contradict, predict	18. spectator, spectacle, inspect
9. conduct, introduction, educate	19. contain, obtain, retain
10. generate, genealogy, genesis	20. terrestrial, terraqueous, terraceous

PRACTICE LISTENING

1. c	3. d	5. c	7. a
2. b	4. c	6. c	8. a

PRACTICE TAKING NOTES

Practice Exercise 1

I. What can I expect to learn?
II. What are some of the things to be covered?
III. What will the author say about the subject?
IV. What is the author's method of presentation?

Practice Exercise 2

The Nature of Comprehension

I. Student view of reading: reading is a mechanical, passive process.
II. Parent view of reading: children must be able to pronounce words; emphasis on phonics and oral reading skills.
III. Madison Avenue view of reading: emphasis on reading speed with "satisfactory" comprehension.
IV. Realistic view of reading: a combination of the above — (1) read actively and spend time; (2) know phonics; (3) have high-speed skimming skills.

Practice Exercise 3

Vision and Reading

I. Visual acuity: ability to see small objects clearly.
    A. 20/20 is normal, but those without 20/20 do not necessarily have faulty vision; must test.
    B. Three optical defects.
        1. Myopia: nearsightedness; blurred vision; corrected with glasses.
        2. Hyperopia: farsightedness; severe cases require glasses.
        3. Astigmatism: symptoms are blurring or discomfort; corrected with glasses.
II. Fixation ability: the ability to aim eyes at motionless objects, to follow a moving object, to shift eyes from one object to another.
III. Accommodation skill: the ability to adjust the eye's focus between objects at different distances. (Ex. looking from book to blackboard)
IV. Binocular fusion: ability to combine images.
    A. It's the brain's function to fuse the two pictures received from each eye into one image.
    B. If faulty, double vision occurs.
V. Adequate field of vision: peripheral vision; being aware of surrounding movement while looking straight ahead.
VI. Form perception: ability to recognize shapes; perhaps most important visual skill.

EDITING

Line 2   hand,

Line 3   office, becoming the; Principal

Line 5   relatives,

Line 6   immigrant; brought

Line 7   among Indians; Cherokee, OR Ross, who thought of himself as a Cherokee,

Line 8   to leading the people

Line 11   accomplished

Line 12   churches.

Line 13   Through

Line 17   would be removed from; In 1822,

Line 19   Council

Line 20   United States. Neither

Line 21   commissioners

Line 22   Cherokee opposition. OR Cherokee resistance.

Line 23   Since Georgia maintained that OR Since Georgia insisted that

Line 25   tribal

Line 26   sealed. Answering the demands

Line 27   Congress appropriated $50,000 OR Congress authorized $50,000; for the removal

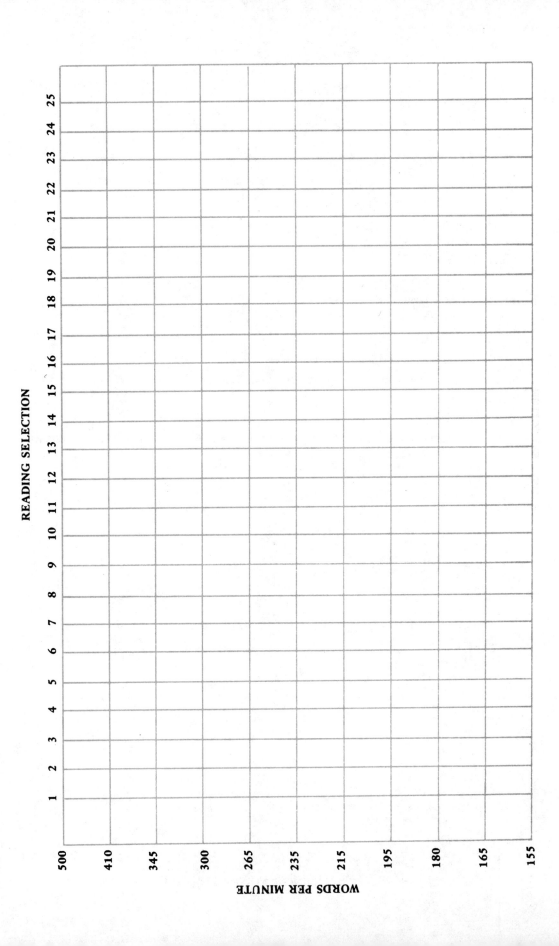

READING SELECTION

1 2 3 4 5 6 7 8 9 10 11 12 13 14 15 16 17 18 19 20 21 22 23 24 25

WORDS PER MINUTE

500 410 345 300 265 235 215 195 180 165 155

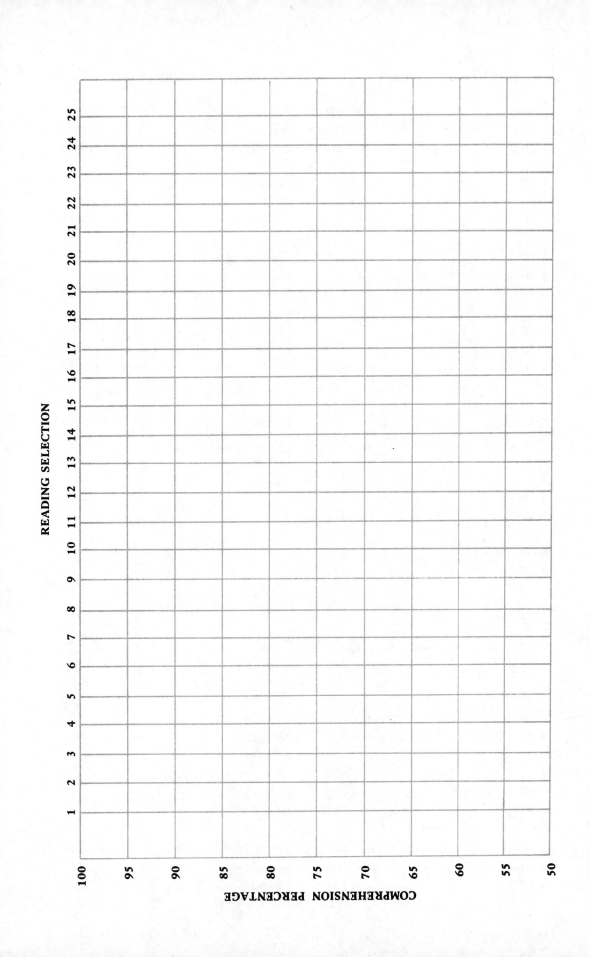

READING SELECTION

COMPREHENSION PERCENTAGE

TIME-RATE CONVERSIONS

Minutes and Seconds	Words per Minute
1:00	1500
1:20	1125
1:40	900
2:00	750
2:20	645
2:40	560
3:00	500
3:20	450
3:40	410
4:00	375
4:20	345
4:40	320
5:00	300
5:20	280
5:40	265
6:00	250
6:20	235
6:40	225
7:00	215
7:20	205
7:40	195
8:00	190
8:20	180
8:40	170
9:00	165
9:20	160
9:40	155
10:00	150
10:20	145
10:40	140

TIME-RATE CONVERSIONS

Minutes and Seconds	Words per Minute
11:00	135
11:20	130
11:40	128
12:00	125
12:20	123
12:40	120
13:00	118
13:20	115
13:40	113
14:00	110
14:20	108
14:40	105
15:00	100

CLOZE CONVERSIONS

Cloze Scores	Comprehension Percentages
10 – 14	50
16 – 20	55
22 – 26	60
28 – 34	65
36 – 40	70
42 – 46	75
48 – 52	80
54 – 60	85
62 – 66	90
68 – 72	95
74 and above	100